Cambridge Studies in Social Anthropology

General Editor: Jack Goody

27

DAY OF SHINING RED

*For a list of the titles
in the series, see page 235*

Day of Shining Red

An essay on understanding ritual

GILBERT LEWIS

Lecturer in Social Anthropology
University of Cambridge

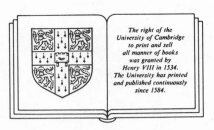

*The right of the
University of Cambridge
to print and sell
all manner of books
was granted by
Henry VIII in 1534.
The University has printed
and published continuously
since 1584.*

CAMBRIDGE UNIVERSITY PRESS

Cambridge
New York   Port Chester
Melbourne   Sydney

Published by the Press Syndicate of the University of Cambridge
The Pit Building, Trumpington Street, Cambridge CB2 1RP
40 West 20th Street, New York, NY 10011, USA
10 Stamford Road, Oakleigh, Melbourne 3166, Australia

First published 1980
First paperback edition 1988
Reprinted 1990

Printed in Great Britain at the
University Press, Cambridge

Library of Congress cataloguing in publication data
Lewis, Gilbert.
Day of shining red.
(Cambridge studies in social anthropology: 27)
Includes bibliographical references and index.
1. Gnau (Papua New Guinea people) – Rites and ceremonies.
2. Puberty rites – Papua New Guinea – Sepik Valley.
3. Sepik Valley – Social life and customs.
4. Rites and ceremonies. 5. Symbolism. I. Title.
DU740.42.L477   301.2′1   78-68354

ISBN 0 521 22278 8 hard covers
ISBN 0 521 35888 4 paperback

CONTENTS

v

To Ariane

ANALYTICAL TABLE OF CONTENTS

vii

Chapter 3. Views from one village

Chapter 4. The rites of puberty seen

Chapter 7. *Moon, river and other themes compared*

Chapter 8. *For success in life*

Analytical table of contents

Analytical table of contents

xiii

PREFACE

Prospero speaks to Caliban: 'When thou didst not, savage, know thine own meaning, but wouldst gabble like a thing most brutish, I endow'd thy purposes with words that made them known.' An anthropologist has not the magic art of Prospero that he may dare to speak like that; yet some would almost seem to. It is easy to think about other people's rites and symbols in terms of our own preoccupations. We have received ideas. Questions put by other anthropologists influence what we ask about in fieldwork, how we listen to answers and observe. Strange customs tempt an anthropologist more strongly to interpret them when he feels the people have not given him a good enough reason for following them. The question of what should count as a good reason runs through this book.

The anthropologist cannot escape from the complexity of his subject matter. Rather than suppose that one idea or theory should singly guide my comments, I have tried to find which ones help in understanding a rather short rite performed by the Gnau of New Guinea. In chapter 2 I present a general view of the problems and then in subsequent chapters take up various aspects of them for further exploration, in the light of what the Gnau had to say. I take extracts of Gnau conversation in chapter 3 to show what sense they have of ritual, and how they come to learn about it and how to do it. Next I describe the rites and mention some aspects of my impressions of them. These have no doubt influenced how I later evaluated the rites. It seems to me false science to disguise the selective personal component that enters willy-nilly into some field observations by an anthropologist, in the hope that the reader will be duped by impersonal phrasing. Some kinds of ethnographic data and observation may be collected, with appropriate effort, both systematically and objectively, but others, by their nature, cannot achieve a like status as 'hard' fact. The subjective impact of the different things I saw is partly what directed and motivated my efforts in inquiry and analysis.

Chapter 5 is about the rules of participation in the rites, and some further inferences that may be drawn from them about the intentions and motives of the actors. I relate it to questions of genre, address and style in ritual. Chapter

6 argues that we may mislead ourselves when we think we naturally understand a representation or a symbolism. I also discuss here some anthropological uses of the term 'metaphor'. The aim of chapter 7 is to see whether comparison within a limited ethnographic area helps to adjust the balance of commentary, partly in regard to the question of how relations between the sexes bear on interpretation of the rite. The long chapter 8 tackles the detail of what is done in the rites, going into issues of response, expression and meaning, especially with regard to differences in what the actors perceive according to sex, age and experience. I have tried to present a full account of a Gnau understanding of human development through life. Chapter 9 looks at how emotion may affect people's perception of symbols and chapter 10 takes up the idea of token, type and variation to examine some further aspects of the functions of the rites and how they have been affected by social change. The final chapter is an inventory of themes in the book.

My apology for the detail of this study would be that it tries to work right through a particular case and be accurate to my understanding of Gnau views, rather than to offer another new theory or to show how well one theory works for some of the data. I have been influenced by the books of Gombrich (1960, 1963), Wollheim (1970), Frye (1971), Cherry (1966), and Huizinga (1965). None of them was intended as a work for anthropologists and perhaps for that reason it is easier to single them out. Within anthropology there are too many different sources for my ideas, coming from friends, books and articles, to acknowledge all of them justly, and so, uncertain as to how I should do it, I do thank them, and single out only Bateson's *Naven* (1958), A. I. Richards's *Chisungu* (Faber and Faber, London, 1956) and Leenhardt's *Do Kamo* (1947) for their closeness in subject matter and the influences of the ways they handled it.

For all their kindness and tolerance, and for the help they gave me, I owe the people of Rauit village a deep debt. I hope they might find this book true to them.

I thank the Social Science Research Council for funds enabling me to visit the Gnau from December 1967 to November 1969 and again from July to December 1975. Some of the text used in chapters 5 and 9 previously appeared in 'A mother's brother to a sister's son' in *Symbols and Sentiments*, edited by Ioan Lewis, Academic Press, London, 1977.

Naumas   G. L.
August 1977

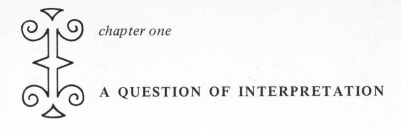

chapter one

A QUESTION OF INTERPRETATION

A sentence of Nadel is quoted from time to time to be criticised for the limit he set on interpretation: he wrote, 'Uncomprehended symbols have no part in social inquiry, their social effectiveness lies in their capacity to indicate; and if they indicate nothing to the actors they are from our point of view, irrelevant, and indeed no longer symbols (whatever their significance for the psychologist or psychoanalyst)' (1954, p. 108). Nadel can be understood to limit 'symbol' to those situations where the relationship between something and what it stands for is intended, conventional and can be put by the actor into words. It points up the distinction between the communication of meaning to people within the society (actors) and items of social behaviour or belief which express in an indirect or obscure fashion some principle, value, conflict or problem occurring in that society. Expression is not the same thing as communication. You can express your feelings to a stone, yet it is unmoved. You could also, like the mystic Henry Suso (Huizinga 1965, p. 148) eat three-quarters of an apple in the name of the Trinity and the remaining quarter in commemoration of 'the love with which the heavenly Mother gave her tender child Jesus an apple to eat' and unless you or Henry Suso told me, I would not, though I watched you twenty times, discern your symbolism or even that what you did was symbolical.

There is little consensus about the definition of the word 'symbol' or about the distinctions between sign, symbol, and other candidates for inclusion in this complex. But we trade often in such words, especially 'symbol'. They are convenient for they allow us to float over the troublesome issue of whether we speak of expression only, or also of communication, and, if the latter, whether that communication was between actors within the society, or from these people, unwitting, to the ingenious and deductive mind of the anthropologist.

Hard, fascinating problems of interpretation are often posed by actions or beliefs which the actors do not explain enough to satisfy the anthropologist's curiosity. He goes on to say they are expressions of something else: they have another meaning. But his curiosity is selective, both according to the theories which preoccupy him and his individual leanings: one anthropologist may be ready to accept at face value the reason given by the native actor when another

1

finds it inadequate and proposes a more devious, his deeper, explanation. As Leonardo said of the blot of paint on a crumbling wall, 'You may see whatever you desire to seek in it.' With brilliant imagination, another has perceived, and perhaps seduced many a dazzled reader to see too, the imagined social institutions of a Caduveo Golden Age, drawn in patterns on a woman's face (Lévi-Strauss 1955, p. 203). There in brief lies the problem of selection and interpretation.

These reflections were prompted by two things connected with my findings in the field which I mention now. I worked among the Gnau, a people living in the West Sepik Province of New Guinea. On certain occasions Gnau men secretly and apart from women cut their penises to make them bleed. The first time for someone to do this was during his puberty and on this first occasion he did not cut his penis himself in the new style with a sliver of glass or broken razor blade but instead was cut — stabbed or bored into is more accurate — with a sharp awl of cassowary or wallaby bone. On other and subsequent occasions men cut themselves and most prefer now to use the bottle or the razor rather than the bone. The Mountain Arapesh, a people who live about seventy miles away, also bleed themselves. Margaret Mead reported at length on this (1970, part II) and wrote that the penis-bleeding was equated with menstruation. Even more to the point, she quoted Hogbin on another people of the island of Wogeo, which is off the Sepik coast, who refer to incision and bleeding the penis as men menstruating; indeed Ian Hogbin has called his latest book *The Island of Menstruating Men* (1970). But the Gnau when asked directly whether to bleed from the penis was like menstruation, answered, 'No, it is not like menstruation.' The first point, then, which interested me was what significance to attach to the finding that Gnau men did not equate their similar practices of penis-bleeding with menstruation, while some other peoples in the area, or at least their ethnographers, did so equate it.

The second point emerged from reading accounts of puberty and initiation from elsewhere in the Sepik. I found some close parallels to various Gnau rules and practices in these accounts. In some instances, a reason was given for a custom which the Gnau shared, but for which they gave no reason but tradition, that it was the right thing to do, one that their forefathers had taught them. In a few cases, elements of the reasoning which the other people used were also stated by the Gnau, but they did not overtly link the custom and the reason. When I chanced on an explanation which fitted, it was tempting to infer the link which would enable me to put some practice or belief, seeming before isolated and wayward, into place according to the logic of a system. Two examples may make what I have in mind plainer.

The Gnau have complicated food prohibitions about kinds of animal. Among many prohibitions for which I collected no reason but custom was a rule forbidding young people to eat any of the eleven kinds of fish in their rivers except for one. In Whiting's account (1941, p. 68) of the Kwoma, he notes that the

2

Kwoma prohibited fish to young men for the months which followed initiation, for the reason that they bled their penises into a stream where fish might eat the blood, and since a man must not ingest his own blood, he must not eat fish, which could have eaten this blood, until he was sure that his blood had flowed far beyond his country into the great Sepik river. Like the Kwoma, the Gnau bleed into water. In addition the girls have their buttock scars cut over river boulders at initiation so that the blood flows into the river and, as with the Kwoma, an individual (but male *or* female) must not ingest his or her own blood — it is one of the cardinal Gnau rules regarding blood.[1]

The second example concerns bleeding induced from the mouth and chewing betel and areca nut. Mouth-bleeding was done by the Gnau after homicide, in the major male initiation rites called Tambin, and at a culminating rite of hunting by which a man, usually in his middle or late thirties, who had shown his prowess at hunting, became entitled to full knowledge of hunting magic and entitled as well to chew areca nut with lime which makes the betel juice bright red. Neither women nor young men were allowed to use lime. The Gnau explained their cutting of the men's tongues and gums as something to make them fierce or 'teethed men' (*baniŋɔtasel*). To chew betel with lime was the privilege of men; they said if young men did so it would interfere with their success in hunting. Women chewed areca nut with ash as the young men did, until their reproductive life was over[2] and they had grandchildren, when the women too were allowed to chew with lime and spit bright red. As with smoking, where permitted use exactly paralleled the use of lime with areca nut, I obtained no particular explanation of why women should be forbidden lime except on grounds of custom and privilege. Privilege, scarce lime and selfish pleasure seemed adequate to explain the rules which favoured senior men without looking for some recondite symbolic explanation.

However a number of other peoples in the Sepik (Kwoma, Wogeo, Iatmul) also bleed men's mouths and the other sources mention it as part of the male initiation ritual. On Wogeo, the island of 'menstruating men', bleeding the tongue is the cruellest stage of initiation which precedes the time when a man first incises his penis. Hogbin, guided by his Wogeo information, explains that tongue-bleeding is done at puberty; it is, he says, 'in a sense a youth's first artificial menstruation, corresponding with the initial menstruation of a pubescent girl. The tongue is selected for the bleeding because hitherto he will have absorbed the worst of the pollution orally with mothers' milk . . . In a few years, when he is sufficiently mature for sexual intercourse, the penis will be the agent whereby

---

1 I was able to ask them, in 1975, whether the taboos on fish had anything to do with bleeding into streams or water, and they answered 'No'.
2 The Gnau have a phrase *wap wutaləm wutaləm* which they use of a woman whose reproductive life is coming to an end or has ended; she has had many, many menstrual periods, and they are ending now. *Wap wutal* refers to something which has been hung up out of reach or put on a shelf high up.

contamination is transferred. Accordingly in later life this is the organ that receives menstrual treatment' (1970, p. 114).

The Gnau do use occasional similes between copulation and eating, between mouth and vulva; a woman teased another who was slow at her work, 'You go on sitting there and teeth will come up in your vulva!' and female images are made in which the vulva is painted red and open and is lined by two rows of white Job's Tears seeds just the way the mouth and teeth of the figure are represented. But neither they nor I produced the simile which Abelam men do, so Anthony Forge tells me, who liken the blotches of red juice they spit on the ground to menstrual blood. The old women among Gnau may, like men, chew the areca nut with lime and spit red, and they no longer menstruate.

In both these examples, it seems possible to play with logic of a kind, and place an isolated observation in a context to which it had not seemed previously to belong. Tidiness, order and system please (as in Stephen Daedalus's version of Aquinas, *ad pulcritudinem tria requiruntur – integritas, consonantia, claritas . . . Pulcra sunt quae visa placent*), and they tempt one to select what will fit, rather than to remark what would not fit if one were as ingenious as a sceptic finding evidence to contradict the proposed system. There is certainly this hazard in the appeal of order, but if we discount it for the moment, the question remains of saying what use it is to suggest, by comparison within an area, possible or perhaps tendentious links of this sort; to find them where the people concerned ignore them, do not know them. A student of diffusion and survival might well be able to show a constellation of elements in the Sepik rituals of puberty and initiation which commonly recur, though variously assembled, sometimes with, sometimes without, the same interpretation. He might study the distributions of the elements because he was interested in their dispersal. Or another might follow Lévi-Strauss, with a hypothesis about how the human mind works, which justified or indeed required this manner of comparison to develop or test it (Lévi-Strauss 1958, ch. XI). Alternatively, a justification for comparison might be that a grasp of the common elements over a wide area enables one to discern the particular stresses, gaps or reformulations which are dependent on, or consistent with, the particular social constitution of one society compared with others in that area. To know what is ignored, *not* done or *not* recognised by one people, when other peoples around them do recognise it, may be to gain an illuminating perspective on those whom you have studied.

Expression in any medium draws on choice or selection from a limited set of possibilities; the more precisely you know what possibilities there are and what are the limits of the system, the more exactly you can understand the significance of a particular selection or performance, or of a departure from convention. You appreciate fine shades of expression in an actor, a piece of music or a painting, as you know well the conventions for restraint or flourish, say, in some gestural or artistic style. The analogy from interpreting expression in an artistic medium parallels quite closely the problems facing an anthropologist when he wishes to assert that some ritual action, or some other behaviour, expresses a principle or value or a contradiction which is unstated, unrecognised by those who act, and is not directly apparent from the bald description of what happened. Gombrich (1960, 1963) has exposed with convincing wit and care the gross limitation to interpretations of artistic expression which are based on, or assume, a theory of natural signs or, as some name it, intuitive natural resonance. For my purpose, I would have you note especially his comments on the image in the cloud, and on how possible it is at some level of association to assign almost anything towards one or another pole of almost any clear dichotomy — his choice was ping or pong. Indeed, if it were not for this, how else could Osgood measure his semantic differentials? Gombrich argues that expression, and its interpretation, depends on choice and selection within a particular context and structure. The human body and its parts may be 'natural' symbols used to express things which we can guess to some degree intuitively, but only because we share with those we study some perceptions of the form, the senses and the limitations of our common frame.

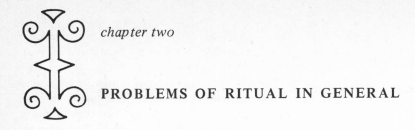

chapter two

PROBLEMS OF RITUAL IN GENERAL

To begin with

Let me begin by summarising how I shall develop the argument of this chapter. I shall seek to relate the problems of defining ritual to problems of understanding the symbols and expressions of other people. Part of the argument is on questions of interpretation in which the anthropologist may think it right to go beyond what his informants tell him.

The attempt to set ritual apart from other kinds of activity and define a clear boundary round it has not gained general support. I put first the reasons why no adequate case can be made for separating ritual sharply as a special kind of action distinct from others. To avoid these objections, others have put forward the view that ritual is an aspect of many actions, not a kind of behaviour. The ritual aspect of behaviour is its expressive, symbolical or communicative aspect. By this view, the identification of ritual comes to be inextricably bound to the ability to recognise expression, symbol and communication. In some cases, the people who perform these behaviours do not or cannot put into words what they express, symbolise or try to communicate by them. Then if the anthropologist makes an interpretation, he is the only one who has been able to put that interpretation into words. If he had not done so, then perhaps neither he nor we nor the people who performed it should have distinguished that aspect of the action. But that aspect is required for the identification of ritual according to this second view. And sometimes we feel almost sure something is ritual before we know or can think of any meaning for it.

Some people are quick to see the point of a joke, others are slow. Some see a suggestiveness about it which others miss. Some have fertile, inventive and daring imaginations; others more stolid remain earthbound, literal, and poetry is lost on them. But even such earthbound, prosaic people do sometimes see more than meets their eyes and they can be taught how to understand a symbolism or expression seen by others but not natural, familiar or intuitive to them. With effort and attention they can learn to see it, just as someone could learn from an expert by dint of patience and application how to interpret the tracks of animals in the snow. Or someone might learn to accept the meanings for his dreams which, though perhaps patent to his psychoanalyst, seem at first so strange to him that he would ridicule and deny such an understanding of himself. The point is that the ability to see or respond to symbols and expression varies with the cast of individuals' minds, their flair, their learning and interests, and the degree of attention they choose to give to something that presents itself to them. And anthropologists are in no way exempt from such human variations. If the anthropologist needs to be able to recognise symbol, expression or communication to identify ritual, must he then count towards ritual only whatever contains the symbols comprehended by the people and stop there, or go on and add whatever in the things he witnessed happened to feed his fancy; or are there other reasons by which to guide his attention and control his search and efforts at interpretation, if he would go beyond the part explained by the people?

If ritual may be the expressive or communicative aspect of almost any action, it becomes difficult to identify an unknown as this view makes the potential field for ritual encompass almost all behaviour. This seems odd on first acquaintance. To those who have not tried to work out a definition of ritual and not tried it against objections and the difficult test-cases, as to those who have not tried to fathom the technicalities of anthropology, 'ritual' and 'rites' are words of common speech that are readily enough applied to some conspicuous kinds of performance, for example, ones to do with religious worship. Even those anthropologists who rack their brains to define it agree that certain kinds of performances are ritual if anything is. There is a central area of general agreement; it is the periphery and the boundaries that are in dispute. I take the central area first, where there would be easy general agreement, and try to see what there is about such kinds of performances which make for this immediate, intuitive recognition. If it is possible to see what leads to this response in the central area where there is general agreement then we may be able to unravel some of the difficulties that lie towards the periphery. At this stage in the argument I am concerned with what produces such an immediate response in the anthropologist. He recognises the peculiar fixity of ritual, that it is bound by rules which govern the order and sequence of performance. These are clear and explicit to the people who perform it. It is a form of custom. The fixity, the public attention, the colour and excitement or solemnity that go with such performances are what catch the anthropologist's attention. He responds to this peculiar quality in ritual performances. It can guide him as to where to concentrate his efforts at interpretation. It may be present in great or small degree. For the time being it is the anthropologist who concerns me and the effect of the peculiar quality of ritual on him. At a later stage in this section I will return to the effect this quality has on the performers and participants.

I emphasise this quality so that the horse shall go before the cart and not the cart before the horse. The anthropologist would like to identify and interpret the symbolism in ritual. But this is often the hardest part of his work, the part he last understands and only after much effort and learning. He does not witness a performance and say to himself, 'Ah! this stands for that, and this for that, etc. Therefore these are symbols, therefore I have seen a ritual performance.' What he says is more likely to be, 'This is odd. This is ritual. Why do they do it like that? There is more to this than meets the eye. I must try to find out what.'

The alerting quality is variable, a matter of degree. Sometimes one may be unsure whether it is there or not. This fits with our immediate recognition that there is a central area which we nearly all would clearly recognise as ritual and then more and more doubtful instances peripherally. Ritual cannot be demarcated by a clear boundary from other kinds of custom. The numerous attempts to classify and distinguish different kinds of custom (for instance, into etiquette, ceremony, magic, religious ritual, etc.) appear to be attempts at distinguishing ideal types of custom from the standpoint of their chief intention or address. These genres of custom are formulated as ideal types. So we often find that an actual particular example does not fit surely or securely into just one such genre or category. But recognition of the chief intention or address in the custom is nonetheless important for a just and proper interpretation.

From this discussion of where to search and where to make an effort to interpret, I go on to the grounds by which we may come to understand expression and representation. I borrow many of my arguments from writers on aesthetics where the problems of interpreting the silent objects of art offer parallels to the problems which face the anthropologist who would go beyond what his informants tell him. In developing these issues, I come back to the performers and participants and discuss the peculiar quality of ritual from their point of view. A ritual may not be explained by the performers. Or the anthropologist may sometimes be told a great deal about it. Ritual performance may aim at clear, explicit symbolism or aim at mystery. I look at some of the methods by which mystery or clarity is achieved and suggest some guides for finding out what is aimed at.

Throughout this section, I try to maintain the distinction between expression and communication. I stress that if we wish to speak of communication proper, an intended and successful imparting of information is required. To liken ritual to communication by code or language gives some insight into it. But this simile, I think, has been taken to distorting lengths. It is more accurate to look on ritual as a performance, like a play, which is responded to in various ways: communication is only a part of it. To seek to explain ritual as though it were language or code, with methods appropriated (or misappropriated) from the disciplines that deal with them, carries the risk that we shall miss some of what is distinctive to ritual. Ritual is not exactly like language; it is not exactly like communication by means of a code nor can it be decoded like one. The complexity and uncertainty about a ritual's meaning is not to be seen just as a defect — a code too obscure, too hard to decipher, too easily garbled. It can also be a source of that strength, evocative power, resilience and mutability which may sometimes sustain and preserve ritual performance.

Ritual is hard to define just as art is

The word 'ritual' like the word 'art' does not have one commonly agreed definition; nor, if we resolve to avoid the uncertainty entailed by using it, is it easy to find a better or a satisfactory substitute. We find we have to use it and in many circumstances we do not doubt that we use it rightly even though it is hard to say exactly what it rightly means. Ritual and art pose some similar problems. We are sometimes uncertain how to distinguish a ritual act from a technique or a game; and we are sometimes uncertain how to separate an art from a craft or an amusement. So we may choose to say there is a ritual aspect to many actions; and we may choose to see artistry in many artefacts. What are those aspects that we point to by calling them ritual or artistic? Are they something to be found either in the action itself or the object itself as facts presented by it (which we either see or are blind to), and separable both from the intentions of those who do the action or make the object and from the interpretations of those who behold them? If fact cannot be in a clear way separated from interpretation, must we then decide on the presence or absence of these peculiar aspects by means of the purposes of those who do the actions or who make the objects, or by some recognition and interpretation on the part of those who behold them?

It has been argued (Collingwood 1938, p. 5; Tatarkiewicz 1963) that the Greeks of antiquity did not distinguish art from craft, and had no concept of art as we employ it; it has been argued that the Dobuans did not distinguish between what resulted from magical, and what from technological, ability in the accomplishment of their various ends (Fortune 1932, pp. 97–8). But we speak of the achievements of Greek art or of Dobuan technology and sometimes distinguish them from those of Greek crafts or Dobuan ritual. As for the beholder's part it could happen that as we walked along some familiar street we were asked to stop and look again at one house in it, and to recognise it as a work of art; or as Firth did with the turmeric paint-marks in Tikopia (1951, pp. 24–5) we might stop to look at something seen before and passed over casually, and recognise it for a ritual act. We might attend to something closely and see that the action we had taken no previous notice of had a ritual aspect, and that the house we had passed by, seeing it only as a habitation, was also an artistic achievement.

As with art so with ritual: they have both been likened to language and held to express or to communicate. With both there are performers (makers and doers), performances (action, objects, media) and beholders and interpreters. Is it just this expressive, communicative aspect that we point to when we say we recognise a ritual aspect in some action or an artistic aspect to some object? Or is this not enough?

Despite these parallels, we feel no temptation to substitute 'art' or 'artistic' for 'ritual' in most of the contexts where either one or another of the words occurs. What then do we mean by the word 'ritual'? If 'ritual' refers either to a particular kind of behaviour or a particular aspect of it which demands special attention for its description and analysis, we must first decide what kind or aspect this is to be, and learn to recognise it so that we can know where to exercise this attention, lest otherwise our efforts be misplaced and futile.

Ritual refers to conduct or performance but not just any kind

It is common now to find in an anthropological piece written in English that the word 'ritual' appears as an adjective used for convenience instead of 'magical' or 'religious', having the sense of either or both, avoiding the cumbersome 'magico-religious', and evading an otherwise forced decision which may be impossible to make that some belief or some action is either 'magical' or it is 'religious'. Goody (1961) discusses the attempts to differentiate magic from religion. He shows that 'ritual' has been used quite often as an adjective of compromise. When it is so used, it may 'designate the whole area of magico-religious acts and beliefs' (Goody 1961, p. 158). Such adjectival use is undeniably convenient: but it is a special kind of use in which ritual is made equal to exactly what 'magico-religious' is held to mean. Certain kinds of idea or feeling (belief, value or sentiment) are by such usage as rightly called 'ritual' as are certain kinds of behaviour or action.

But this goes against our traditional and unreflecting application of the word to conduct rather than ideas and feeling. It is odd to note how 'ritual' rather than 'rite' is the noun in common usage now in English; I think the reverse used to be the case for French. It is a word we apply essentially to performance. 'Ritual is not synonymous with the whole of a religious or magical system. It is, so to speak, the executive arm of such systems' (Fortes 1966a, p. 411). And indeed wherever the focus is primarily on defining the word 'ritual', we find action or behaviour made part of it.[1]

1 (a) Enfin les rites sont des règles de conduite qui prescrivent comment l'homme doit se comporter avec les choses sacrées' (Durkheim 1912, p. 56).
(b) 'a kind of patterned activity oriented towards the control of human affairs, primarily symbolic in character with a non-empirical referent, and as a rule socially sanctioned' (Firth 1951, p. 222).
(c) 'Ritual denotes those aspects of prescribed formal behaviour which have no direct technological consequence' (Leach 1964).
(d) 'When we speak of "ritual" we have in mind first of all actions exhibiting a striking or incongruous rigidity, that is, some conspicuous regularity not accounted for by the professed aims of the actions. Any type of behaviour may thus be said to turn into a "ritual" when it is stylized or formalized, and made repetitive in that form' (Nadel 1954, p. 99).

But not every action, nor all kinds of behaviour, are part of ritual: we breathe, blush, eat, walk, sleep, and there is usually nothing ritual about their happening, although, in certain circumstances, there might be. Simply to observe some general habit, some statistical regularity of behaviour, such as sleeping at night and rising in the morning, is not enough to mark the activity by its quality of repetition or routine as ritual. To say the action is prescribed, that there is some ruling about the circumstances for its performance, moves closer to an answer. In all those instances where we would feel no doubt that we had observed ritual we could have noticed and shall notice whether the people who perform it have explicit rules to guide them in what they do. This is also the case for custom, etiquette or ceremony, whose definitions have long been tangled up with that of ritual. If the answer 'Yes' is or would be given to the question 'Must x do y in z circumstances?' then what he is to do at least *may* be ritual: if the answer given is 'No, not necessarily', then it cannot be ritual. What is always explicit about ritual, and recognised by those who perform it, is that aspect of it which states who should do what and when. It is practical. It guides action. And phrases like 'prescribed routine', 'standardised behaviour', 'behaviour with incongruous rigidity', which appear in most of the definitions given in note 1, refer to this. Guidance on what to do is explicit, but the reason for doing it, the meaning, motive or interpretations of the action may not be. The explanations for what is done may be clear, or complicated or uncertain, or multiple, or forgotten: but what to do is known. And words, speech, spells may just as well be part of prescribed ritual performance as non-verbal behaviour – Leach (1966) and Tambiah (1968) have driven this point home.

What ritual and custom share

Like ritual, custom too gives explicit guidance on what should or should not be done. I have not gone further than repeating that ritual is one kind of custom. Custom, though the term has fallen out of favour with anthropologists, implies behaviour guided by rules whose claim to validity is based upon the general acknowledgement of those who practise them that these rules are theirs and proper to them, ancient and to be observed because things should be done in that way, as they were done before by their forebears: tradition justifies their practice. Custom is binding on those who acknowledge that they are members of that community to which the custom belongs. As Leach noted, 'For the ethologist, ritual is adaptive repetitive behaviour which is characteristic of a whole species; for the anthropologist, ritual is *occasional* behaviour by *particular* members of a *single* culture' (1966, p. 403; my emphases). Custom and ritual share then this feature: the rules are not binding on all people of a group

(e) 'Ritual, like etiquette, is a formal mode of behaviour recognised as correct, but unlike the latter it implies belief in the operation of supernatural agencies or forces' (Royal Anthropological Institute 1951, p. 175).

11

but on particular people, or on one type of person in a particular situation. To conform to them is to acknowledge that one is that kind of person. They have limited validity. We can speak of performance entailing a recognition of this, of loyalty or obedience, membership, an assertion of status or identity. If the rules for performance are explicit in this respect, then it seems that the inference that ritual may express something about social relationships — or more loosely phrased, that social relationships may be symbolised in ritual — is neither unwarranted nor imposed by the observer beyond the evidence of his observations. To take part in ritual properly demands knowledge of the conditions for performance and demands attention to social status and identity. The actor may not openly say that through ritual something about social relations is expressed, but nonetheless he must know the rules which permit or constrain his participation.

'Montaigne a tort: la coutume ne doit être suivie que parce qu'elle est coutume, et non parce qu'elle soit raisonnable ou juste' (Pascal, *Les Pensées*, Lafuma 525; Brunschwicg 325). 'Custom' is a term that has fallen out of favour. The reason for this lies in the argument that for something to be custom it must be justified essentially by an appeal to tradition: our ancestors did it like that and therefore so must we. If this is taken to mean justified *solely* by tradition or justified solely by general convention — a sense implied in the phrase 'I don't know why they do that. It is just their custom' — then clearly much of what was taken first in ignorance to be 'just custom' turns out as one comes to know a people better to be not 'just custom' but to have a rationale, be it religious, moral, legal, political or whatever. And it becomes part of religious observance, legal custom, etc. As one aim of the anthropologist is to understand the organisation of another society and its culture, to learn how what may have seemed so strange as to be mere nonsensical convention is not so, but fits some social requirement or purpose, so his growing understanding erodes more and more of what seemed at first just custom. Then to speak of some observance as 'merely customary' comes close to admitting his failure to grasp the situation and understand it. But the element of justification by tradition remains with custom as it does with ritual.

If I should wish to show respect to the king or honour to the god in some society, I could not do so unless I had learned the conventions for politeness or worship of that society. To cover or uncover my head, to crawl, stand, bow or kneel would not convey my intentions unless some significance for these actions were established there. Uncovering the head does not indicate respect as spots do measles or a blush embarrassment. The convention which makes head-uncovering a mark of respect is artificial or arbitrary; neither reason nor common sense suffices to make it significant, but tradition can. Convention explicitly guides conduct (see Ladd 1967). It tells me how to show respect. If I wish to be pious, polite, good, honourable, law-abiding, it tells me how, within limits, to conduct myself. Without the guidance and expectation so introduced, I would be bewildered, I would not know how to fulfil one or other of these intentions, or how to put what my ideals required into practice: social life depends on some degree of order and regularity so that an individual can foresee the responses of others to his own actions. The ideals or motives that are, or were, connected with these guides for conduct may be implicit or unstated in them. Statement of the rules is often not of the form 'You must eat' but when, how, with whom and where to eat. For instance, what people say is 'Normally we eat three meals a day' and not 'We must eat regularly to grow strong and stay well so therefore we eat at these three times during the day'; custom dictates 'When a lady comes into the room, you should stand up' — and not 'Because they are of the weaker sex and must be respected and protected, a man must show a lady attention by standing up when she enters the room.' If the forms of action dictated are often wholly, or in part, artificial, they may be justified by the appeal to tradition. This is so whether or not the actions are also on other grounds appropriate to the circumstances which call for their observance.

Technical skill, rationality, efficacy are not sure guides to what is not ritual

Mere custom and ritual have both been seen as having something unreasonable or arbitrary about them which distinguishes them from craft, skill and technique. Indeed, to feel unable to make sense of an action in terms of an intrinsic means—end relationship, a reasonable cause-and-effect nexus, is often what alerts the observer to the action. Words that recur in discussion of the distinctions between ritual and craft or skill are 'irrational' or 'non-rational' where 'rationality' implies Weber's sense of the 'methodical attainment of a definitely given and practical end by the use of an increasingly precise calculation of adequate means' (Gerth and Wright Mills (eds.) 1948, p. 293). It would be convenient for the anthropologist in a strange society if ritual were a special *kind* of action or behaviour which lacked rationality in this sense. It would be convenient if he could study the action, record his observations objectively as facts about it, examine them and then, with due regard to the means available in that society and the stated purpose, say with confidence that that kind of action was or was not rational. The kind of 'rationality' that we are supposed to be looking for here, in our attempt to distinguish craft or technical skill from ritual, is clearly something pragmatic, empirical and concerned with the consequences of ideas that can be tested out and shown to work by experience. The fine School-men's art of logic, of reasoning from a set of stated premises, may be exercised upon the question of how many angels could dance on a pin-point. But demonstration of this kind of rationality or logic is not what we seek. Behind definitions of the type: ritual refers to a category of standardised behaviour in which the relationship between the means and the end is not 'intrinsic', i.e. is either irrational or non-rational, there lies the hope of specifying how ritual may be identified by the observer on the grounds of certain properties which are

13

presented in the action which he can take as objective facts about it. But the boundary between fact and interpretation may not be sharp or simple.

An example from the treatment of illness can show some of the problems well (cf. Nadel 1954, ch. 5). Consider three instances in which a patient with a pain was put into trance by a specialist in healing. The healer intended to make the patient better and in all three instances he did: the treatment worked. In the first instance, it was Pierre Janet, a self-critical medical practitioner, who used hypnotism to treat certain people; in the second, Franz Anton Mesmer who used animal magnetism; in the third, a shaman who cast out a spirit. In each case, the healer and the patient had grounds to be well satisfied with the treatment. Judged solely as an activity with its purpose demonstrably achieved, we could not tell between them whether one were ritual, another craft. We cannot decide between them on the basis of the facts observed by the pragmatic test, nor on the basis of the actor's rationality. Janet did not claim to know why his treatment worked[2] any more than a native canoe-maker might know why most woods float but some sink. Mesmer, on the other hand, promulgated with passionate conviction his theory conceived in an analogy to magnetism and many took it for a great discovery (Ellenberger 1970, pp. 57–83). And the shaman with his theory of illness, and his power to heal shown, would not have cause for doubt of the reasons he gave for his success more insistent than any other of a great number of medical practitioners whose erroneous theories are part of the long history of discarded science in medicine. Neither the test by experience nor an inquiry as to the reasoned and logical links between a man's actions and his theories allow us to see why we do tend on impulse to put the shaman's work with ritual, Janet's with science and the canoe-maker's craft, and hesitate to explain Mesmer until we know more about the man and the history of his times.

Were the function of menstruation thought to be release of impure blood, which men do not do spontaneously and therefore must bleed themselves, in one society all men might do this. If their health was as good as that of the women in those respects which impure blood was believed to harm, they would have no grounds for doubt of their theory. If we are told some hocus-pocus theory to account for the empirical success of a technique, should we therefore call it magic? The change of attitude in our present attention to acupuncture is an odd case in point. Indeed we continue successfully to do many things for which we can give no full explanation — the adequacy and fullness of our explanation depend on how far our questions probe — but we continue to do them because, like aspirin, they work, although we do not know why. We may think we know and be shown wrong by later knowledge or subsequent dis-

2 To make my point, I have rather grossly misrepresented Janet's wisdom. 'Janet described all these peculiar facts in a metaphorical way as the "dissociation of psychic material" . . . It is of course, only a metaphor, which Janet developed very clearly, in order to cover certain cases' (Jaspers 1963, p. 402–3).

covery: yet we should not therefore say in retrospect that what we did was magical or ritual.

The anthropologist observer reliant on the evidence of 'facts' presented, and on some general view of what would be acceptable to Western science as an adequate 'intrinsic' relationship between the means and the end, must teeter sometimes as he faces a decision between ritual and craft — for he is on no sure ground. The error is partly that he has hoped to distinguish a *kind* or category of action, partly that he has tried to make the decision his own and not that of the people who perform it. There are also other difficulties in the way of his endeavour. The motives or intentions behind many actions are not simple or necessarily explicit. So the stated purpose of the action may alter with perspective, time, mood and individual, as the answerer widens or narrows the circumstances he takes into account in answering, as he fixes his attention on one element or another in the action. If there are many purposes of differing saliency and explicitness, so the judgement of efficacy is complex and may be equivocal. If the anthropologist looks for a kind of action, he is obliged to segment the flow of behaviour and asks his question about bits of behaviour or action. When he says for instance: that is a gardening ritual, or that an initiation ritual, he may find a multitude of small bits of behaviour within the action he has bounded as a ritual which are practical, straightforward, effective solutions to some technical requirement; or as Malinowski did, he may find that rite and technique are interdigitated in the ordered accomplishment of some task (cf. Tambiah 1968, p. 198).

The view that ritual is a *kind* of action distinct from craft or technique imposes on the anthropologist a decision between them which he cannot always make. The view implies that an action cannot be both of the ritual kind and of the craft kind, both rational and irrational. Barth pointed this out when he stressed that we are prone to assume, if an activity is clearly practical and effective, that it therefore cannot be ritual. This may blind us to the possibility that an action has both aspects. He was struck by what seemed a poverty of ritual among the Basseri nomads of South Persia. But it dawned on him that their spring migration, which was a triumph of adaptation to a harsh environment, might also be the great central rite of their society (1961, app.). I have tried to indicate that I think the either/or position comes from the anthropologist's attempts to treat action as a kind of object with facts about it which putatively will enable him to distinguish between ritual and craft. His attempt parallels that position in aesthetics which equates art to its objects and looks to explain the nature of art and understand it by sole attention to what is given in the objects. This position is fallacious (see Wollheim 1970) and the reasons for saying so of art I believe have some bearing on problems in the interpretation of ritual. Put baldly, art is neither solely in the head or intentions of the artist (the Croce—Collingwood ideal theory) nor solely in the object (the presentational view — although without the productions we would have no art) nor solely in

15

the eye of the beholder (we do not normally speak of a beautiful sunset as a work of art). We require all three, and we also require there to be something peculiar about the intentions that went to make the object and the attitude in beholding it. The previous sentence indicates, albeit barely, those lines of Wollheim's intricate discussion which I will try to apply to ritual in later sections of this chapter.

The alternative view: ritual as an aspect of action

Unable to accept the view that ritual is unambiguously a different kind of action from craft, some anthropologists have suggested that we should say instead that ritual is an aspect of action. Leach has said this clearly: 'Almost every human action that takes place in culturally defined surroundings is divisible in this way: it has a technical aspect which does something and an aesthetic communicative aspect which says something. In those types of behaviour labelled ritual by any of the definitions so far discussed, the aesthetic communicative aspect is particularly prominent but a technical aspect is never entirely absent' (Leach 1968). When he defined ritual in 1966 he distinguished three forms of behaviour which are not genetically determined:

(1) Behaviour which is directed towards specific ends which, *judged by our standards of verification*, produces observable results in a strictly mechanical way . . . we can call this 'rational technical' behaviour.
(2) Behaviour which forms part of a signalling system and which serves to 'communicate information' not because of any mechanical link between means and ends but because of the existence of a culturally defined communication code . . . we can call this 'communicative' behaviour.
(3) Behaviour which is potent in itself in terms of the cultural conventions of the actors but *not* potent in . . . itself . . . we can call this 'magical' behaviour.
. . . For complex reasons which cannot be developed here I myself hold that the distinction between behaviours of class (2) and behaviours of class (3) is either illusory or trivial so that I make the term *ritual* embrace both categories (1966, pp. 403–4).

If we take this as it stands, it is clear that we must consider all signalling and language as ritual. But Fortes commented: 'If ritual is wholly subsumed within the category of "communication" then the policeman on point duty is performing a very explicit and efficacious ritual . . . It is a short step from this to the position that there is no such thing as ritual *per se*, no actions, utterances, ideas and beliefs that belong specifically to a domain we can identify by the term ritual, as opposed to everything else in social life that is non-ritual' (Fortes 1966a, p. 410). Some agreed with Leach's position: Turner for instance gives it assent at the outset of his book *The Drums of Affliction* (1968, p. 1), but he also implicitly responds to the objection which Fortes raised and which is also the objection of our unreflective impulse to categorise some things as clearly ritual and others not. He describes in his book what, by this unreflective impulse,

16

are clearly rituals, and they are not all forms of communication. When he comes later in the same book to say what he means by 'rite' and 'ritual' when referring to Ndembu culture, he writes: 'Prescribed formal behaviour for occasions not given over to technological routine, having reference to beliefs in mystical (or non-empirical) beings or powers. But I shall also define a ritual or *a* kind of ritual as a corpus of beliefs or practices performed by a specific cult association' (p. 15).

The distinction between the instrumental and expressive aspects of human behaviour had been seen by others too as crucial for an understanding of ritual: for Firth when he spoke of ritual as a 'kind of patterned activity oriented towards the control of human affairs, primarily symbolic in character' (1951, p.222); and for Beattie when he wrote: 'Now the chief difference between what we call practical, common sense techniques for doing things, and ritual or "magico-religious" ways of doing them lies basically in the presence or absence of an institutionalized symbolic element in what is done' (1966, p. 202). And he goes on to say with regard to rites: 'This means that the whole procedure, or rite, has an essentially expressive aspect, whether or not it is thought to be effective instrumentally as well' (ibid. p. 203).

A virtue of this view

One persuasive element in this view of ritual is that it gives us insight into what sustains belief. The formality of ritual lies in the fact that it is not simply a solution of immediate technical problems by the most economical means, but the solutions are regarded as having in themselves a certain validity irrespective of their technical concomitants. 'Because of their general validity, apart from the individual situation, they tend to be given a repetitive routinized character which in itself is regarded as strengthening their significance' (Firth 1967, p. 12). If the whole procedure is essentially expressive, as Beattie says, whether or not it is thought to be also effective instrumentally, this expressive aspect makes performance an end in itself. In so far as it is essentially expressive, to have said whatever it expresses is worth while and centrally important, whatever other reasons there may be for believing its purpose accomplished.

The hazards to interpretation

If there is an expressive aspect to almost every action, as there is colour in every object, and that expressive aspect equals ritual, we should not accept the view I gave before (p. 11) that not every action nor all kinds of behaviour are ritual; nor accept the impulse to call some procedures ritual, others not. But I do accept this. If we say rituals are 'essentially expressive' or 'primarily symbolic', we must find out how to know or recognise this essential or primary attribute in some action or procedure. We cannot and we do not just read it off: Henry Suso,

17

silent, would have eaten his quartered apple and we should not have seen his symbolism. And we can read meaning *into* what we see (where it does not belong) and this may tell more about ourselves than about what we have seen. 'The finest view I ever had of a lammergeier occurred today. I came on him but a few feet away silhouetted against a gold-red sunset, magnificent against an horizon stretching for miles and miles into golden infinity. He was quite unconscious of my presence. He sat on a rocky pinnacle facing the setting sun, wings slightly drooping and half-stretched head turned up towards heaven. Was this the phoenix of the ancients, Pliny's "bird of brilliant golden plumage around the neck, the throat adorned with a crest and the head with a tuft of feathers?" Was this lammergeier conscious of his sacred relationship with the sun? The phoenix of the ancients presaged peace everywhere in the land. What I saw this evening seemed to foretell war, a long, bloody war. It was the finest, most beautiful and yet most terrible, the most romantic view of any bird I have seen at any time anywhere' (Colonel Richard Meinertzhagen: My Diary, 26. vii. 1914, Beluchistan).

People may express things unaware that they do so; they may express through action things that they find hard to put in words. When either of these is the case, unless we look attentively, we well may miss the significance of what they do. For they cannot tell us. A madman can fabricate a meaning out of senseless circumstance, a detective piece together the silent evidence of tiny clues that show a significance we should not see unless we looked with that same minute attention and ability he brings to bear on them. If ritual is the expressive aspect in almost every action, on what grounds should we decide to limit or expend our effort, knowing that the rewards in understanding derive so much, but so uncertainly, from the quality of our attention? When we analyse expression, we may choose to stress either the active, indicating side which shows it, or the respondent, passive, perceiving side. With expression, we deal (in anthropology) with people, those who express things and those who understand, interpret or respond to them. The means or vehicle of expression, whether object or action or state − so to speak, the thing recognised as the expression − may be referred to as the sign or the symbol. As we have objects or performances in art, so we must have performance or actions in ritual; and so we must have signs or symbols in expression. The study of ritual is thus, for Turner, tantamount to the study of symbols. But whether we consider an art object, a ritual performance or an expressive symbol, we cannot neglect the terms on either side, viz. who (or possibly what) expresses something, who (or again what) responds to it. When we talk of 'communication' we deal with all three terms (the emitter, the message, the recipient) if we take note of that element of sharing or distributing information contained in its etymology. We must further take note of the intention to convey information, and its successful reception, if we are to distinguish communication from expression, a message from a symptom. The blush which betrays the blusher, the lammergeier portending war, the madman's gibberish are not examples of communication except by a special or loose use of the word (see MacKay 1972): neither the blusher nor the lammergeier intends to convey a message; the madman may intend to convey one but he fails.

The actor may certainly tell where there is a meaning expressed or symbolised. For Nadel this was required if, as anthropologists, we should speak of social symbols. But Goody (1961, p. 156) and Callan (1970, p. 104) have pointed out that we are likely to attribute a 'symbolic' or 'expressive' element either to conspicuously strange behaviour which thereby happens to catch our attention, or to actions we can make no sense of. We cannot make sense of them in terms of an intrinsic means—end relationship and so we assume that the action in question stands for something other than it appears to. 'Symbolic acts are defined in opposition to rational acts and constitute a residual category to which "meaning" is assigned' (Goody 1961, p. 156). This is surely hazardous as a way to recognise the 'essentially expressive' or the 'primarily symbolical' element that characterises ritual. But many anthropologists have felt that there was more to the meaning of what they recognised as ritual than what the actors told them.

What is clear and explicit about ritual is how to do it — rather than its meaning

I noted certain features shared by custom and ritual. First there was the presence of imperative rules. They were explicit and guided action in the sense of constraining or enjoining it. Behaviour that might seem arbitrary was made significant by tradition or convention, at least as far as recognition of identity and the obligation to obey went. The convention or tradition was seen as particular to the community of people to whom it belonged. It was specific to the circumstances that demanded its performance, to the people bound by it: the ruling was not self-evident, or intrinsically dictated by the requirements of the situation. The rule was overt and communally recognised. It might also have an elaborated explanation to account for it or its meaning, but it might not. We recognise immediately that this view at least is consistent with the reports of many anthropologists that people know clearly how to perform their rituals, assert that they know right from wrong performance, yet they do not necessarily provide an explanation in words of what they express, what they communicate or what they symbolise by their rituals. The ruling is explicit but its meaning may be implicit; may be esoteric, or established for all to know, or forgotten and unknown; tolerant of interpretation on many levels and by many individuals, or intolerant of any but the single 'true' meaning established by tradition within that culture. The ruling is public, clear and social; its meaning may be so, or it may be indeterminate, private, various and individual.

The alerting quality of ritual

A constraint is introduced into the ordinary flow of everyday life which limits

19

freedom, requires alertness and attention: the presence of rules bounds or marks out an area as significant. Failure to recognise the situation until too late, failure to conform or the actions done wrongly, may be expected to be met by sanction or misfortune, and a lapse prompts embarrassment, shame or anxiety.

That the rules are not self-evident in the circumstances, but artificial and requiring to be taught and learned, that they gain their validity essentially by reference to tradition, is the basis of that quality which we discern as the arbitrary or irrational in much ritual. It alerts us, the observers, as it does those to whom the ritual belongs that they are within a peculiar arena, peculiar in the intransitive sense, where gestures, actions and behaviour may have significance which they would not otherwise have. Elements that are often to be observed in ritual — the aesthetic side of colour, noise and smell; the decorations, singing, the aromatic plants, the formality, stiffness or strangeness of gesture; and the tension translated by a great volume of excited chatter or by a constrained silence; or the very secrecy which I have mentioned in connection with penis-bleeding, the presence of esoteric or hidden knowledge, the irrationality or non-sense of what would seem arbitrary action (*omne ignotum pro magnifico*) — these are all elements which alert the attention and make ritual peculiar, saying 'Look and listen', not simply 'see and hear'. We respond to these elements as observers: they are the real grounds for that unreflecting impulse which convinces us immediately, intuitively, that we deal with ritual. It is not by a process of reasoning out the rationality of their actions, and being left with a residuum unaccounted for, but because we sense the positive alerting peculiar aspect of ritual which calls to us for attention as it does to the performers, but to them more variously and subtly than to us for it comes within their culture.

I have presented the argument for peculiarity and attention-identifying ritual as though it were something we would feel confident about being sure to recognise. But such confidence as this is clearly not what our experience offers us when we ask whether we know surely how to distinguish between the different varieties of custom — for instance between etiquette, ceremony and ritual. I rejected earlier the argument that there was an either/or distinction between ritual and craft. My dissatisfaction with the view that ritual constituted the expressive, communicative aspect of almost any action or behaviour (though it contains an important and persuasive insight) arose from its inadequacy in showing us where to look for something expressed or communicated, given that there is much we are not told by the actors in the society to satisfy our curiosity, and given that we may be able to understand some expression or communication only if we look into it very carefully. The view as it stands does not tell us how to direct our efforts. Nor does it explain why it is we feel that some procedures are so clearly ritual, even in the absence of interpretation by the actors.

The quality of seeming out of the ordinary alerts us, but it is present in varying degree in different rituals. There are rituals which have this peculiar arresting quality and come clearly in the centre of the field we recognise as ritual. Others seem to have it less and lie towards the periphery or far from the centre, and we are uncertain whether to take them as ritual or mere ceremony or etiquette. We can appreciate the quality and it is this that encourages us to say of some rituals that they contain a 'primary' or 'essential' expressive aspect. The decision is not one about whether some behaviour has or has not this quality but about the relative degree to which it shows it. For didactic purposes we may speak of polar or ideal types and with Firth agree that ceremony is 'a species of ritual in which the emphasis is more upon symbolic acknowledgement and demonstration of a social situation than upon the efficacy of the procedures in modifying that situation . . . Whereas other ritual procedures are believed to have a validity of their own, ceremonial procedures, while formal in character, are not believed in themselves to sustain the situation or effect a change in it' (1967, p. 12). But in granting this distinction 'between theoretical types, we recognise that in practice they may merge into or alternate with each other' (ibid.). My purpose in dwelling on the peculiar quality in ritual, however, is not to claim that it allows us to distinguish between the different varieties of custom but to point out that it acts as an indicator showing us where to concentrate our efforts in interpretation, especially in those situations where we would think to go beyond the information of actors from within the society. Almost inevitably as observers we respond to it though we may not pick out explicitly or precisely, even to ourselves, how our attention was caught. I shall come back later to consider the peculiar quality of ritual from the point of view of the actors and audience within the society.

The field encompassed by what any anthropologist would accept as ritual has great variety. It would range from the brief act of a single performer alone in his garden to the great occasion when, before a multitude, the priests perform their solemn duty. In what is general to such a range, from the most private to the most public, many particulars must for sure be lost to us. We cannot say that every ritual performance has an audience. But we can say there is a public aspect to performance in the sense that the ritual (which anthropologists study) is ruled and taught and learned. The rules require recognition and transmission by some community, whether or not a restricted one within the society. Not all have equal access to the creed or dogma which may go with the ritual; not all have equal access to its performance. But as there are rules recognised by a community, so there is a public social aspect to ritual which exists independently of the particular individual in a particular situation who performs it (cf. the quotation from Firth (1967) cited on p. 17). An obsessional neurotic man may express his fears through private ritual and we may come to understand his ritual as symptomatic of these fears. With this understanding we may learn about the personality and experience of the performer but learn little about the society in which he lives. As we examine the rules guiding ritual action in a community we learn about the society and the performance, but not about the individuals who perform it. But we may also learn something about the individuals from the way they choose to work the rules and from what they say about the ritual where this goes beyond what is established as public or esoteric knowledge. The elaborated interpretations of ritual by men like Ogotemmeli (in Griaule 1965) and Muchona (in Turner 1959), I would suppose, are partly revelations of their personal experience of their culture; they tell us about themselves as individuals, as well as telling us about their culture.

The idea of type and token applied to ritual performance

The explicit side of ritual lies in the rules for its observance and in any dogma that may be attached to it. These are public, not personal or individual. Without this acknowledged formality, neither performers nor observers could identify *a* ritual, or speak of its performance as the enactment of the ritual, or identify the same ritual repeated on another occasion. We recognise the performance of a ritual as like the performance of a play or a piece of music: the performance is related to the ritual as a token to a type. Not every property that can be predicated of the performance must necessarily belong to the type. The rules establish the type of the ritual as the score does the symphony or the text the play, but in their performance there is essentially an element of interpretation; the performance (token) may have properties in excess of those of the type. As Wollheim has pointed out (1970, pp. 90–100), we have various terms for generic entities and the things which fall under them, viz. general and particular, class and member, universal and instance, type and token. 'With types we find the relationship between the generic entity and its elements at its most intimate; for not merely is the type present in all its tokens like the universal in all its instances, but for much of the time we think and talk of the type as though it were itself a kind of token, though a peculiarly important or pre-eminent one' (p. 92). And he goes on to note that perhaps the central set of circumstances in which we postulate types 'is where we can correlate a class of particulars with a piece of human invention: these particulars may then be regarded as tokens of a certain type . . . At one end [of the spectrum] we have the case where a particular is produced, and is then copied: at the other end, we have the case where a set of instructions is drawn up which, if followed, give rise to an indefinite number of particulars . . . There are many ways of arranging the cases — according, say, to the degree of human intention that enters into the proliferation of the type, or according to the degree of match that exists between the original piece of invention and the tokens that flow from it' (p. 94).

The setting of a type and its interpretation: recognition of intention and genre

As we read that the type is thought of or spoken of as though it were itself a kind of token, though a peculiarly important or pre-eminent one, we hear again echoing that concern in ritual and its exegesis with origin or first performance, with charter and first cause (cf. the *aition* in Greek drama; Murray 1946, p. 41). The type of a ritual is given. It is an invention yet it does not self-evidently fit the circumstances. And the type is often seen not as a human invention, but as an ancestral or divine invention for the ordering of human conduct in certain social affairs. The ritual type is a blueprint which ideally will fulfil its promise when repeated in its tokens. As Tambiah has written; 'It would be more in line with [Malinowski's] evidence to say that Trobriand magic is a testimony to the creativity of thought, that its logic is anticipatory effect . . . The Trobrianders regularly enjoy good harvests and *kula* success . . . [They] practice prospective magic because they have engaged in systematically conceived activities in the past and because they intend to engage in them in the future. But when fate does withhold the regularity of events . . . the Trobriand system deals with misfortune *ex post*, not in terms of "laws of nature" but in terms of deviation from an ideal order of social relations' (Tambiah 1968, pp. 200–1).

In the performance of a ritual, we allow for an element of interpretation by the performer. In responding to it, we must further note that there may be a range of ways in which the spectator or audience can take the performance. But to mistake the 'intention' of the ritual performance may seriously distort the meaning we extract from it. To attend to the kinetic play of red and green and yellow traffic lights and indicators and experience it aesthetically is to go against their 'intention' and crash; to see the policeman's gestures as droll mime is also not wise. The older classifications of custom into magical or religious ritual, ceremony, etiquette, etc. are classifications of different genres in custom, particularly from the standpoint of their 'intention' or 'address' to spirits, the achievement of a specific purpose, placation, public demonstration, or acknowledgement of a situation, etc. The genre may be more or less closely defined but always as an ideal type. It is not the case that any and every particular custom will fit easily or unambiguously under only one heading in these classifications. And anthropologists have come to no general agreement with the fiat of one classifier over all the others. But this does not mean that we can neglect the 'intention' or 'address' of a ritual if we would make just interpretation of its meaning. As the 'genre is determined by the conditions established between the poet and his public' (Frye 1971, p. 247), so in one ritual the performer addresses a demanding spirit, while in another he may copy the plan established by some ancient precedent, solitary and bent to his purpose of faithful repetition, addressing himself wholly to the proper and successful achievement of his task. There are rituals which cannot be performed without an audience as there are declarations which cannot be signed without a witness.

If we would speak of communication in ritual, we must recognise that in some instances there is the actor's intention to communicate with a watching, listening spirit and there are known ways in which the spirit may be recognised to answer, to make demands expecting an appropriate ritual answer. There are rituals in which the performer addresses his audience, and others in which he is overheard. There are rituals whose invisible and jealous creator is thought to oversee the proper performance of his invention, and there are others whose creators are concealed, absent or unknown, but which must be performed before the acknowledged guardians of a tradition. We may wish to speak of communication but we must be concerned to distinguish the differences in intention and the direction of sharing information; the modes of statement and reply; the sense in which the performers in ritual, like those in a play, cannot be answered by their audience, though the performance of the peculiar series of events is intended to work on the audience by means of a complex of signs and stimulations. I will return later to this issue of communication in ritual. For the present, I have only wished to suggest that a recognition of the genre or style in ritual is intrinsic to its proper understanding.

The problems of an analysis that goes beyond what the anthropologist was told

One way to phrase the general problem of the anthropologist's interpretation of ritual is to ask whether it is a matter of discovery or persuasion. Should we expect reasons to be offered in justification for some interpretation? Or to put it crudely, are we sometimes convinced by the eloquence of the anthropologist recounting the thoughts, intuitions and associations aroused in him by the performance? In other words, is it sometimes to be purely a matter of taste whether we accept or reject his interpretation? The question, of course, arises when his interpretation either goes beyond what his informants say or overrides it. Nadel's answer or ruling about social symbols is not satisfactory to most of us, particularly if we extend it to the general issue of understanding ritual. Things may be expressed in complex ways and it is often hard for the actor to put them exactly into words. There is the further argument that they are sometimes expressed in complex ways because it is the only way or the best way they can be expressed. There is no way except through music for some to express certain things: we cannot put a perfume into words. This argument, like that on the heresy of paraphrase in art, would assert that it may not be possible to translate some expression adequately into another medium, or into words. We must expect our informants to be at times inarticulate or silent about part of what the ritual means to them, or does to them, or makes them feel. But we can get closer to it by careful study and analysis, just as we could convey something about the identity of a perfume if we paid it close attention and had skill with words.

We are simple-minded if we think that we can give 'pure descriptions' of ritual

There is the additional problem of the description of ritual observed. Both we, the observers, and they, the performers, say that the ritual has properties which are incompatible with the physical actions and material objects involved. What we say is that the ritual action expresses something more than it seems to, or that it represents something other than it is. What I see, for example, is a man spit into the air: what I learn is that he is about to invoke a spirit or he is attracting its attention. The fronds of a coconut leaf are tied in a particular way around the stem of a tree; they brush me as I pass; but, if I were a Gnau man, as I noticed the touch I might feel anxiety and foreboding. Without recognition, it is only the touch of a leaf, or the man spitting. As the songs of birds or a strange language are only sounds or noises in our ears, expressing nothing to us, so the ritual gestures or acts or objects have only their directly perceptible properties unless we recognise them for what they are. Gnau men often spit, but not all their spitting is anything but spitting; not all tied leaves mark something protected by a spell. We, and they, require additional cues to recognise that a particular man spitting is doing something more than just spitting. Without the additional cues, it is just a spit, as it is if we fail to recognise the cues. But if we know them, the spit may express something more to us or mean more. Without the element of attention, awareness or recognition that something is a work of ritual, those expressive or representational properties which are not simply given by its perceptible properties may be lost on us. A minute description of observed ritual limited to the properties it presented and excluding any element of expression recognised would be something parallel to the minute description of a canvas as the concatenation of particular oily pigments in different-sized patches on a flat surface, when that canvas was a painting in perspective of a landscape. But it is hard to see it so flat and meaningless, as it is almost impossible to hear the words of our own language as pure sound. The 'facts' can not be simply or sharply separated from their interpretation, nor description kept 'pure' and unaccompanied by recognition.

The alerting quality in ritual acts on the participants

The peculiar quality of ritual, which I emphasised earlier from the point of view of the outside observer, is also important to the members of a society. The things like formality of ruling, rigidity, decoration, special gesture, serve to alert them and create that expectancy intrinsic to the recognition of ritual expression, the recognition that what goes on within the arena marked out by these accredited signs may have a special meaning, that the actions involved may be taken at more than their face value, may express something beyond what they would seem to. But the cues may be mistaken. We might suppose meaning or expression where there was only error. We might suppose a whole symbolism to bloodletting where there was only an erroneous medical theory concerning the accumulation of putrid humour. If we were to learn that swabbing the arm before the injection made no difference to infection at the site, we would not then have reason to look for the expressiveness of swabbing. The lammergeier on a rock before the sunset itself expresses nothing. We require positive grounds on which to search out expression, and so do the members of the community.

The grounds on which we understand expression

I now turn to the question of how actions or physical objects become expressive. The human face and limbs and gestures are first among the things we would hold to be expressive, and we are quick to see, and to respond to, the tiny signs which betray a certain state of mind or feeling in someone else. Such tiny signs are just the sort of thing we recognise most subtly and respond to without being able to say clearly why or being able to analyse them precisely. Ritual involves human actions and performances with objects. At first sight it might seem that we might escape the difficulty of answering how it comes about that we attribute expressive properties to things since we deal with human actions. But the paradox is this: although ritual involves human gestures and actions (the prime medium of expression) it is conventionalised. Indeed a main feature of ritual is its formality. Malinowski mistook this and looked to see the performer's emotions let out, translated into ritual action or canalised in response to it. At the end of a public lecture, I may be expected to clap to show my appreciation and gratitude to the lecturer. I will be taken to have expressed this if I clap, however inauthentically my clapping corresponds to my real feelings of disagreement or displeasure with what he said (see Gombrich 1966). The expressiveness of clapping cannot be accounted for in terms of my condition when I do it. The expressiveness of ritual does not lie exclusively in the mental condition of the performer when he performs it. The ritual act is not necessarily a symptom of the performer's mental state. Nor does the expressiveness lie, as a second view might have it, in its capacity to produce a certain state of mind or feeling in the spectator or performer. The cacophony of clapping may sound hateful to me, not appreciative. In England the fans might whistle if they liked it, in France they would whistle to boo. A ritual of mourning is not expressive of grief because the performers must necessarily feel sad to play their part in it, nor because it necessarily arouses sadness in those who watch it. Just because ritual involves human actions and behaviour, we do not have a sure short-cut to understanding, through asking either the performers what they feel when they do it, or the spectators what they feel when they watch it.

In consequence the problems in interpreting ritual expression are not so different from those of interpreting expression in a work of art which is purely a physical object. The performance, just like an inanimate object, may itself be held to manifest expressive properties independently of the emotions or responses of particular individuals in their dealings with it. This argument is linked to my earlier distinction between the social nature of the ritual which anthropologists study and the private ritual of the obsessed man. In the social case we learn and understand about the performance and the culture rather than

26

the mental state of the individual performing it; in the obsessional's case we learn about the performer as an anxious, scared or unhappy individual rather than about his society. The second aspect of this point is that it supports the stand taken earlier that there may be things in the ritual of a society which lie outside the immediate awareness of the current particular performers or spectators within the society. I will come back to this later in connection with the view that ritual may serve as a code or device to transmit and recover information.

But despite what I have written about the state of mind of a *particular* performer or spectator, we should not accept the claim that a particular ritual was expressive of grief if we learnt that no one had ever felt grief when he performed or watched it. 'For our confidence that a certain kind of object was what we would produce if we experienced grief would be shaken by the fact that not one (or very few) had actually been produced in grief: equally our confidence that in other circumstances we should feel grief in looking at them could hardly survive the fact that no one (or scarcely anyone) ever had' (Wollheim 1970, p. 43).

Expression is essentially symptomatic or indicative. Our understanding of expression is grounded in our perceptions of the human body as the outer sign of an inner state (mental or emotional). Certain gestures or tears are so directly linked with our experience of grief as to seem naturally produced by that inner state. We may think of an object as expressive of sadness because, when we are sad, it seems to match or correspond to what we experience inwardly. When our sadness passes, the object may remind us of it poignantly or revive it in us. On the one hand, we can endow an object with expressive meaning because 'we credit it with a particular look which bears a marked analogy to some look that the human body wears and that is constantly conjoined with an inner state' (ibid. p. 49). We find a mirror to our mood and come to speak of objects or things done which match it as being expressive of that mood. Or we may make the link artificially and establish it by the repeated conjunction of that inner state with exposure to some outer object.

Our observations of the human body are the source of what we understand as 'natural expression'. Because we share with those we study some perceptions of the form, the senses and the limitations of our common frame, we can understand to some degree intuitively the expressive meaning of human gesture, and by extension other forms of human expression. This may be true in the weak sense that once we know what a gesture or a ritual action expresses we can see that it does so; but not in the strong sense that from simple observation we can invariably know what it expresses. Even tears may not be a sign of grief, as Radcliffe Brown was to learn among the Andaman Islanders (1922, p. 239); even tears may not be so spontaneously, so naturally expressive as we might suppose (cf. Nadel 1951, pp. 64–8).

If even with tears we may still need collateral information to establish their significance, what intuition of 'naturally' expressive meaning can hope to stand established if it be nothing else than the conviction of the anthropologist? Gombrich (1960, 1965) has put forward a powerful argument concerning the way we come to understand expression. To understand it aright, if we are not told by the performer, or if we would go beyond what he says, we must have some knowledge of the range of alternatives from which a choice was made. If I have only one tie in the world, and it is red, I cannot show that I mourn by wearing a black tie; nor would some man be right to assume I flout another feeling because I wear it: if I would wear a tie, I must wear a red one – I have no other. If I had only two ties, one red and one blue, my choice of the blue one might be understandable as the fitter match to my mood, for there is some basis in natural expression underlying the communication of emotion in terms of an ordering relationship of the type 'darker than' or 'lower than'. The move towards one end of the series correlates with specific inner states.

But as I widen the gamut of colours to include dark brown, ultramarine, deep crimson, purple and indigo ties, my particular choice becomes harder to make, harder to predict, harder to understand intuitively. Clearly one important thing that a ritual ruling does is to narrow my field of choice and the consequent uncertainty which would attend the wide spectrum I might otherwise have to choose from: in fact, in this instance it narrows it down to one proper colour, black, whose expressive meaning is clear and unambiguous. This point is an expansion of the earlier one that custom explicitly guides conduct; the narrowing of the field of choice or the inflexibility introduced by convention may bring significance where before the meaning of an action would have been more arbitrary and unclear.

Now suppose I decide to play the game of matching colour to mood with someone of another culture, and, to make the point more clearly, suppose that we must indicate the colour by naming an appropriate English wild flower. While the person from another culture may know the names of only three differently coloured English wild flowers, I may know ten. I would quite possibly mistake the significance of his choice of a particular flower to match a given mood if I suppose he selects one from the same range of flowers as I do. In a more complex game of such correspondences, the degree and intensity of assent we gave to each other's choices of, say, what flower, animal, colour or bird best matched some mood would provide a measure of our common culture (cf. Gombrich 1965). To understand the significance of some expression we need to know something about the range of alternatives from which a choice was made, the repertoire. As well as this, the example illustrates how we depend on collateral information to understand expression and suggests (what is anyway obvious from experience) that such understanding, in the context of another culture, depends on learning. Learning, not intuition: the anthropologist is more a true connoisseur as he learns more about the range of expressive modes and media used in the ritual of a society, the ritual styles and genres, and how they relate to other aspects of life and experience in that society.

The understanding of representation

Similar arguments apply to our capacity to see one thing as like another or to see it as resembling another; in other words, our capacity to understand representation. I began with the case of expression in ritual rather than representation, because it seems to me harder to provide the grounds on which we might, as outsiders, attribute expressive meaning to ritual, since the response we are concerned with is feeling rather than recognition, affect rather than cognition. We and they can feel something intensely without being able to understand clearly why: the intensity of the response bears no necessary relation to the clarity with which we or they understand it or can talk about it. Gombrich's argument that we require collateral information and knowledge of the repertoire applies also to representation. A cowrie-shell does not naturally represent something else: placed in the eye-socket of a skull, we have no difficulty in seeing it as an eye. With only cowrie-shells at my disposal, I may use cowrie-shells for both the eyes and ears of the skull. But if I have pebbles and cowrie-shells, I may choose pebbles for the eyes and cowrie-shells for the ears. I look for the best match in the circumstances. For the maker of a representation, his activity involves looking ahead among the range of possible alternatives (so to speak, the media available to him) for the thing which will best serve as a substitute for what he wishes to represent, a substitute that will do for his purpose and be seen as he intends. If he intends to represent something clearly he will try to establish it by setting it round with clues which reduce the uncertainty as to how an observer will take his representation. When we see a cowrie-shell as substitute for an eye, we are prepared to neglect a large number of features which the shell has and the eye has not. In the eye-socket of a skull, the setting prompts us to see what in the shell is like an eye and neglect what is not.

The part played by intention in these substitutions is rich and strange. If I intended to represent an eye, I could try to make sure that you would see my choice as I intended by silently giving it a setting that reduced ambiguity as much as possible. I could, of course, also tell you what it was meant to be. In some exposition, for example, I could draw a circle and tell you that this was to be taken as an eye, and, indeed, for my particular purpose it might do quite well to stand for it. Later as we talked, I might change and say that the circle now represented a woman. Again it might serve my second purpose adequately. What is to count as a representation can be established by a convention. Even if I had chosen a bold black X to stand for an eye or a woman, you might still have been able to follow my exposé. But suppose that I had drawn genealogies before an anthropological audience and had presented this black cross and said to them it stood for a woman. Even then they might have understood my exposé, but they would, I am sure, have been curious to know why, before anthropologists, I chose a black cross to stand for a woman.

Clarity or mystery

The final point put into the example above is there to lead into an attempt to show how symbols may gain mystery. A preceding part of this account has been primarily concerned with the difficulty we face in attributing expressive or symbolic significance to ritual when the actors tell us nothing or we wish to go beyond what they say. But of course they often tell us something, or there is an obvious straightforward meaning or use attached to what they do, or some object is involved that is quite ordinary and recognisable. But the action or the object is inappropriate and out of place: it makes no ordinary or obvious sense put in the ritual as it is. It confuses. It invites speculation, just as my use of a black cross to stand for a woman in a genealogical diagram would disconcert an audience of anthropologists. By purposefully going against a convention, or ordinary practice, or common knowledge, I can mystify or make something ordinary peculiar.

Now it may be my purpose to make a representation that is clear and un-ambiguous; or alternatively I may seek to mystify; or I may try to intimate a mystery so that it seems graspable by the mind by investing it with perceptible form. If clarity is my purpose, I will set my object round with clues to its meaning; if I intend mystery, I will isolate it. A single straight line drawn on a sheet of white paper might represent a match or a distant horizon: we would need further clues to decide. Thus it may be a device of ritual to isolate some familiar object or action, as though within a frame, by means of those special features which alert the attention of the spectator, and so invite him to discover relations or aspects of that object or action which he would not otherwise or ordinarily see. As a connoisseur recognises the style, so the anthropologist can learn or seek to judge whether what is aimed at is clear, unambiguous rep-resentation; or whether he, just like those within the society, is being asked to speculate and perceive something familiar in a new light. Isolation and cognitive dissonance may be recognisable as techniques at work in ritual.

Huizinga wrote in his beautiful chapters on the religious imagination and symbolism in its decline in the later Middle Ages: 'Symbolist thought permits an infinity of relations between things. Each thing may denote a number of distinct ideas by its different special qualities, and a quality may also have several symbolic meanings. The highest conceptions have symbols by the thousand. Nothing is too humble to represent and glorify the sublime. The walnut signifies Christ: the sweet kernel is His divine nature, the green and pulpy outer peel is His humanity, the wooden shell between is the cross. Thus all things raise the thoughts to the eternal' (1965, p. 198). This idea of the deeper significance in ordinary things is familiar to those who take part in and those who study ritual. The ambiguity of things isolated or out of place may rouse the imagination to make a leap which will resolve what has been made enigmatic about them. By setting ordinary things within a ritual field, contrived and peculiar, asking

30

for attention, the mind may attend to the thing as a sign or symbol which may yield up information about a mystery that seems to come within grasp when invested with perceptible form. 'Instead of looking for the relation between two things by following the hidden detours of their causal connexions, thought makes a leap and discovers their relation' (ibid. p. 195). 'For now we see through a glass darkly: but then face to face.' Instead of seeing the object or action in a conventional way, we 'ungate' our vision and search its different special qualities, which have no relevance in the ordinary economy of our perceptual and practical dealings with it, but which with close attention, by some sort of short-circuit of thought, may provide an intimation of a mystery.

The lines demarcating different concepts are broken down so that we tend 'to incorporate into the notion of a definite something all the notions connected with it by any relation or similitude whatsoever'. The very notion of metaphor demands that two concepts are distinct, but despite their separateness are yet linked by some quality common to them both. It is on the ground that they share this quality that we say they are the same. But it is only as we recognise that the two concepts are distinct that we can speak of their *metaphoric* identity. The virtue of metaphor is that it isolates and emphasises the quality which provides the ground of some identity between the two, for it is only by neglecting or disregarding those other features which force them into separate categories that we can speak of their identity. Though we accept the identity on one level, or see it as a revelation, we are troubled by a multiplicity of features which in other ways conflict with that identity; and perhaps we seek to reconcile them. The feeling of richness, discovery and elusiveness that goes with certain symbols seems to me to be in part psychologically accounted for by this troubled insight.

Gombrich (1965), from whom I learnt of Bruner's notion of 'gating' and 'ungating' (Bruner 1957), also describes how the spectator may attend to a main sequence of meaning in some representation or performance, following it by ordinary logical thought, but as he does so his attention is suddenly deflected by some echo to the meaning, or by some cluster of associations or potential contexts. By the device of making certain things in ritual the objects of peculiar attention, the spectator is prompted to speculate, he is invited to 'ungate' the way he sees some object so that he is free to look for further and further echoes to its sense. And this also contributes to that feeling of meanings richer but less precise than those to be talked of clearly which some have said is the hallmark of the 'true' symbol.

But after all this has been said, I would reassert that the anthropologist is not free to assume that everything occurring in ritual aims at mystery and has many meanings. The style in ritual may tend towards clarity, overt meaning and lack of ambiguity; or for certain purposes aim to disconcert, confuse or fascinate. There are suggestive indications when the spectator is invited to 'ungate' through the isolation and situational oddity of some action or object in ritual. The emphasis I gave earlier to the peculiar quality in ritual has been altered by these reflections on how it acts on members of the society to set a frame around certain actions and to arouse their attention.

The analogies with language, code and communication

I have discussed some of the difficulties we face in attributing expressive or representational properties to rites. The burden of these difficulties is that we are not able to say for sure, nor do the actors in the society always assert clearly, what message some rite carries. Its meaning is often stated variously by different interpreters, although in broad terms they may tend towards the same general sense. We read detailed and minute analyses of ritual with curious, sometimes surprised, attention, for the meanings are rarely obvious, and we follow the reports of varied and differing interpretations of the same events undisturbed by any pressing sense that we must reconcile these differences or judge one right and another wrong. In effect, we allow or expect a latitude, variety or complexity in the interpretation of ritual meaning which is different from what we would expect of language. To speak of ritual communicating messages as language does is to suppose to be resolved a series of special problems which are not. The analogy with language was perhaps not intended in a strict sense; instead it would turn us away from linguistics towards sprouting semiology for guidance, and have us take as our objective to describe and analyse the means of communication involved. For the moment we must be concerned with the means by which messages are passed, for we cannot yet perceive what entities in ritual would be remotely parallel to lexical or phonemic units or discern stable rules governing their combination when some message is to be transmitted. If eventually we were to distinguish something like units or entities of a code and the rules for using them, we might come to speak of the system or systems involved.

Is it easy to identify a symbol?

Turner has regarded ritual as a configuration of symbols in which the symbol is 'the smallest unit of specific structure in Ndembu ritual' (1965). He considered the symbol as the atom of ritual behaviour overloaded with meaning and efficacy. If we were sure when something (an action? an object? an idea?) was a symbol, we might be able to identify these units. But it is just the doubt surrounding this identification of symbol which I have discussed in relation to selective attention, and the task of identifying expressive and representational properties. Also, we are not much helped in identifying these units by being told that they are symbols — e.g. is the initiation rite taken as a whole a symbol of rebirth, or some specific item in it, or a sequence of gestures and body positionings selected from the whole? The symbolism often can only be grasped through a complicated interplay of relations and stimuli. I am not clear what unit Turner would refer to: for instance, if rebirth is symbolised, is the unit to

32

be the complex of relations and stimuli which manage to convey this single idea, or some action such as crawling out from between another person's legs, which is the symbol unit having perhaps different meanings in different situations? Symbols are not discrete objects. 'There are strictly speaking no symbolic objects, only symbolic relationships' (Firth 1973, p. 245).

Is ritual really a form of communication, or a code?

The notion of communication is popular now, but it is difficult to use except loosely. There is, as I have said, some uncertainty about the messages conveyed by ritual and this uncertainty tends to increase as the analysis becomes more fine and detailed, and the rite taken part by part. We may suppose there is communication by means of a code, but we have little or no sense of the conditions in which we might consider it to be misused or garbled. If we assume there must be a system to it, implying rules to organise its operation, we might expect to recognise 'ungrammatical' or wrong usage of the code: but instead obscurity or uncertainty about the message is tolerated, even valued. *Omne ignotum pro magnifico*. The use of the term 'code' does not seem to imply the expectation that we should eventually be able to decipher any message in the code and put it straight and true *en clair*.

If we neglect these difficulties, we have still to face the question of who communicates to whom in ritual. I have already noted that there are varieties to the direction of address and response in different ritual genres according to the intentions and beliefs of the performers. I have already noted how the rules governing proper performance may involve a recognition of social identity, and in this way the performance may be taken as asserting loyalty, obedience or a claim to certain rights; in limited ways the audience of the performance can show that they accept and understand it thus. If the communicative aspect of ritual meant only this, then the sense of a message intended and received would be apt. In this respect the 'communication' of performers to spectators, just as in the theatre, is often overwhelmingly one-sided because the audience can respond only in severely limited ways to the performance. Transmitter and receiver cannot reverse roles using the same code. The similarity of ritual performance to theatrical performance is obviously close.

The likeness of ritual to the performance of a play

When we watch a play we are affected by the words of the text, the gestures, movements and intonation of the actors, the costumes and the décor, and the lighting. The play is a contrivance of great complexity in which most varied stimuli work on us to produce or spark off a complex response. The varied stimuli of light, colour, gesture, movement, voice, language work on us in different ways to set up this complex response. As Mounin (1970, p. 92) suggests

33

for the theatre, it may be more helpful to think generally of what happens in ritual in terms of stimulation rather than communication. Both performers and spectators are acted on or affected by a performance, although in different ways. But the 'meaning' of a ritual performance or a play is much further off from the meaning of a purely linguistic message than it is from the 'meaning' of an event. We interpret a ritual or the performance of a play rather in the way we interpret an event at which we are present or in which we take part: we do not 'read' the event as we experience it or as we reflect on it; we do not 'decode' it to make sense of it or understand it. We are affected by it. It may set us thinking. Rituals, like plays, are contrived usually as a very special sort of sequence of events, and designed to produce an effect on those present at their performance. By notions about code and the communication of messages or information, we are led to a preoccupation with the intellectual aspect of the response to ritual, so that other aspects of the response which ritual brings about are neglected. But these other aspects are also part of what ritual was contrived to bring about.

If we choose to concentrate on the tripartite notion of communication (emitter, message medium, receiver), we should need to distinguish (1) whom the performers believe they communicate with or intend to communicate with, and what expectation of answer they have; (2) the sense in which the performer communicates with his spectator—audience; and (3) the sense in which there is an author, originator or creator of the ritual who, though not present and perhaps unnamed, just as the author of a play is not present at its performance and may have been dead for three hundred years, through the medium of his text and his instructions for performance, may be said loosely to 'communicate' with those who perform or see his design realised. Again this is a quite one-sided kind of communication. In the case of ritual, as I sought to bring out in the discussion of type and token, and the special stress on origin or inventor, the originator is often seen as a spirit, an ancestor or that unnamed collectivity of those who passed before and left behind what we would call a tradition. The anthropologist and stranger sees an author such as tradition, or a spirit, or an ancestor, as the product of innumerable and uncountable and unknowable past exchanges between people of decisions, ideas, evaluations and experiences which over time have been reformulated, selected, refined, transmitted to eventuate in some formal and accepted ruling to guide action in a certain kind of situation. In effect we call this authorship that of society or culture; and the acceptance of the tradition, its own mostly unknown history, the agreement to abide by these distinctive rules, is part of what characterises a particular society or culture. So what would seem to be argued in the case (3) of 'communication' in ritual is that the 'author' is society or culture and is 'communicating' with its present members. Phrased like that, it sounds mildly absurd, or at least a very partial account of ritual: for those who perform it, the ritual is more clearly something practical providing guidance on how to cope with some particular situation of difficulty or importance, and it is correspondingly valued. The ritual offers a contrived and complex experience; the view of it as stimulation would include both those aspects of response which give it value as a means of coping with some situation and also its communicative and expressive elements. To limit ritual to its communicative aspect would exclude and falsify its significance for those who perform it. Ritual is not done solely to be interpreted: it is also done (and from the point of view of the performers this may be more important) to resolve, alter or demonstrate a situation.

What features of a code can we find in ritual?

With this said, we can return to the analogy of ritual with communication, as it were, between an author (society) and its present members, and especially to the attempt to see the particular content of the rite as carrying messages of diverse sorts as though in code. There are a number of features that might be required or implied in the analogy of ritual to a code. A first feature is to be able to paraphrase or understand it (as for instance with semaphore). If we claim to understand a coded message and are then asked what it says, we should be able to say. This feature does not seem to fit well with the experience of those who perform ritual or the evidence of anthropologists who observe it. The second feature has to do with the notion of code as a means to transmit information in a systematic way that involves ideas of likelihood or probability. On the basis of one sign or set of signs we are able to make a preferred guess as to a subsequent sign or signs. The code has constraints or rules which give rise to some expectancy about what will follow. If one sign inevitably follows another, the following sign does not convey new information: it is redundant. On the other hand, if it represents a choice between a limited set of alternatives, the particular choice made is informative; it resolves a preceding doubt about what would follow (Cherry 1966, ch. 5). The elements of constraint, of limited choice, of rule-bound sequence, of expectancy all fit with those features of ritual which I have discussed earlier in relation to the significance introduced into actions by limiting their arbitrariness, to the narrowing of the range of appropriate sequences, and to setting it round with alerting signs. The third feature of a code is that it serves as a device to economise in transmitting information. A code enables one to fix, transmit, recall and retrieve more complex information by means of certain ciphering and deciphering rules. By adopting certain conventions, I can draw a scale plan of a room which stores condensed information to be drawn on later when I have gone somewhere else and my memory of the room is blurred. The ideas of restricted codes used by Bernstein (1965) and Douglas (1970, ch. 2) and of symbols as condensates with many meanings used by Sapir (1934) and Turner (1965) belong with this feature of the code.

Leach (1966) provides a clear short statement exemplifying how ritual coding may serve in the economy of primitive knowledge.

I think it goes almost without saying that concepts such as Nature and Culture do not occur in primitive languages, yet primitive people must still be aware of the distinction between Nature/Culture . . . But how? . . . Raw meat, cooked meat, fresh vegetable, putrid vegetable are all explicit concrete things, but placed in a pattern these few categories can serve to express the highly abstract idea of this contrast between cultural process and natural process. Furthermore, this patterning can be expressed *either* in *words* (*raw*, *cooked*, *fresh*, *putrid*) and displayed in a myth, *or* alternatively it can be expressed in *things* with ritual manipulation of appropriate objects. *In such ways as this the patterning of ritual procedures can serve as a complex store of information* [p. 406] . . . The more condensed message forms which are characteristic of ritual action are generally appropriate to all forms of communication in which speaker and listener are in face-to-face relations and share a common body of knowledge about the context of the situation. In these restricted circumstances, which are normal in primitive society, the condensed and multifaceted concepts to which I have been referring do not lead to ambiguity. In any event in ritual sequences the ambiguity latent in symbolic condensation tends to be eliminated again by the device of thematic repetition and variation. This corresponds to the communication engineer's technique of overcoming noisy interference by the use of multiple redundancy. (p. 408)

One of the aspects of economy in this view is that to do with meeting the need to ensure that useful knowledge will be passed down over generations. People who cannot fix all that has been found out by writing it down *in extenso* yet manage to preserve and transmit it encapsulated in another, condensed, more surely memorisable, code form. A second aspect of the notion of economy is that the practical demands of life and survival have tended to limit the kind of elaborated, reflective thought which develops special words for concepts of an abstract sort. So the languages of non-literate peoples are not cluttered up with words for concepts of no practical or everyday relevance. But from the lack of identifying words for them, it does not follow that these concepts or distinctions have all gone unrecognised: certain of them have been sensed and have seemed important. In the absence of words to name and isolate the idea, it can still be brought out by contrasting and juxtaposing actual objects or ordinary actions, perhaps reinforced by showing a like contrast repeated in other concrete terms, and so, by a process rather like the one I distinguished in my remarks on metaphor (p. 31), emphasise and isolate the quality or idea sensed through relations of contrast and juxtaposition. Phrased in general terms, as in Leach's article (1966), both these ideas are suggestive and appealing. But applied to particular cases in detail, they pose problems and prompt doubts over how to apply them. It is, I think, harder to go through a single ritual and show the useful knowledge it encapsulates in various details than to suggest the ways in which it stimulates and directs activity in some situation, providing perhaps at the same time some 'imaginative, prospective and creative understanding' (Tambiah 1968, p. 200) of the situation, the technological operations and social activities involved. The second aspect (that of a way offered to apprehend ideas sensed as important but not easy to isolate without leisure to reflect on them or words to name them) might be sought in those elements of ritual which clearly carry the invitation to interpret them or discover their meaning, rather than in any or every element of ritual: I have hoped to suggest in the earlier sections of this essay, which have dealt with interpreting expressive and representational properties, some guides to where to look.

What features of communication can we find in ritual?

There is still some strain to the analogy with message and information if one thinks in terms of communication between 'society' (tradition, the ancestors, etc.) and its present members. Spelled out, the notion implies that in the past some individual or individuals have sensed an idea and tried to tell others about it, perhaps without formulating it other than by showing it in terms of the relations of contrast and juxtaposition between certain things by which it first presented itself to them. The way they did it (perhaps then its meaning seemed clear and overt) so caught the attention of those whom they told or those who learnt about it afterwards, that they repeated it to preserve it, because it caught their fancy, seeming worth doing even though perhaps later no one could say exactly why this was so or elaborate on what it meant in words. Perhaps there never was anyone who could, but still they did it, and at some time the doing of it became fixed by rule. The analogy of a message intended and communication blurs. The argument is either that in recognition of its value the message was intentionally fixed by rule to be transmitted in a special way that would preserve it; or that at some level other than that of intellectual recognition of the message, the people who continued to do it responded to it and felt its worth, though they did not understand it. The question is partly: what was the message, and was it ever the message elaborated and articulated as some anthropologist may suppose from his 'decoding' it; in other words, did anyone at any time intend to communicate that information? The question is also whether a forgotten message, or a sign that betrays some meaning, or a message that no one under-stands, is an example of communication, in any strict sense. To say that people in the society continue to do it because they feel an obscure appropriateness or satisfaction in what they do is to speak in terms of stimulation and response rather than in terms of communication and message.

There must often be a fortuitous side to the precise form and detail of ritual that will remain unknown to the inquirer in a society without written records of its history. And this side cannot be known by intuition or reflection on what is done. Even into our time, a man should raise his hat if he wears one when he greets an acquaintance or a superior: the message of the gesture is salutation (a greeting and acknowledgement). To know that 'This form of salute is peculiar to the Western world and is a residue of medieval chivalry: armed men used to remove their helmets to make clear their peaceful intentions and their confidence in the peaceful intentions of others' (Panofsky 1970, p. 52) does not alter the message now conveyed by the greeting; to learn the precise intentions that originally lay behind this action which has come down to us so slightly modified does not lead to a truer understanding of some 'real' message that is still there to be decoded. But such a derivation does seem to account for the particular form of the greeting in a way we can not aim to match for a people without records of their past.

The ways in which ritual differs from communication are not its defects

The recognition of communication and of coded message provides an insight into ritual: there are, in some senses, elements of both these there. But to go from that to the view that ritual *is* properly communication (by coded messages) is to turn one's back on the nature of the original insight, and require oneself to alter and force the sense of communication and code contained in the original insight into a new and much looser form. It is a paradox of art that what the artist tried to put in his painting — the perceptions, feelings, thoughts that lay behind his work — has always been more than any particular beholder does draw from it; and yet that the ideas, impressions and feelings that the painting calls forth from the beholder always go beyond what the artist intended. To talk of understanding in art or ritual, there must be some kind of match or correspondence between the deviser or creator or performer's activity and the spectator's reaction, but the match will not be complete (cf. Wollheim 1970, pp. 135–6). In ritual as in art, he who devises or creates or performs is also spectator of what he does; and he who beholds it is also active in the sense that he interprets the performance. The value of ritual lies partly in this ambiguity of the active and passive for creator, performer and beholder: the sense of an arena of constraints within which the individual is free to some extent to search out, interpret and discover implies an indeterminacy about the full significance of what is done which is not to be taken necessarily as a defect of communication; it also contains a way of seeing that ritual may survive, still seem worth doing, offering some feeling of continuity, message and enrichment to those whose circumstances and experiences have changed from what they were for the people who first formed and performed the rites.

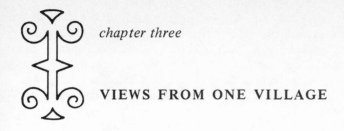

chapter three

VIEWS FROM ONE VILLAGE

After so long a disquisition on ritual in general, I would like now to look at one particular people's ideas of ritual, the Gnau's. As I wrote the preceding chapter, I thought that I would be hard put to find much clear in my field notes that would help to test or confirm some of the standpoints I had come to. I do not recall sitting down with a Gnau and trying to find out from him his view of the nature of ritual in general; or even if he had one. In talking about an event or procedure, people often said things that implied the way they thought, or they explained some detail and in doing so made clear some of their assumptions. Part of the problem I would have faced had I attempted to ask about ritual in general would have been the words to use. If, simple-minded, I expected a specific term for the concept I hunted, I would not have found exactly what I wanted. This will, I hope, become clearer below. A dictionary does not contain the sum of concepts in a culture, for some concepts may require a phrase, a sentence, a paragraph, even a book for their isolation. If a technical term or a neologism be devised and gain currency, the idea now dignified by naming does not thereby emerge winged as a concept, having been before something other and less fully formed. The Gnau have many ways to indicate what they are referring to when they talk about what I take to be 'ritual'; perhaps most commonly they speak of 'doing things', using the verb root *-bari-* which has roughly the range of the verbs 'work', 'do' and 'make' in English, and a neutral plural direct object suffix *-əm*. But 'doing things' was not limited to ritual, and there were other ways to talk of it.

Towards the end of my first stay with the Gnau in Rauit village, one hamlet, Wimalu, built a men's house (*gamaiyit*) to replace the dilapidated one they had destroyed. I watched the events to do with this, which were complex and took many days, and also I used a tape-recorder and sometimes left it going, set down beside groups of the people involved in what was going on. They were used to the tape-recorder and paid it no special attention. Afterwards I spent many hours with helpers who had taken part in the work, transcribing and translating what had been recorded. I have chosen some extracts from this long recording to show how the Gnau talk about ritual. These extracts are not of talk to me nor of answers to my questions (I was quite often somewhere else while they were talking), but are extracts of conversation between the people involved in the proceedings or commenting on them to each other, or come from the proceedings themselves. Thus obtained by eavesdropping, not inquiry, the extracts show how they talked among themselves: talk unaffected by any need to make allowance for my ignorance or expectations, or to cope with odd, perhaps inept, questions.

Months before the opening night, they had spoken of building the house. Most hamlets of the village had spent between four and six weeks at distant bush camps, hunting to prepare for it; in the preceding month or two, they had also helped to collect most of the building materials and other things they would need: posts, beams, rafters, slats, split bamboo, thatching leaves, rattan for lashings, food, decorations, certain special plants, etc. On 22 August 1969, all Wimalu returned at last from their hunting camps and on Monday the 25th they cleared the site and dug the holes for the main posts. At dawn next morning the log *garamuts* (slit gongs) announced that the main posts were to be placed upright in position. These and then the beams and rafters — the skeleton of the house — were set up. On Thursday the 28th, all the hamlets of the village went separately to collect and bring back the plant materials, the scented herbs, bark, tubers, fruit, coloured leaves and flowers which would be used for the figure to be formed on the main post of the house — a figure which has many names, among them Wɔlpawei, Panu'ət, Ləgin (which means Man), Masipə (which means Face). On Friday the 29th, in the early morning, the whole village gathered to thatch the house. Towards noon, with *garamuts* beginning to signal that the roof was nearly done, with the women bringing the feast food, everyone gathered. They exchanged food; they ate some, kept some; the women fetched their sago-processing equipment, the men took up position holding onto the posts; the women were outside ready. Then, suddenly, a crashing wave of triumphant voices and *garamuts* rolling broke into a single verse of song, which they sang as they shook the house, some of the women striking the newly made thatch with adzes and sago-pounders. Then everyone dispersed for the afternoon away from the still-unwalled house where only the senior men remained to fashion the figure on the main post in private and put in its sculpted face. By the late afternoon, this was completed. The house floor was swept and the herb materials to be burned into ash later — the hunting ash (*nawugəp*) — were laid out ready. All over the village people were making themselves fine and decorated.

When it was dark, just quite dark, all of the village assembled at the new *gamaiyit* without walls. The men and youths with bows and arrows and hand drums all crammed within the square formed by its four angle-posts; the women and children were underneath the roof, but outside the square. No fire or light of any sort was left alight as Saibuten, senior and main instigator of the rebuilding of the house, pulled fire by friction, and, when the first lick of flame caught and set fire to the dried herbs laid to make the hunting ash, the voice of the whole company of men burst out into the tremendous noise of the first word which opens the first verse of the great song sung at the building of a new *gamaiyit*: *Simarei*! *Simarei*! *Simarei*! ('It flares! It flares! It flares!').

The great song is a series of many verses[1] which must be sung through until the dawn. As the song begins, fire taken into a half coconut shell on a split-ended arrow-shaft is thrust and jabbed up to sear and singe the Face and, carried round in a circle, to sear all the posts and beams of the house. The assembled men sing holding their undrawn bows with their arrows in position, all following the aim of the arrow-shaft containing the smoking coconut bowl of fire as it circles round the *gamaiyit*. The herbs laid out are burned and turned into the hunting ash. The song goes on right through the night until the low oblique beams of the early rising sun slant into the house without walls. Then the people go off to eat and rest. I have called this night the opening night.

The singing and gatherings and visits of people from other places to see the house continued sporadically after this for many weeks. They had not ended the rites for this new *gamaiyit* when I had to leave New Guinea in November.

Gnau men and boys do not sleep in a house with women, but in their *gamaiyit*. The hunting ash (*nawugəp*) can only be prepared when a new *gamaiyit* is built. Later in the months and years that follow it is used, and gradually used up, in hunting rites held intermittently for individual men and youths, and for dogs, and also in some other rites. The great song sung at these rites is only sung through for the building of a new *gamaiyit*.

The extracts which follow come from two different days — the first lot (extracts I–IV) were recorded on Tuesday 26 August in the early morning just before they put the two main centre-posts into the holes in the ground which had been prepared. The second lot (V–IX) were recorded on Friday 29 August near noon when the roof was nearly ready and the feast food being brought.

The *gamaiyit* is built according to a complex and strictly ruled procedure, and to say in Gnau 'they will build a *gamaiyit*' (*lyila'ap gamaiyit*) is to imply both the technical ways in which they will do it and, necessarily, also all that is obviously ritual about it. As the series of events proceeds there are different ways to refer to specific parts or aspects of what is to be done. In many instances the same particular event can be distinguished by more than one phrase, by referring to its technical side, to some characteristic gesture involved, to the intention behind the action, or by the use of some quite specific idiomatic phrase. For instance, the complex of things that happen on the opening night can be indicated in the following ways:

1 Words in the song are thought to be in the language of the ancestors — the general sense of each verse is known and what it is about — but the words are rarely those used now for what they are supposed to be about. For instance, *simarei* is translated 'it flares' and is said to be an ancestral way of saying *mərərə'a*, which is Gnau for 'it flares' (literally 'they flare', because *da'ag* 'fires', is a plural).

(1)	*lirag gamaiyit*	they sing and dance for the *gamaiyit*
(2)	*lirag Madən* or *Bulti*	they sing and dance Madən or Bulti (names for the song)
(3)	(a) *lagəl lagəp*	literally (a) 'they break the long (shin) bones'. (b) and (c) use emphatic forms
	(b) *lagəlil lagəp*	of the verb. The phrase in context
	(c) *lagəlilam lagəp*	means quite specifically to sing–dance the Madən song, which has a characteristic *garamut* rhythm called *lagəla lagəp*
(4)	*Lasəlilup gamaiyit* or simply *lasəlilupa*	they swing dance for it (the *gamaiyit*). The verb root *-səlilu-* means to swing and the men dance back and forth only a few steps as they sing this song, some indeed hanging onto a bit of creeper tied onto a beam
(5)	*ləgə'ai nawugəp*	'they fire the hunting ash'
(6)	*liyelilyiwam*	'they singe or sear it (the *gamaiyit*) by fire'
(7)	*latao da'at lugati*	'they hold fire in the arrow-shaft'

Clearly the different phrases single out different aspects of the events, but in ordinary conversation any of the phrases might be used to indicate the whole inaugural night by naming a part or aspect of a part of the ritual. In many instances, then, both of important rituals like this one, and of lesser ones, I was struck by the variety of ways in which they could refer to rituals, and by the occasionally mystifying specific idiomatic phrases for them. There was also the lack of a single name for each distinctive ritual in the way that we identify occasions by name, such as Christmas, Passover, Easter, a christening, etc. Flow and sequence are in the ancient heart of the word 'rite', which is said to come from the Sanskrit *riti* 'a stream', 'a running', and the verb *ri* 'to flow', and the Gnau remind me of this by their incontinent use of metonymy to identify their rituals. A part may serve to imply the whole: a technical aspect — 'throwing down the posts' to stand upright (*litau sulaŋ*) — just as much as a ritual 'frill' — 'spit-anointing', rubbing and decorating the posts (*lasigət sulaŋ*), because in ritual the rules lay down a fixed sequence of procedure and if one part be done, so must the other.

The extracts have been chosen to illustrate different points: they come embedded in a variety of conversational themes, in comments on how things are going, in bits of boasting and joking self-assertion, and in much shouted instruction on what to get, what to do next, how to do it and so on. I have set each extract down with no cuts in the flow of talk; each speaker is identified by name. I have tried to translate the words they spoke as closely as is consistent with intelligibility. Brackets indicate words or sense implied but not spoken where the sense would have been obscure to a non-Gnau person without the additions. It is difficult to convey in translation the assertive, rhetorical tone of the many statements introduced by the conjunction *ba*, which implies a question or a viewpoint that must obviously be denied or refused assent. It will soon be clear that Gnau men in animated conversation prefer to make sure that what occurs to them gets said rather than risk forgetting it or losing it by waiting for someone else already speaking to finish first; the other man will probably continue anyway, so it is often their practice to say out their added opinion on top of his by means of greater voice power. This of course can become competitive. I regret that the reader cannot hear some of these exhilarating tapes: he will miss the direct experience of a quality in many gatherings of the Gnau for ritual which conveys their delight in them. The speakers in all these extracts are married men, nearly all fairly senior men with grown-up children. The numbers (suffixed) refer to explanatory notes which follow immediately on the text of each extract.

Extract I: To show the direct address of the ritual; the recognition of custom; the hope of a successful outcome

This first extract begins by a direct address to the immediate patrilineal dead of the man speaking. Such speech is prefaced by spitting, in most cases before each name is called; the speech is loud (*nant bu* 'big voice', 'loud speech'), declaratory and spoken usually with the face slightly raised up to the sky. It follows the whispered or choked secret spells blown into and over the gathered herbs and plant materials, which will be used to rub and anoint the main posts with betel juice before they are put in position and decorated with some of these same plant materials. Such loud speech says out what is being done, what motives and hopes are involved, and demands or asks for successful results. It is directed aloud to the spirits of the dead and is heard by all present. It is explicitly said by the actors, and said repeatedly, in all such declarations, that they are following the customs or ways of their ancestors. The recurring phrase for this is *dau wǝgatǝm bigǝp adjip*: it means literally 'we (inclusive) follow your hands'. The declarations, though often cliché-ridden, do not have a fixed form; the speakers say what they choose to; two different speakers, both from Wimalu hamlet, address the ancestors at the same time, interrupting each other. The last speaker brings up the theme of learning: this will appear more fully in later extracts. He does not address spirits of the dead but the people present.

Text I

Saibuten: (*spits*) I.1 Father! Grandfather! I am building this house for your grandchildren (descendants),I.2 I am building a little *gamaiyit* for them to sleep in . . .

Marki: (*spits*) Wormei! Dalpǝti! Sǝwani! Tupan! I am following your ways here. What! Could I lose them, throw off these things and leave them? I am following your ways . . .

Saibuten:	We have no game, no food. We are doing (all) these things. May we hunt and kill game . . .
Marki	We are to make the figure[I.3] well here. May we shoot pig, game. Our people have nothing . . .
Saibuten	. . . nothing, nothing left to us. I follow your ways. Do the things for our children so that they may shoot game.[I.4]
Daikun:	We used to ask our (fathers and) seniors[I.5] to sing out clear and strong to help us (so that we could learn well). Do we just know these things?[I.6] No! They are their things, the things of our ancestors.[I.7]

Notes

I.1 The Gnau use most often the ordinary verb root *-su-* ('spit', 'blow' or 'smoke') to refer to the spitting, but sometimes they use the root *-iao-* for this specific kind of spitting which prefaces an invocation. The root in question has the ordinary meaning 'to stand something upright'.

I.2 The kinship terms which I translate as 'grandfather' (*mami*) and 'grandchild' (*baluan*) may refer to any relative at two or more generations remove. In plural forms they can have the sense of 'ancestor' or 'descendant'.

I.3 The 'figure' referred to is the figure of the spirit which has many names and is fixed with a wooden painted face on the main post. Its body is made chiefly of plants contained in a bark skin; it also contains bits of ancestral skulls. The word I have translated as 'figure' (*tambit*) means 'skin' in the sense of whole outside skin and appearance; it is also the word used for 'self' in emphatically reflexive verb constructions. As individual identity is apparent in appearance so this link of appearance, the whole skin, identity and self is, I think, understandable (see Lewis 1974, p. 65).

I.4 The 'things for our children (*ta'aləmdəm* — one word in Gnau) so that they may shoot game' are things that are brought about by the performance, or through the effectiveness of its appeal to the ancestors. In many of the later extracts, as in Daikun's remarks later on in this extract, 'things' will also appear as a way in which they indicate a recognition of some collective entity, or entities, which, though without a name to identify them specifically, yet seem to me clearly to be what we might mean by 'ritual' things. Later on we will see how 'things' of this general sort have by implication certain curious attributes.

I.5 The word in the text is *gatagəm*. In Gnau, there are a number of odd collective terms for people in certain relationships, having a plural sense but no regular singular forms. The kinship term *dai* (father's younger brother) has the collective form *gatagəm* as its only plural. It means men standing in the general relationship of 'father' or senior. The word *gatagəm* is linked etymologically to the adjectives *gatəgil*, *gatəgilda* 'huge', 'big in size'. In reference to the dead, it can mean male ancestors.

I.6 'Do we just know these things?' The sentence carries the implication that these are things which could not be just reasoned out, found out by common sense or experiment, deduced. This theme comes again more clearly in later extracts.

I.7 *Bawul-gatagəm* is the collective form used here: it includes female and male seniors. *Bawul* is the collective term for womenfolk standing in any relationship. Etymologically the word ought to mean 'big human beings' as it is the adjective for 'big', 'many' with a plural, human ending: in fact it means 'women'. As the compound used here, in reference to the living, it means 'grown ups' or 'parents', but with reference to the dead, it should be translated as 'ancestors' or 'forebears' (implying male and female ones). C.f. n. I.5 above.

Extract II: To show that the ritual must be done publicly before an audience; that there is concern for public registration and opinion of what they do; that there is concern with the precise detail or order of procedure

This extract is taken from part of the recording shortly after the first one. The materials were ready for the men to spit betel juice on the posts and rub, anoint and decorate them (*lasigətəm*), but they say they must wait for some of the men from other hamlets to come before they throw posts down into the holes made ready. They are concerned that they shall be seen to have done it right. Perhaps also the concern is more explicit at this particular point in the proceedings, although it is not the sole or prime reason for it, because it is thought that very serious destructive magic against other persons can be accomplished, by placing certain materials in the bottom of the post holes at the moment when the posts are thrown into them to stand upright. At the moment when the posts are thrown upright, the *garamuts* beat out in the rhythm which announces a killing — they said they would formerly have beaten the rhythm for a man killed, but in these times and on this occasion they decided it would be proper only to beat the rhythm for a pig- or cassowary-killing. Towards the end of the extract, there is a contested point about the proper order of procedure.

Text II

Marki:	(*spits*) Father! Wosin! Sɔwani! . . .
Silmai:	We are making a (new) *gamaiyit*, (the old one) had holes in it. We stayed on using it, on and on. (*spits*) Grandfather Wamukan! We are building this *gamaiyit*. We are following (the ways of) our ancestors so you must bring us pig, game, for us to kill. For are you worthless things, no use, no good, that we can break up the old house? that the things (we are now putting up) can just hang there and nothing (come of it)? that they can just break up (the old *gamaiyit*) anyhow?[II.1] We have told people to come so that they shall not talk about us (to our shame), but they have not come yet. We are going to make (the posts) ready and blow— spit (the spells and betel juice) on them. We are going to put the things down into the posts.[II.2]
Sakai:	No! Go on and do it even if they've still not come! Let's get on and throw them (posts) down into position.
Silmai:	But we've got to wait for them. When they come, well, then we can put the posts in, for (remember) these are my things, the things of the ancestors . . .

Sakai:	All right, wait, leave the rub—anointing (of the posts). Not time yet, then, when the others get here, all right, then . . .
Patik:	You must get the leaf and tear it.[II.3]
Wɔkapət:	The rub—anointing, the tearing of the leaf — they must wait (can't do it yet).
Silmai:	You can rub—anoint your own ones [i.e. the posts you cut] but then put them down and wait . . .
Sakai:	When most of the others come, then you can pick (the posts) up and (throw them down) *gəgru*! [onomatopoeic] (into the post holes) . . .
Wandi:	Yes! We must wait for the others first.
Marki:	We can rub—anoint them and wait, then when everybody's here, then you can pick them up and throw them (into position).
Silmai:	That's right! What you're saying! You do that! You do the posts, (the things) down onto the posts, tear the leaves, we must rub—anoint them.
Saibuten:	Make the cigar and get the hearth ashes!
Patik:	Rub—anoint it, recite our words[II.4] there. Bring the tobacco, make the cigar, blow it over the things and then you can rub—anoint the post, and I'll . . .
Sukadel:	Yes! Go on! (Someone) go and get the hearth ashes so that we can blow—bespell[II.5] the things for them.
Wɔkapət:	Tear the leaf, then you rub—anoint them . . .
Samo:	(yelling) No!! Listen! First you rub—anoint them, then you tear the leaf!
Silmai:	Rub—anoint them straight, right at the place you hold them to throw them (into position), that's the right place.
Samo:	That's it! That's just what I say!
Galwun:	Rub—anoint them straight there! In the middle there! That's it!

Notes

II.1 This sentence, as do certain phrases which appear in later extracts, explicitly contains the notion that what is done is not ordinary, but special or peculiar. The things which are done are not done just anyhow. This idea can be put over perhaps most clearly by use of the phrase *yida tambit*; it is used to mean something done without bothering, thoughtlessly, just as you wish. It often appears in comment on ritual as the injunction 'You must *not* do it in this thoughtless way', that is, you must do it with care and pay attention. The phrase *yida tambit* is an important idiom for the opposite of that alert, intent approach in ritual which I discussed in the preceding chapter. The idiom is made up of a verb *yida* for which I know no other use except as it appears in this phrase; and *tambit* which means 'self' (see n. I.3). Its Pidgin English translation was given to me as *mekim nating*. In Gnau to do something *gipi'i* or *gipi'im* ('emptily', 'nothingly', 'just anyhow') also means to do it ordinarily.

II.2 Here again a sentence in which 'things'refers to ritual things (i.e. rub—anointing, spit—blow—bespelling) and speaks of them as a kind of entity. The verbs used (*lauwəm məwag*) literally mean 'fill up with the things so they go down into or inside' (c.f. n. I.4).

II.3 Tearing the leaf: this is perhaps the most obvious, characteristic, ident-

46

ifying act in Gnau ritual. At almost any point of special importance in ritual proceedings, a certain leaf is held over the person or the things or the materials for or by which benefit is sought and it is torn. The leaf is a *lyimaŋgai-* banana leaf; it has two hibiscus flowers stuck in it at either end just by the midrib of the leaf. It is spat and bespelled with two betel-juice blotches to each side of the midrib in the middle. It is held at one end by the officiant over the person or things; someone else again has put some white ashes of a hearth-fire on a small patch of leaf and holds it roughly under the *lyimaŋgai* leaf too. Then as the officiant whispers or chokes the secret spell, a puff of tobacco smoke is blown over the leaf and ashes, and the officiant, with one motion, tears the leaf completely lengthwise down the midrib as he holds it over the person or things. In this instance, the leaf was to be torn over the two main posts after they had been rub—anointed, and just before they were stood up in position. In the extract there is some brief dispute about whether they should be rub—anointed first or the leaf torn first. Extract IV contains, in fact, the moment at which the leaf was torn over the two posts. Extract VI contains an elliptical speech referring to the myth in which is to be found the origin or first performance of this act of tearing the leaf.

II.4 The phrase *wiyapəp nʌnt* 'we recite the words' is one of many in which *nʌnt* 'mouth', 'speech', 'language', 'voice' is used for the secret spells. The root *-iap-* (*-iapəp* is an emphatic form with a reduplicated syllable) in other contexts means 'to dig up': in this phrase, I think, the particular verb used always implies words whispered or choked out in a tiny voice, i.e. secret spells. They also commonly say they 'blow' (*-su*) the spells (*nʌnt*), or they 'throw them down' (*-tau*), or they 'do' or 'work' them (*-bari*), or they 'take' or 'carry' them (*-tao*) to do something, or they 'follow' or 'come along' (*-ʌg*) with them to do something, or they just 'speak' them (*-sa*). There is a very large class of spells called *bəlyigap* 'spells' which are ones which are also sung out loud, very loud, as verses of different great songs. When used in magic, they are, however, often whispered or choked out secretly, but then they usually also have special sound trills and particular secret names which must be added for their magic to work. The verses sung aloud in the song are spoken of as the 'spells' (*bəlyigap*) and they form important long sections of the song. The singing through of the song on great ritual occasions (such as this one for building a *gamaiyit*) is repeated sporadically on many nights before the ritual comes to an end and it is the chief way in which young men learn the main body of the spells they use for diverse kinds of magic. We will hear more of this in later extracts. Not all secret spells are also sung; such ones are covered by the term *nʌnt* 'speech', 'voice', etc. although they are not strictly *bəlyigap*.

II.5 The root *-su-* (*supəp* emphatic) which I translate as 'blow—bespell' is almost as frequently used as *-bari-* 'work', 'do' in reference to performing ritual. In almost any context in which *-bari-* is used of magic or sorcery, it could be replaced by an appropriate construction using *-su-* (see Lewis 1975, pp. 189—92).

Extract III: To show a direct request to the ancestors that the things they left to their descendants will be effective so that other people will speak well of them because of what the ritual performed will enable them to do

This extract is of what Saibuten and Silmai called out as they were rub—

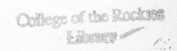

anointing the main posts. They ask for success in hunting so that they can repay their women and children for their help and work, and can also give generously to people of the other hamlets who have helped them.

Text III

Saibuten: *(spits)* Aah! Sɔwani! *(spits)* Father! You showed[III.1] me these things; you showed me the (ritual) plants;[III.2] you told me which things . . .

Silmai: We are doing the things according to your customs here. *(spits)* Ulibel! When we do the hunting at the end,[III.3] Ulibel, may we hunt well truly. The women and children have worked hard for this and they have sweated. Let us kill so that we may make return to them for their work; so that no men may speak (with scorn) about us. May we kill so that when we give them game there is enough to give to every *gamaiyit* (hamlet).

Notes

III.1 *Dji bədapilpəgam* 'You were showing to me/these things': the verb root *-apil-* means 'to distribute' or 'give out', e.g. food; 'put down'; or 'leave behind'. There is a derived word *napil* which means 'orphan'.
III.2 *Lu-lambət*: literally 'tree-liane', but as a compound it refers to the many plant materials specially used in rituals, and primarily people speak of them as things that must be obtained from the bush (*tuwi*), either garden land (*tuwi gargitasa*) or forest, wild bush (*tuwi sinapə*), but especially wild bush.
III.3 Before major ritual occasions (i.e. those in which the great songs are sung through as well as certain others) can be brought to a close, the men who have taken part in initiating and performing them must hunt, going out on day-long hunts until they have a day of conspicuous success and kill at least one large pig or cassowary. The specific verb which refers to this kind of hunting (root *-watəp-*) was usually translated for me into Pidgin as *traiimem*, that is, 'trying it out' (for success presumably). The root is, I think, in fact *-watə* + *-p* the indirect-object marker.The verb root *-watə-* means 'to bury'. The Gnau use *-watə-* for burying dead in the ground, but the same word was used also for the traditional method of disposing of the dead in which they laid out the corpse on a platform like a table and smoked it dry. Thus *-watəpəm* may have a sense of final disposal of the rites, but I think the Pidgin translation meaning a testing out of their efficacy is suggestive of how they think of this hunting.

Extract IV: To show statement of belief in the efficacy of the rites, and that men without knowledge of them would be as nothing, ignorant and incapable

This extract comes from just about the moment when the leaf was torn over the two main posts before they were taken up to be placed in position. The second of Silmai's speeches begins with the trill 'Pr-r-r-r' he made as he tore the leaf.

Text IV

Silmai:	Ah! You stand strong and firm with these things of yours to work dogs (for hunting), or to work men (for hunting) or for the main post (of the *gamaiyit*). Without them, what would you have to accomplish[IV.1] things? Are you so great that you could just take things and accomplish things?
Wɔkapət:	What! Can children do any such things? Are you so great that you can just set to and do them? No!! No, we are (like) children here. We are ignorant. But then these children, their eyes will follow everything you do and they will (learn to) do them for themselves.
Marki:	(*spits*) Father! (*spits*) Tupan! We are carrying out[IV.2] your customs here, these things – Hey! move those things over to the middle of the leaf there![IV.3] – We are building the *gamaiyit*, something that belongs to us here [i.e. the customs].
Sakai:	You mustn't eat the things[IV.4] there yet! Leave them fastened up! You watch first.
Silmai:	Pr-r-r-r . . . (*spits*) There! For the hunting to end them (the rites) – a terrific kill! There! That's so you are going to kill – big! little! plenty! everything!
Marki:	You [i.e. the spirit addressed] bring to us (game) of the tree tops, of the ground below. Let us kill it then so that no man can say of us that we built something rotten. Is it a house? No! (It is) a *gamaiyit* we build!
Saibuten:	I have nothing (left) now! I am building it, building it well. I am following your ways, these things are your things!

Notes

IV.1 'Accomplish' may be too flowery a translation. The verb used is again *-bari-* 'word', 'do', 'make'.

IV.2 He says: *wɔgai bigəp beiya djip*, literally 'we take your hands'; c.f. *wəgatəm bigəp adjip* 'follow your hands', i.e. follow your ways.

IV.3 Note the way he interpolates this instruction to someone in the middle of his invocation to the dead spirits: as I mentioned at the beginning of extract I, the invocation is made in a relatively free and unfixed, though rhetorical, manner.

IV.4 The 'things' which must not be eaten yet are the raw dry magical substances, called *gəplagəp*, which are made from scrapings or shreds of special plants of the *lu-lambət* kind (see n. III.2 above). They are eaten with areca nut by those who are to spit on the posts and rub—anoint them, and also by Silmai as he tears the leaf. *Gəplagəp* distinguishes the general kind of prepared magical substances which are finely scraped and shredded and pounded, used in tiny amounts, containing also with them scrapings of animal substances such as bits of dried blood, scrapings of tree-phalanger scent glands and of human skull or jaw bones. The other general kind of prepared magical substance is cooked and wet; it is typically like a thick stew. This kind of prepared magical substance is called *wa'agəp* (or, sometimes, *wə'ati*, the singular form).

Extract V: Expresses the idea that the ritual is a source of knowledge of how to do things, especially spells, learnt from the ancestors and held in trust by senior men for their descendants; there is a duty to teach it and pass it on

With this extract, we move on to the Friday noontime when they were approaching the moment at which the house with its thatch just completed would be shaken. The extracts to come are from discussion and comment by the men talking excitedly shortly before this took place. In this one they speak of the duty to teach or pass on knowledge held in trust. It makes clearer their view that learning comes from experience. So far as I was able to find out, the dominant way by which knowledge of how to do rites was passed on was by taking part in their performance. Some rites and knowledge were shown in progressive stages, which means that those who were learning were allowed to hear and see more of how they were done in successive stages; in some cases, this progress depended on the postulant showing his ability in some field, or fulfilling some requirement first. I was not given to understand that now or in the past were there periods of formal instruction apart from practice, or that, for example, during the long period of seclusion in the *gamaiyit* for men's initiation rites (in which the rites and song called Tambin were done), the older men were required to explain and describe the way of doing them, the myths that went with them and their meaning. They did them and in the course of doing them, as we shall see, they said things about them which were explanatory or served to interpret them.

But the teaching method is not that of the school, with theory and explanation rather set apart from practice, with a curriculum intended to establish some common body of knowledge for all those who take the lessons. Instead what is learnt through any particular performance is to some extent fortuitous and dependent on what happens to be said and heard on that occasion. In all the important rituals I witnessed, there were moments at which someone senior spoke didactically about why they were doing them or what they symbolised, but these interventions were brief and there seemed no pattern or direction to them. The mode of explanation was often elliptical, not exhaustive. When I questioned people about how they had learned or failed to learn about something, for example, a myth, genealogies, the meaning of some ritual action, they sometimes mentioned individuals who had told them, often their fathers, or they said it was the sort of thing men used to talk about in the evening in the *gamaiyit* when they were lying on their beds before going off to sleep, or on rainy days when they hung around by the fireside. In similar circumstances, although rarely, I have heard men by some chance get round to a myth and tell it, or go into some explanatory point about the meaning of a rite. At the stage of my inquiries when I used to harass so many people with requests for them to go through their genealogies, I found that there were some men who were just ignorant, as there were others who were acknowledged to be outstandingly learned and accurate. These differences were put down, first, to interest and innate ability, and secondly, in respect of ignorance particularly, to the death of a man's father while he was still a child and before he could have taken in the kind of thing a father would normally tell his son. I think this view is of interest more as a rationalising statement that follows from the expectation that most men should learn from their fathers than as a statement of what necessarily follows from losing one's father during one's childhood. Some of the most knowledgeable men had in fact lost their fathers in early childhood. A fatherless child has an upbringing which is very like that of any other boy; he sleeps in the *gamaiyit*; his father's brothers or elder classificatory brothers treat him with an affection, care and concern which I could rarely distinguish in any way from that which they showed for their own children.

None of my inquiries or observations suggest that either in the past or now Gnau people had 'courses' of instruction. But they learned set things about ritual by taking part, that is, by experience. The set things they learned were the procedures — how to do it — not the interpretations, the 'meanings'. These were accumulated much more haphazardly and were not learned as 'set' things in the sense that the procedures were. For the Gnau, then, learning about the meaning of their rites is subject to a very different level of injunction and constraint from that of learning how to do them.

Text V

Dukini: Your grandfather, the younger brother one [literally the little one], he came knowing nothing at all of these things. His elder brother knew them, the younger brother, well, he was too young (at the time his father died) so he knew nothing. You build this (*gamaiyit*) of yours but you must not do it just anyhow. No! You do it properly and right in every detail[V.1] for these are things of the ancestors. You must look after the children's things so that they, the children, their eyes may follow these things here; so that when some boy has grown up and he builds a *gamaiyit*, a house, and then he tries to think of what to do to fire his hunting ash — these things here, you sing them for him so that he shall know them, and will sing them.

Wutilkai: Without the spells (*bəlyigap*), if he does not know them, he will stay empty-handed, with nothing. The spells, these are the things we are going to tell [i.e. to teach] them so that they, grown up, will be able to sing them, so that they shall know them. They shall not be ignorant of these things. No! They shall know them — these grandchildren of yours. We must lead them in the singing[V.2] of these things and go through them. They shall know them.

Samo: These things are there in care for[V.3] the children. When they grow up they will come to know them so that they can speak them too. We must wait a little (until later in the day) but then we will sing them for them, (the things) of the great song-spirit,V.4 so that they will know them.

Notes

V.1 The idiom *galapəm baniŋgətap wɔləm* could be translated literally as 'you clench tight your fierce teeth for the things', but it has the sense of doing something with determined effort and concentration to get it done quite right.

V.2 In the context of singing, *taupeldəm* 'throw things down before them' is used specifically for the action of leading the song on into a new verse; that is, each new verse is sung through once by a single man and then all the others join in and take it up as he reaches the end of the line and the repetition begins.

V.3 The verb root *-narəp-* used here means to 'watch', 'look after' or 'take care of'. For instance it is used of someone who inherits a tract of clan land; he has stewardship over it. It is used of someone who fosters or cares for a child he did not father, such as a step-child. It also means simply to 'watch' or 'look at'.

V.4 The word *bəlyi'it*, which appears here in an adjectival construction (*beiya bəlyi'isa*), means both 'song' and 'great spirit', i.e. the great spirit associated with these rites. In a sense it is a universal spirit. I have elsewhere discussed the Gnau idea of great spirit and the sense by which 'spirit' and 'song' are called the same (Lewis 1975, pp. 158—61, 169—76).

Extract VI: To show their pride in their ritual; their trust that by it they will be admired and amaze others; that what they do is not ordinary; that it could not be discovered but only learnt; that this knowledge has an origin or first cause; that it is peculiar to the people who practise it.

The first part of this extract, in which they say that they expect to startle and amaze their friends and visitors by the magnificence of the ritual, speaks for itself. The idea that the things are not ordinary leads them on to point out that a stranger would not know what to make of what was going on, and in keeping with their own suspicious regard for those things other people do which are incomprehensible, they suggest that he would assume their purpose to be nefarious and evil — implicitly, sorcery. But no, the man speaking (Dukini) answers himself, it is because they are things peculiar to us, the Gnau. At this point, his elder brother (Səlaukei), a man of recognised and outstanding learning in matters to do with traditional knowledge and practice, immediately refers them to Dəlubaten, the site of the most ancient first settlement of men who were ancestors of the Gnau and other people. Dəlubaten is a domed hill close to the village of Rauit, covered now with forest; and the people will not make gardens there. Dukini says something next and then Səlaukei elliptically tells a fragment from the myth of Dəlubaten without saying any of the names of the protagonists in the myth. The fragment refers to the moment when the mother who had only one son — her husband was dead and there were no other men then — had gone to pound sago in the bush, and she heard a noise as though men were singing in the *gamaiyit* with her son. For her son in the *gamaiyit* had taken the feathers of many, many birds, certain scented plants and other herb materials and crushed them and mixed them in together. He fashioned bows and arrows and stood them in the ground, one bow, one arrow, one bow, one arrow, round in a circle in the *gamaiyit*. He took a *lyimʌŋgai* leaf, stuck hibiscus flowers in it, spat betel juice on it, spat betel juice in the crushed feathers and plants, held the leaf over it and tore it lengthwise (see n. II.3 above). He thumped the sole of his foot on the ground and . . . a man stood by every bow and arrow round about him. In extract II as Silmai said 'Pr-r-r-r' he too thumped his foot on the ground. Both the tearing of the leaf and the thumping of a foot on the ground, actions which in certain rites go together but in others are done separately, have their origin explained in this myth. The peculiar forms of the ritual actions are thus accounted for, to the Gnau who know — these are explanations for the precise form of the actions, in type not unlike Panofsky's explanation for why men lift their hats (p. 37 above). As they say in the text, if it had not been done like that then how could they have known it, how could anyone have known it? From this point Səlaukei goes on to relate that, strange to say, he found that the people in another village, Womil, which is about four or five hours' walk from Rauit, did exactly these ritual actions, which he refers to by an identifying idiom 'they work the birds' ('work' in the sense 'work magic, wonders', i.e. work birds into men) as part of the puberty rites, and his surprise then sprang from his assumption that the ritual of Rauit was peculiar to Rauit, yet he found the same actions done at Womil. Perhaps I should note here that tearing the leaf does not appear as the focal point of the puberty rites at Rauit.

Text VI

Tawo: When they have finished doing that (the thatching) then we've got to shake it. That over, then we will fill (the figure of) Panu'ət properly. We will put in the Face (*Masipə*). We will do it really well and stick the pig tusks [nose ornament] in standing upwards like this. People from everywhere around are going to come and see it. Then we will start the singing. Ah! How we're going to sing! The *garamut* will be beating out the Wɔləp[VI.1] rhythm. We'll be singing. Yes, that's it!

Wɔkapət: First all our (village) people have to come, there will be the giving out of the feast food,[VI.2] give them all the food, then they will clear off (for the afternoon) while we do the work on filling (the central figure) . . .

Dukini: And some young woman — when she gets inside and sees what's there! It's not time yet, but when the *nʌndat* frog starts his piping[VI.3] and we've finished making it and then she comes in, she'll stop amazed.[VI.4] She'll call out Udei![VI.5] What a husband for me there! that man there![VI.6] — with the *garamut*

	and *kundu* drum beating and beating away. She will come inside and stand amazed.
Wutilkai:	We'll get ready and set fire to our hunting ash. It's going to be really strong and powerfully done[VI.7] this time so that they will talk about it — pig, cassowary, whatever — we will shoot them out, kill everything, finish them off! crowned pigeon, brush turkey, phalangers, tree wallabies — anything left? Nothing! Empty! Finished!
Tawo:	Our dogs (when they've had the hunting ash) they will just about go mad (into fierce trance).[VI.8] And the others when they get inside not knowing what (to expect), they are going to say, Wut! What have they been doing? Magnificent!
Səlaukei:	They won't know what (to expect) and then we'll pull away until the fire catches and we'll put fire into the arrow-shell standing outside, bring it into the house there and then . . .
Dukini:	Then when all the women and children come and get inside and see the things we've done . . .
Wutilkai:	Yes! They'll be out there in the dark, the fire going back and forth, and their eyes — stuck wide open! coming out of their heads!
Wɔkapət:	Eh hei! He (the figure) splendid! And your grandson, your son, he said he thought you were just going to make it (the face and figure) plain, simple. I told him, No, not at all — that you would get black paint by burning the *gablit* creeper, would give it teeth, paint it up with bright marks, put pig tusks through its nose. And he said to me, will he just get the stuff and set fire to the hunting ash? And I said to him, What! Just do it as though it were nothing! No, we are going to do it properly and well. We can't have other men talking about us (with scorn).
Tawo:	Yes, you are going to do it properly and then you'll go off (to the bush to hunt) and it (the spirit) is going to catch hold and bring it (game) to you so that it falls down *tur*! [onomatopoeic, i.e. 'dead at your feet!' This is followed by a chorus of whistles and shouts *Ei! Ei! Ei! Ei!* signifying agreement and strong approval.]
Wɔkapət:	His things (rites)! Going to do them properly here!
Səlaukei:	His things! He's[VI.9] going to have his spells and things covering him over![VI.10]
Wutilkai:	Aah! We know about these things and we keep to them. You must not do them wrong and mess them up. No! We must follow exactly what our parents did.
Səlaukei:	We must follow our ancestors.[VI.11]
Dukini:	Suppose some stranger came, well, he might say, Ah! What are they doing? Something evil and wicked there, some devil's work.[VI.12] (Then we'd say) What? You think it's devil's work? Look, these things here are our things, our things for hunting and killing game!
Wutilkai:	*Waŋgapida*!!! [In the recording, this is a tremendous shouted oath of approval][VI.13]
Səlaukei:	Because (these things) were at Dəlubaten, for they first stood there and then they came here, these things, and they went about.
Dukini:	If they were to be left behind, (think of) some young boy here standing, stretching out his empty, begging hand and saying, Oh?

What? And think of him. What could he know? How could he know? Think! If he could only watch, and his eyes follow these things, he would know them. If not, then he would just stand (empty-handed and) ignorant.

Səlaukei: His mother[VI.14] went and she went down to (the bush called) Lagiwut to pound sago and she heard something. He had stayed (in the village), but she heard him, the *garamut* beating — kir! kei! kir! kei! kir! [onomatopoeic] and she said to herself, What? That son of mine? But he's alone sitting waiting in the village. Who can be with him? Who sings with him? And he there, he was sitting. He made the things, bow, *talwut* arrow, *garamiti* arrow[VI.15] He made them and he thumped his foot before them.

Wutilkai: Ah! Us, our ancestors knew these things, so we can thump our feet in that way — but if we (our ancestors) had not been then, how could we have known?

Səlaukei: They did them, so we do them. About thumping our feet, exactly! If they hadn't then, we could not have known about it. Listen! At Womil, they 'work the birds' for the puberty rites[VI.16] of their young people. Listen to this! I went there once, stayed there, sat there watching. I said, Wut! These men are doing our things, the bird things, they're doing them! So I told them and they said, Look, we are not doing just anything, no, we are 'working the birds' for their puberty rites so our young people grow fine and our village is stocked full of them. So I said, We do them too, these things, they belong to the village of Rauit, and here I am, sitting, my eyes following the things you do — Well, they were doing them for the puberty rites for the young. They were 'working the birds'.

Wutilkai: They do them just as we do our things.

Səlaukei: They crush, rub and mix all the stuff, they get the special, good leaves and herbs, they come and crush and mix them. Yes, they do them as the Womil way there.

Notes

VI.1 The Wɔləp rhythm is the name of the staccato *garamut* beat which is used to announce the killing of a pig or a cassowary on return from a hunt.

VI.2 At gatherings for ritual occasions, meat rather than leaves or vegetables is eaten with sago jelly. The food of an ordinary Gnau meal is referred to as *teltɑg—təbəgan* (*tulip* leaves—sago jelly) but the food of ritual occasions is called, as it is in this text, *digi-təbəgan* (a contraction of *digap—təbəgan* — game—sago jelly), and on important occasions, such as this one, the different contributions are first laid out in packets, and then the different families providing them give them to certain relatives and receive what they will eat from others.

VI.3 The piping of the *nɑndat* frogs begins just before 5 p.m. It heralds the approach of every evening in the year (Rauit is 3° south of the equator).

VI.4 *Wɔgəlapə waiyi* 'she'll stop amazed'. This verb is used for trembling or unsteadiness in the legs, and it is also used to convey the sense of sudden weakness accompanying a shock or a surprise. The emphatic expression for fundamental shock is this, indeed: *nəmbət wɔgəlapə waiyi*, literally 'arse trembles unsteady'.

VI.5 'Udei!' is the commonest Gnau exclamation of surprise, consternation or pain. I have also left certain other exclamations unchanged in the text, viz. Wut! (surprise, doubt), Eh hei! (pleased, approving surprise), Ei! Ei! or Elei! lei lei! (agreement, triumphant ululation); but I have translated the strongly nasalised crescendo negative exclamations Aãã̃ã! and Nyəə! as No!

VI.6 'That man there!' is meant to refer to the figure on the post with a sculpted painted face, accoutred, as it should be on that night, more splendidly than the finest dancer or fighter.

VI.7 The idea I have translated by 'it's going to be really strong and powerfully done' was conveyed by the phrase I explained in n. V.1. They said *migə'ai nawugəp adap migəlapəm baniŋgətap wɔləm*, literally 'we will set fire to our hunting ash we will clench tight our fierce teeth'.

VI.8 In hunting and killing, some men go into a fierce state of trance in which they are less aware of their surroundings and of danger to themselves. In certain rites for hunting and killing, they seek to arouse this state called *wuna'at gipi'i* (empty or blank consciousness) and it may be shown by some men. The Gnau say that it is in part an effect of the hunting ash, which is given with certain powerful herbs. The idea of the sentence quoted is that the dogs will be driven into a like state of crazed zeal to hunt and kill when given the hunting ash. *Wuna'at gipi'i* is discussed in Lewis 1975, pp. 208–14.

VI.9 'His' and 'he' in the translation refer in these two sentences to the image of Panu'ət on the post, and the speakers use human male affixes. They are in the middle of talking about the likeness of the image to a magnificent-looking man — the aspect of Panu'ət as Ləgin (Man). This may be why they use the infix appropriate for a man. Spirits and shades of the dead should take neutral verb agreements (in the singular these are the same as for a woman); for example, in speech about the shade of a dead father or about Panu'ət the neutral agreements should be used. But it is also a trick of Gnau idiom to indicate or emphasise the size, growth or splendour of something admired by using male human agreements. They may be used of a girl or a woman admired just as of a house, a spirit, a tree or a dog admired (for instance, the sentence 'that daughter of mine has grown up big' would normally be translated *niŋgi gadəg eita biwatətiyi bu*, but it could be said with a proud emphasis indicated by the male agreements: *niŋgi gadəg eitan minatətiyi bun*). So the stress on the magnificence of the image may be the reason for the human male agreements here.

VI.10 As in the words I commented on in nn. 1.4 and II.2 above, the sense of ritual things as a collective entity is strong here, for the words I have translated as 'going to have his spells and things covering him over', *bətau bəlyigap bətalidəm*, might be put more literally as 'about to throw down the spells to lay them out or spread them out on it'. The verb roots *-tau* and *-tal-* mean 'to throw down and lay out' as gifts are laid out to be displayed before they are given out, as a leaf frond is thrown down to cover something and shield it from the rain, as a cloth is spread out on a flat stone and left to dry in the sun.

VI.11 *Mələt adao* 'our ancestors'. The word *mələt* is the most general term for 'spirit' in Gnau and it is in the singular here. It is also the only word of theirs I know for a story, or a myth or a genealogy (cf. n. V.4 on *bəlyi'it* 'song' and 'great spirit'). A request *Dji sap mələt adji* 'You tell your *mələt*' is met by the telling of the myth linked with a lineage, its history and the account of the man's pedigree. Very commonly, as here, *mələt* is used to refer to a man's ancestors as a collectivity, and is said in the singular with this reference intended. I have discussed how the Gnau use *malət* and their other words for spirit in Lewis 1975, pp. 156—64.

VI.12 In this sentence the notion of bad and evil things, implying sorcery, is first conveyed in the Gnau by 'they are doing bad things, bad things, these things', *ləbari wɔləm wɔləm yitəm*; then he says, *Satan yitəm* 'Satan these things'. The devil is called Satan in Pidgin, and the word *Satan* has been adopted into common speech in Gnau where, as in this context, it can serve to identify something seen only as evil. The Gnau do not have a spirit that matches our Satan. They consider in general that the power of spirits is ambivalent and may appear in either the good or the bad. They have adopted *Satan* as the word for evil, for bad unalloyed. It identifies that perhaps more simply than any alternative Gnau phrase.

VI.13 *Waŋgapida*!!! This great shout of praise is the word for a 'bow' (*waŋgapə*) given an adjectival suffix. The bow and the hornbill (*wamələn*) are proud emblems. A hornbill, the head and upper parts mounted, the cropped wings splayed, is worn with the great beak jutting out between the wearer's shoulder-blades by those men who have achieved the right to wear it through killing game and, formerly, men. The quality of a bow or a hornbill is included in a number of idioms to express admiration.

VI.14 The speech is dropped like a pearl into the rush of conversation flowing past. The speaker refers only to 'he' and 'she', the questions running through the mother's mind, and the son there making things, thumping his foot. To someone ignorant of the myth, the few phrases are almost meaningless: to someone who knows, the whole myth is called to mind in a flash by these few allusive fragments, and the origin of the ritual action that men do now is picked out. In the myth is the first performance, the creation of a type of action that men do now.

VI.15 *Talwut* and *garamiti* are the names of different kinds of barbed arrows used in warfare.

VI.16 'The puberty rites' is a translation that serves to identify what they refer to. In the extract, the phrase *latel nəŋgadil* is used. It is one of a number of phrases by which they may identify the puberty rites. This one is idiomatic and contracted. *Nəŋgadil* means the young people or children, *latel* is a contraction of the idiom *latel bigəp wuyi*, which is also commonly shortened to *latel bigəp*. The idiom means 'they make beautiful'. Someone might say of the way they will decorate the men's house that they will do it *tel bigəp wuyi*, that is, beautifully. I do not know how the idiom is derived. The words are literally *-tel-*, a verb root meaning to cut across or cut off, to clear a new garden site, to mark a boundary, to cross a river; *bigəp* 'hand'; *wuyi* 'well', 'beautifully'. With a direct-object suffix as *latela bigəp*, it is frequently used as the identifying phrase for a girl's puberty ceremony, having the sense 'they beautify her', but for the boy's ceremony, they might say *lisarkaki'en* 'they decorate him', but not *latelen bigəp*. *-isarkaki-* is often applied to the girls' ceremony too. The short form *latel nəŋgadil* refers here to the ceremonies for both girls and boys. There is no cutting of arms in these ceremonies.

Extract VII: To show how the symbolism of a particular action is publicly explained

These last three extracts show different aspects of the way the Gnau speak and learn about the meaning of their rituals. This first one is the most explicit and easy to understand. Senior men, excited and expectant, shout out directions to the women about where they must stand and what they must do when the house with its thatch just completed is shaken by the men to *garamuts* beating out and the men crashing into song for a single verse. The men are to be inside the house holding the posts to shake it, the women are to stand outside, carrying their sago-processing equipment (sago-pounders, palm-spathe sheets and containers, the coconut-leaf-base-fibre sieves, their adzes) and strike at the new thatched roof. One important aspect of the spirit Panu'ət is its concern with sago. In the performance of major ritual, many benefits are sought. In this short episode of the rites, the women are to come with all their sago-processing equipment before the spirit to show themselves and be recognised so that it will know them, reward their efforts to produce sago with success, and not harm them as strangers or stealers when they do it. Wutilkai names the more senior women present, telling them where to stand, and Səlaukei explains how an old woman would strike an adze right through the roofing and thrust her equipment through into the house to show it to the spirit. From this perspective of the women, they liken the whole new-thatched *gamaiyit* to the trunk of a spiny sago palm with entangling creepers, mosses, ferns and epiphytes growing on it, litter which must be cleared before work on pounding the sago can begin. The women as they beat the roof are doing something to the house parallel to clearing the outside of the trunk of a sago palm before they set to work on it. The image of the *gamaiyit* as being like the trunk of a sago palm appeared clearly here in this short episode but not in any other part of the ritual so far as I know.

Text VII

Selpak:	And you stand up, you must stand with your bundles, your palm-spathe containers, the coconut-leaf-base strainers . . .
Various men	(*shouting*) Yes, Yes! with all the things for pounding sago! the pounders! the palm spathes you use for it!
Wutilkai:	The pounder, your best pounders (you must have them with you) to get success in your work and get plenty of good food. You, here, go and stand on this side. Bərau, Wapərik and some others, you go and stand on this side! Daukas, Meini, Bagi, Səwarbo, Maikət, you go and stand on that side. Get your pounders and come to pound the sago palm. Clear away all the dust and bits, the moss and stuff on it for it's a *balbiti* [one spiny variety of sago palm] — it's a *mʌŋgi* [another spiny variety] you're working on!
Səlaukei:	The women from times long long past have always got their things (to do this). The old women would get their things, get them ready, and then one would take her adze and strike it right through (the roofing), take coconut-leaf strainers, take a palm spathe and push them into (the house) so that it (the spirit) saw the things she used. And that done she would go and bash

58

the outside of the roofing . . . (*laughs from listeners*) . . . an old
woman would come, her pounder tap! tap! tap! the stick she was
leaning on tap! tap! tap! Your pounder, adze, stone adze? Where
are they? (Get them.)

Wɔkapət: All the stuff, each woman carry her own stuff for pounding sago.

Səlaukei: You must bring your blunt pounding adze, fasten them up in
your bundles with the other things.

Wutilkai: Because we're going to do the *garamut*-beating bit.

Samo: The men, give it everything! the women, give it everything!
[literally 'men, foam now bubbling boiling! women, foam now
bubbling, boiling!']

Extract VIII: To show how men discuss the order of the song performance in terms which assume knowledge of some of its implicit associations

On the opening night they must sing the whole song of Panu'ət. They sing from
about 7.30 p.m. through the night until the dawn has come at about 6.30 next
morning. During this time they take a few short breaks, each of about ten to
twenty minutes, amounting *in toto* to about two hours. For the rest of the time
they sing. The song is made up of different 'verses', each on a subject they can
name. The 'verse' is identifiable by naming its subject theme, by saying for
instance 'Now they are about to sing Hibiscus Flower' (*lyibərag tapəlut*). In the
one song (for a different ritual) that I tape-recorded and transcribed almost in
full, the night-long performance included just over 150 different 'verses'. Certain
verses are repeated many times before they move on to the next one. The
number of repeats is large if there is evident enthusiasm and delight in the
singing of that verse. The performance and the volume of sound is tremendous
and exhausting. By the time dawn approaches, men's voices grow hoarse, their
throats sore. After it is over, some men can only croak or speak in husky
whispers. The song is repeated, in part or in full, on subsequent nights in ensuing
weeks before the rites are ended. By performance and repetition younger men
learn it.

The words in the verses are said to be archaic and few of them are words of
Gnau though some of them can be twisted to resemble words now used (see
note p. 41). They may also be interpreted because some words are like words
in neighbouring languages that they know, or sometimes even because they are
like Pidgin words. Names of places and persons in the songs are recognisable
though they too often have distorted syllables. There is much sound or syllable
repetition and drawing out. There is a sense-but-nonsense, jabberwocky quality
to the words and language of the verses. It is as if sung speech were being played
on as an artistic medium with sound emphasis and distortion, which yet allows
for likeness to be seen to real language. So wood or paint may be used to create
objects highly stylised or distorted which still have some graspable likeness to
real things like a person's arms or eyes. In one, the medium is voice sounds and

the resemblance is to real words; in the other, the media are visual or plastic and the resemblance is to real objects. Seeing the likeness was an aspect of their interpretations which came to the fore when I sat transcribing the 'words' of the verses and asked them to say what they were about. So I would take a particular verse, say, the Hibiscus verse, and they would pick among the sounds, here and there, such correspondences as would sustain their interpretation of what that verse was about. The interpretation would be given first. For instance, the Hibiscus verse: the Man (the hero of the myth) has come to an ancient site, Raiyas; he stands up close to the stem of the hibiscus plant and picks a twig with blossom and puts it in his headdress; he comes to Raiyas and plants it there and then he dances with the blossom stuck in his calf bands. That is a representative example of the sort of detail a senior man would reach in explanation to me of what a verse was about. In fact the words of the verse as spoken for me to transcribe it are these (there are three strophes):

(A) *bəlim beli witətapi wimba ləgi tatapi wimbələgi witətapi wimba ləgi wimbəli bəli yamba witətapi wimba ləgi* (repeats)
(B) *bəli bəlim bəli witətapi wəmbu Raiyas* (repeats)
(C) *sua agaga aga waləyilpə wɔla waipia ragis siwulapia wula mələla wɔmbu Raiyas* (repeats)

In strophe A the men commented on *beli*, which is the Gnau word for the base of a tree; on *witətapi*, which contains the element *witət* 'it stands up' in Gnau (*witətapi* could roughly be construed 'it stands up beside you' as *-api* is so close to *-əpi* the affixes of /direct-object thing/ + /indirect-object marker/ + /pronoun 'you'/); on *wimba ləgi* as an equivalent for the Gnau *wasin ləginda* 'it sticks something into the (headdress) thing of the man'; on *tatapi* as an equivalent of *tapəlut* 'hibiscus'; on *wimbəli* as the word the myth hero used for *tapəlut*. In strophe B, they commented on *wɔmbu Raiyas* as equivalent to 'he brings it to Raiyas', Raiyas being the name of a known ancient site. In strophe C, they commented on *sua* as equivalent to the Gnau *su'əp* 'thighs'; on *agaga* as 'beating' because it is like *yɑgɑga* 'beating a hand drum'; on *wɔmbu* as 'the bottom' equivalent to the Gnau *nəmbət* 'bottom', in the sense of referring to him kicking his heels up to his bottom as he danced. As I went through the hours of the recording (my example is taken almost at random from somewhere in the middle), the senior men would give the statement of what the verse was about with fair confidence, and then after that, in response to further questions, say what particular words they could interpret for me. The men who did most of the work with me in transcribing and interpreting this tape-recording were two senior men (Səlaukei and Kantyi) who had taken part in the performance and who were both acknowledged by others as men who really knew about that ritual song.

I have dealt at this length on a single verse to bring home two main points. First, it is not because they can understand the words of the verses that they know what they are about, but for other reasons (note for example, that *wɔmbu*

60

in the phrase *wɔmbu Raiyas* receives different interpretations in strophes B and C, that two different words are taken to be equivalents of *tapəlut* 'hibiscus' in strophe A). Secondly, it is a feat of devoted memory to perform such a song, 150 verses long, few verses having any closer correspondence to their real language than the one that I have quoted. They do not perform them as often as they used to and the songs may, I suppose, soon be lost beyond recall. In the performances I witnessed, mistakes in the order of verses, or verses left out, were pointed out. They know it is easy to make mistakes. There is a proper order for a complete, correct performance and it is in terms of this ideal order that they consider they make mistakes.

The extract which will follow comes from a discussion among various men about the order of performance of the song. From one point of view, it reveals some aspects of how they remember this order. From another, it reveals something of the variety of links which parts of the song have to other areas of their knowledge and experience. When I transcribed the song I have mentioned, I asked them to explain the verses and they told me or taught me what they were about. I took it verse by verse. They must have learned what they knew about it by performing it, from hearing myths, from learning the application of verses in it to various other activities outside the situation of performing it, from countless disparate ways in which things relevant to it cropped up in other circumstances. They did not learn it by going through it verse by verse and having it explained to them.

The extract will seem incomprehensible without explanation of the main assumptions that lie behind the performance of such songs as this one. The speakers in the extract share these assumptions, and do not need to explain them to each other.

I have noted that one word for 'spirit' also means 'song' (n. V.4) and that another word for 'spirit' also means 'myth' (n. VI.11). A particular named spirit may be known both through a myth and through a song; indeed it may have more than one version of each. The song of the spirit can be seen sometimes to correspond to the myth of the spirit. I should note that, given the word identity *bəlyi'it* = song = spirit and *malət* = myth = spirit, I could not translate this sentence into Gnau and make it make sense. In the myth, a named person usually with human and superhuman attributes does various things; occasionally the person has more than one name or there is more than one person. He (or they) comes from one village to another one, does something there and then goes on. A myth, therefore, may contain information about place names, names of persons, objects and actions which can serve as reference points. A myth recounts these as a sequence of events.

The first conspicuous feature of the plan of one of these great songs is that it is seen to have direction and location in a geographical sense. At any point during the night's singing, a question such as 'Where is it now?' could be answered by saying 'It [the verse being sung] is at the village of Womil', or 'We are now

61

crossing the river Napigəsa', or 'It is on the path going up into the ancient village of Maru.' The grand design for each of the great songs is this: the song begins at the village Rauit where it is being sung, it goes off in one direction from place to place until it reaches a distant site on the outskirts of the country of which they had traditional knowledge (some place usually not more than about fifteen miles away by the map); there the song is 'turned round' and brought back by a different route, back to Rauit, where it ends with dawn. The song travels in a rough circle back to the point where it began. It can be sung therefore in two ways, either going out by route A and coming back by route B or vice versa. So when they discuss the order of verses for the performance they use verbs of travel and direction, speaking of it going along in an upwards direction towards the higher land lying in the Ningil or Lumi direction, north or westwards, or going downwards towards the south and east. The subject themes of one set of verses may be linked to the place which the song has reached: for example, in one song, as it reaches the river Yakəsu, the verse-subject sequence goes King-fisher, Mayflies, Foam on the Water, Water, Frog (of a particular kind), Fish, Water Snake, River Boulder, Great Cuckoo Dove (seen in great trees of the forest on the river bank). The themes take one through and across the river to the forest on the other side. The myth may tell what happened at a particular place: for example, the hero hid his skin and went away to dance incognito at a certain place, his skin left behind was set on fire, and he went mad turning and twisting as he danced, coming dancing in the patches of moonlight and at each pause in the dance disappearing into the shadows, so that when the song reaches that place the verse subject sequence is Skin of the Hero, Fire, Moon.

Particular verses are closely linked with episodes in particular myths, and so with places. But myths and songs are also owned by particular clans, and some-times even by particular lineages. Members of the groups in question have a right to tell the myth or to perform the song, which they regard as theirs and may consider others to usurp if they use it. They may teach the song and rites to others; in the past this has been done and a transfer of shell wealth given in recognition by those who were taught it and thereby acquired secondary rights to perform it. They are said to hold the rights second (*lalut* 'jaw') while the owners hold them first (*garut* 'hair of the head'). The people who now make up the village of Rauit have detailed traditions of their diverse clan and lineage origins, and places of settlement in the distant past. Their myths are different. Now they live together and the people of one clan know that the distinctive myth and the song owned by another particular clan and specially associated with its performance for a new *gamaiyit* differ from their own. But they see these differences just as versions of knowledge and practice about the same general spirit, in this case, Panu'ət. The different myths that have some link to different verses sung for the making of a new *gamaiyit* are a miscellany. The names, sex, number of protagonists, episodes and actions vary. They are not either in general, or even in almost any single particular, versions or continuations of each other. But they are assimilated, put together by the people and acknowledged all as different things to do with the same one spirit whose most common name is Panu'ət. As the people who now make up Rauit have come in the distant past from different places, from different directions, so the myths associated with their clans come from different places, different directions, and so the verses of the song linked with a certain myth belong to those places or come from that direction.

The whole song now sung at Rauit as a great circle in one of two directions is made up of sections identifiable sometimes by the name of the associated myth (e.g. Gamulti − Bird of Paradise) or sometimes by a special name for that song section (e.g. Bulti Lagəp − Bones of the Snake), and the sections are also linked with particular clans and lineages and their history, and with places. As the village is now the unit made up of people of different origins, so the song is now a unit made up of sections from different sources. When the men of a particular hamlet make a new *gamaiyit* they are assisted by men of all the hamlets of the village. When they sing for the building of a new *gamaiyit*, they sing the whole song, the whole village comes to sing it, and the song sets out in the direction which will take them first to the section of the song linked to the clan or lineage of the men who have instigated and built the new *gamaiyit* for themselves to sleep in. Though the song is made up of parts associated with different clans in the village, a sense of its unity is implied when they speak of the parts belonging to some clans as the 'base' (*beli* 'base' or 'stump of a tree', also 'origin' or 'source') of the song, and the parts belonging to others as its 'crown' (*bəna'at* 'crown of a tree').

The journey of the song from Rauit by one route to a point where it turns round and comes by another route back to Rauit is then one main guide to the plan of the song. A second main feature of its plan is its division into parts that are called (1) the part of the spirit (*lyirag bəlyi'isa* 'they sing belonging to the Song Spirit' or *lyirag bəlyi'it* 'they sing the Song Spirit') and the other parts called (2) the part of the spells (*lyirag bəlyigap* 'they sing the spells'). The basic plan of the song is (A) a song-spirit part − *bəlyi'it*, (B) a spells part − *bəlyigap*, (C) a song-spirit part − *bəlyi'it*, (D) a spells part − *bəlyigap* and (E) a song-spirit part − *bəlyi'it*. The beginning at Rauit is *bəlyi'it*, the journey out is *bəlyigap*, the point at which it turns round *bəlyi'it*, the return journey *bəlyigap*, the end at Rauit again *bəlyi'it*. The characteristic which they say identifies *bəlyi'it*-part verses is that they contain the names of distant places and ancient and distant sites of settlement. These paradoxically are the parts sung when the song is at Rauit or at the point of turn. In contrast they say the *bəlyigap* verses contain the names of land tracts which they regard as coming within present Rauit territory. These are the parts sung when the song is on its journey. But these alleged characterising distinctions do not stand out in the transcriptions I have made. Many verses contain no place names; only occasional *bəlyi'it* verses contain strings of place names. *Bəlyi'it* verses may contain names of persons appearing in the myths, while *bəlyigap* verses more often contain recognisable names of animals, plants or objects; but neither sort of name is exclusively found in one or other part. Nor are all *bəlyigap* verses used as spells.

In n. II.4 above, I explained that young men learn the main body of the spells they will use for diverse kinds of magic through repeated performance of these great songs. Although certain parts of the song are called *bəlyigap* or spell parts, the *bəlyi'it* parts also contain spells. The *bəlyigap* parts contain long sections to do with hunting and gardening activities. The *bəlyi'it* verses tend to be the source of spells used in *rites de passage*. A particular *bəlyigap* section may be identified by saying *lyirag digasəm* 'they will sing of the game things', i.e. spells to do with hunting, or *lyirag wadagəsəm* 'they will sing of the things to do with tubers', i.e. with growing tubers. A verse-subject sequence to do with hunting, for example, goes: Early Morning Mist, Cobwebs (across the paths), String Bag, Pig Noises; a verse-subject sequence to do with taro-gardening, for example, goes Holes for Planting, First Leaves Sprouting, Leaves Trembling in the Breeze. The sequences follow an order familiar to every man from common experience. As the verse on trembling leaves is sung, the singers should shake their heads in imitation of the leaves. At the same time the verse can also be situated by where the song has got to, and it may also be linked to a particular myth, the persons in the myth and what happened to them and to the particular clan who hold the song section *garut* 'first'.

A third scheme of associations also gives some guiding order to parts of the song, although it does not permeate the whole song in the way the other two do. The scheme is set by linking certain verse sections to phases in the progress of the night. Thus in one song, at a point towards the middle of the night, there are verses in which they sing of the moon, and of noises made by creatures of the night; and as the night grows more cold and blue at the approach of dawn, the song, now close again to the village, has as subjects for the verses sago flour, yams and taro, the leaves to wrap them up in, the bark straps for carrying them in bundles to the village, the firewood for cooking, the birds of the dawn chorus − (1) Bell Magpie, (2) Cockerel and (3) Coucal − yams, the water cooking in pots, Pink and Yellow Clouds in the Eastern Sky, the sun. For the singers will eat a meal in the early morning when the song is done.

Thus a great variety of knowledge is associated with verses of the song. Rote and logical memories and reminiscences of personal experience contribute to its evocative power and beauty. A list of the subject themes and correspondences to be found in the various songs would read like a great inventory of Gnau culture and perceptions of the natural and physical environment in which Gnau people live. I have described three aspects of the general design of the song, which couple associative knowledge with the plan. They go a little of the way towards enabling us to understand how the Gnau are able to recall the order and content of such long songs, sung in an 'archaic' unreal language. The Russian psychologist A. R. Luria was able to study a memory giant called S. V.

Shereshevski for over thirty years. The mnemonic devices used by Shereshevski 'consisted mainly in visualising certain items of information, and in arranging others in the form of a scenic story, such as the story of a walk in which various incidents happened, each incident being a code signal for an item of information' (Kräupl Taylor 1966, p. 210). The similarity of his mnemonic device to the Gnau plan of the song as a journey is most striking: he was a hypermnestic celebrity. Some time after I had completed this commentary on the text that follows, I read Frances Yates's study *The Art of Memory* (1966), an invention of the Greeks, which was passed on to Rome whence it descended in the European tradition. I think the Gnau have developed something of the same art by themselves.

Text VIII

Sǝlaukei:	We will sing it to reach this place, and then we should go on to sing it as it goes on up to that place there. We must sing (the verses) of the song spirit. We should go on up towards that place, singing to go and reach Ningil village, its hamlet Wawas, and then we sing the Spider Lily verses and should go on from there and sing and turn (the song) round to come back down with (verses) of (the ancient site of) Maiyi Wɔlgam right over there. When you do these ones you've turned it and following on from there you're returning. We should sing a base (of the tree or origin or source) (verse) just once, and then you can go back and set off in the other direction.
Wɔkapǝt:	You should sing (the verses of the spells) for game and then you can turn it round and you can sing our (clan's) (verses).
Sǝlaukei:	Sing the base spell for game just once, and then you (sing) your (verses) and so go off onto that part.
Dukini:	Yes! I know the (verses) belonging to you lot too! I know. The base one just once and then the crowns (of the tree) part. You go off in one direction, I go off in the other.
Sǝlaukei:	Yours too, what you sing, I know it.
Wɔkapǝt:	These men[VIII.1] here they say — you are going to sing theirs. Well I can sing theirs too. The base (verse) once, then he goes off on his side there.
Sǝlaukei:	One base (verse) done, then off on the (ones) of the crown.
Dukini:	Ah! your part, yes I've got it in my string bag.[VIII.2]
Samo:	Hey! Listen to what I say. The parts for cooking those things, they're not thingummebob — spells part. They go on and on and then I sing Tubers to bring that (section) to a close. I sing Tubers and they go on straight along and then I continue it with the game (hunting spell) things.
Sǝlaukei:	Yes, we should sing the Tuber (verses), the tuber things (spells), go on with those, and then you should link on the (spells) for (hunting) birds and you go on down and cross over the big river.
Samo:	Sing (verses) of the song spirit to break in there and, with some (verses) left out, then I go into the Madǝn[VIII.3] version and set

65

off with some of the game (spells). That's how I lead into the Madən part.

Səlaukei: You do those ones to lead into the Madən part and then go to the ones for firing (the hunting ash).

Samo: Those ones? No, I don't go on like that.

Səlaukei: Yes, when people from all about have come, and have done the firing and dancing[VIII.4] there, you should sing (the verses about) coconuts and bananas first, those ones, then you sing (the spells) for game after them — go on with those until right into the dawn, then we will sing the Chirruping Grub,[VIII.5] sing the spirit[VIII.6] one there, it should be after the other ones. If you sing the spirit, that shade of the dead one (too early), you will draw the night out long. That one must be left until the dawn has come clear, then you can sing it with the Chirruping Grub (verse). If you sing the Chirruping Grub one, then you will draw the night out into a long one. That one belongs to (the ancient site) Sədaugən Gauwatim.

Wɔkapət: Yes and then sing the Morning Mist (verse) (*whistles and calls of agreement: ala! ala! ala!*)

Səlaukei: When the dawn birds are singing away, that's what they used to say, then sing the Shade of the Dead (verse), sing Chirruping Grub. That's the finish. By then the dawn should be spread out over the village.

Wutilkai: You should sing that one *sun sun.*[VIII.7] The bird singing '*kuwei kuwei*' (*whistles the call*), then you should be singing the *Suŋgin* rattan (verse).

Səlaukei: Yes, you should sing (*sings part of the 'Suŋgin' verse*): '*bin bin bin bin wɔla wɔsa Saigaowa a Saiwɔwat*'.

Wutilkai: No, no! that one's the *bin bin* — it belongs right back up over there.

Wɔkapət: That's the one for over there and the *tun tun tap* big liane one should not be done then.

Səlaukei: But that's the Shade of the Dead one; the *tun tun riyei* one; that's the one which belongs at Sədaugən, which is for the Shade of the Dead, for the Staghorn Fern.[VIII.8]

Wutilkai (singing) *Tun tun riyei tun tun riyei wɔla wɔsa taiylalao tun tun riyei eleileilei lei* — then it's over.

Səlaukei: Yes, you mustn't draw the night out long (by singing it too early), leave it until the dawn stands forth and then you sing *run ala rapeiŋga rapeiŋga walilililili* [Chirruping grub].

Wutilkai: *Wɔk wɔk wɔk wɔk wɔk wɔk wɔk wɔk* [onomatopoeia of frogs and crickets piping towards dawn], that, yes, then you can sing those things.

Səlaukei: A bird just beginning to sing, then, they said, that's the time to sing the Shade of the Dead — Chirruping Grub, Mosquito (verses) — and so I sing them that way and it's the way the ancestors used to sing them.

Wutilkai: Yes! that way! that's how we should sing them!

Notes

VIII.1 The word I have translated by 'men' is *ta'aŋ*. It is the collective term for 'sons', i.e. the kinship term for *naŋganin* 'son' in the plural (see n. I.5 above). The men in question are the present 'sons' of the clan to which that part of the song belongs.

VIII.2 Dukini, through this metaphor, claims that he knows that part of the song, has got it remembered, just as he has got things stuffed in his own string bag.

VIII.3 On p. 42 I noted that Madən is a name used quite commonly to refer to the whole performance. But it is also properly the name of a particular version of the rites as one clan performs them, and for the *garamut* call-sign which identifies that clan, and for the *garamut*-beat rhythm distinctive in general of the rites for a new *gamaiyit*. Where I have written 'I go into the Madən version', what the speaker actually said was *gabagəla lagəp* 'I am then breaking of it long bones', using the idiom *-gəl lagəp* for the Madən song which I have listed at (3a) on p. 42.

VIII.4 The swing-dancing movement back and forth with the feet is especially associated with singeing and searing the *gamaiyit* by fire when a man carries fire in the shell round the new house. This is done at the very outset of the song, and again a second time when the song is turned round — also a *bəlyi'it* part. Here I have translated *lyisəlilupa* 'they will swing-dance' by the phrase 'when they have done the firing and dancing' to indicate that he refers to this second singeing with fire when the song is turned round.

VIII.5 The Chirruping Grub (*gilpə'at*) is the source of high insistent, whirring chirruping that is most noticeable in the early and late watches of the night. The people say it is a grub or larva that produces it. It sounded like a cicada to me. They say the grub 'draws' the moon up into the sky and 'pulls' it down too.

VIII.6 The word used here was *malət* 'spirit', but it was understood in the sense of collectivity of the dead, ancestors (see n. VI.11 above). As becomes clear from the use of *gelputi* 'shade of the dead', in sentences which follow, it is a spirit of the dead that is the subject. Chirruping Grub is so closely linked with Shade of the Dead that the song verses are spoken of as a unit, sometimes by one name, sometimes by the other, often by the two names together, for they are alliterative — *gelputi–gilpə'at*.

VIII.7 *Sun sun* referred to a kind of rattan called *suŋgin*. In the recording that follows there is frequent quoting of bits of the song either by singing them, or by quoting the distinctive sound features of certain verses to identify them. I have left these in the form in which I transcribed them. *Sun sun* and *tun tun tap* both refer to kinds of large rattan used for the baskets in which game is smoked and dried.

VIII.8 A huge staghorn fern is tied round the main post of the *gamaiyit* at the top during the decoration of the post. I was not told that the fern had any special association with the dead, although the decorated post does.

Extract IX: To show the ellipsis that often makes what the Gnau say about ritual seem enigmatic; and to illustrate how an event in the ritual is given more than one interpretation

Text IX

Wutilkai: By sunlight now you must shake it [i.e. the *gamaiyit*] so that, carrying fire, it [i.e. the spirit] goes off to sear the things[IX.1] there (in the gardens). For it is the Eagle Spirit. It is the Wind. You know that. We have seen this done before. Now for the present you may eat without taking any special care[IX.2] but when we come to eating the sago jelly and they are sitting round (after the figure has been put on the post) and the inside of the *gamaiyit* is being done [i.e. decorated] you (*addressing the matrilaterally related men present*)[IX.3] must not eat anything. You must not eat. We have seen these things done before.

Notes

IX.1 The word in Gnau used for 'things' in the sense of any material possessions is also the only word they have for 'food' in general. I think this sense is its central meaning. The word *nəm* is often bound to the verb root -*nu*- 'eat' when someone says, for instance, 'I have eaten' (*dəgədanu nəm*, literally 'I have eaten things'). It would, I suppose, be true to say that a man of property, a man of substance, a man of things, in Gnau society would be a man of food. I mention this because the use of the same word both for any 'things' in general and for 'food' in general strikes me at first as curious.
IX.2 'You may eat without taking any special care' – *dji yida tambit yinu nəm*. He uses the phrase *yida tambit* for doing something without special care and attention which I commented on earlier in relation to the notion of the special or peculiar quality of ritual (see n. II.1 above). Also note the phrase *yinu nəm* 'eat things'.
IX.3 At various points in the rites for building a new *gamaiyit*, men who have matrilateral ties to the clan it will belong to are singled out for special duties. At this point the senior men so related are reminded of their special tie and set apart by the duty to be present at the making of the image but to abstain from the food which the others eat to celebrate completion of the figure.

This extract comes in the recording a few minutes after the one used in extract VII. It is also about the shaking of the *gamaiyit*. The first sentence seems to convey some dark meaning, which I could only half glimpse when I first heard it. My attention was caught by *wiyeliliyu nəm* 'sear the things'. The verb *wiyeliliyu* stands out because it is the one used for the action of going round the new *gamaiyit* with fire in a half coconut shell on an arrowshaft, singeing and searing the Face and all the posts and beams of the house. It identifies that part of the ritual, a part that is done by night. But this sentence begins by saying 'in sunlight' and 'it carries fire' and to 'sear' things. The fire is not made until after nightfall. And this shaking is to be done immediately after noon. No fire is made.

When I asked for an explanation, the man helping me with the transcription and translating gave me one easily and without hesitation by spelling out the detours of reasoning implicit but hidden to me. The sudden shaking, the brief crash of song, the banging *garamuts* are to startle the spirit away from the new *gamaiyit*, to startle it and send it back to the gardens. It will be called back to the *gamaiyit* at nightfall by the opening of the great song when fire is kindled into flame. In the interim the main post of the *gamaiyit* will have the image of the spirit (Masipə — the Face — or Ləgin — the Man) put on it and decorated, and the house itself will be decorated. The spirit must be absent (or not concentrated there) when this is done. It will be at the gardens. The spirit, Panu'ət, is particularly associated with gardens as its habitat, and is concerned with sago stands and some other growing foods (see Lewis 1975, pp. 169–80). It watches over these foods and benefits their growth. It must go off with the sun or sunlight to sear the foods growing in the gardens to make them grow well. It uses the sun to sear the plants as men that night will use fire to sear the new house. The way the man helping me put this was by saying that the sun was like 'a shadow' or 'reflection' (*malauda*) of the fire they would use that night!

To see this so clearly and quickly I imagine the man explaining it to me drew on his knowledge of many other circumstances in which spirits are startled off by bangs, blows and noise, on general ideas of spirit localisation and concentration at places, the way spirits are brought from the bush into the village in particular rituals, concentrated in the village and finally sent off. This is a pattern evident in most large-scale rites. In this case, when the herb and plant elements required for making the image on the post were collected in the gardens on the day before the roof was thatched, food was eaten at the gardens, and then the materials collected were carried to piping from two little bamboo flutes into the village, the spirit accompanying them from the gardens. It had to be sent off while the image was fashioned on the post. They say it would be dangerous to have the spirit concentrated with them at a time when they fashion the image and fiddle with the materials to get it made right. To the observer, it seems as though they do not wish to confuse the practical, human fumbling and fashioning activity with the image completed and inhabited by the spirit.

The aspect of Panu'ət as a spirit above the crowns of palms and trees in the gardens is brought out by its name of Eagle Spirit (*malət gəmən*) and Wind Spirit (*malət də'aipə*) or Wind. The eagle wheeling above the trees and striking down at tree-living game is the name most closely associated with firing the hunting ash and with hunting phalangers and tree-living marsupials. The Wind moving and rustling the crowns of the palms, invisible, now here, then there gives to the senses a way of better understanding how a spirit may be present though not visible, sometimes concentrated at a place but able to move or disappear. Wind offers an experience of invisible non-material presence that helps them to grasp the sense of a spirit being there. It serves as evidence or analogy in the way that scent or smell also serves them as another example of invisible presence or power at a distance. Blowing and winds, scents of aromatic plants, sounds and words are all perceptible, yet insubstantial, and without body; and they are all used in ritual in special ways.

From this short extract we learn another interpretation of the action of shaking the house and bashing its new thatch. It is to startle the spirit off and send it back to the gardens to do its beneficial work there. It is also necessary to do this so that the men may fashion the image of the spirit on the post. In extract VII, the interpretation given to the same action was that the house was like a new-felled sago palm to be cleaned and cleared of entangled litter, that the women were to show themselves to the spirit together with their sago-working implements and be recognised by it. The shaking of the house is done just after much food has been brought and exchanged among the people present. They give each other sago and meat in double the normal amounts. One part is eaten, the other kept for later. The men who have thatched the house eat inside the new house under the scaffolding underneath the roof. They stood on this scaffolding of saplings to tie the thatch on. The scaffolding resembles a roof within the house and it is called the '*gamaiyit* child' (*gamaiyit niŋgi*). When they shake the house, and shout out the verse of song, they say they are shouting out in praise of the food just given. And just before they do it, they put the leaves, coconut shells and other containers from which they have just eaten on top of the scaffolding, the '*gamaiyit* child', so that when they shake the whole house structure, all the containers, shells and things fall down off the scaffolding, bang, bang, bang, on to the ground. The closest anyone comes to explaining this aspect of the shaking in the tape-recording is again Wutilkai (just before the shaking is going to happen). He says: 'Eat the food. You must put the things [i.e. the shells, leaves, etc.] up on top (of the scaffolding) so that when you shake it all the things come tumbling down *ru! ru! ru!* Our Eagle, Our Spirit that!' All that I gathered in direct explanation was that this was of benefit for food. But if I take Wutilkai's reference to 'Our Eagle, Our Spirit' together with the other interpretation of the spirit going off to the gardens to sear and benefit the plants growing there, I see a possible comparison between the Eagle above the palms in gardens making the food abundant, and the moment of shaking in which the things, just before full of food, fall down from high up. But alternatively, I could see the things falling down as debris, as the entangling litter cleared off. The things to be done in the rites at the moment of shaking the *gamaiyit* are clear and well known. The interpretation is not simply, explicitly and coherently set on a single theme.

The object of this succession of extracts has been to find whether something like a view or views on ritual could be made out for one society. I believe it is of particular interest in that the extracts are taken from conversation between the participants or from the proceedings themselves and are not responses to the questions of an alien observer. I chose the extracts from a long tape-recording transcribed and translated in the field, but my selection was made after I had written chapter 2. I chose passages to illustrate Gnau views and reflect my argument. By paying close attention to the way they express themselves to each other and to spirits, I have shown something of how they recognise a peculiar character in actions that should take place in the rites. They do not have special

70

words that can be translated by our words 'rite' or 'ritual'. In explaining the texts, I have been able to say something about how they learn these ways of 'doing things'.

To recapitulate: the succession of extracts was designed to show direct address to spirits in the ritual and the recognition of custom, and the hope of a successful outcome, and to show that the ritual must be done publicly before an audience, that there is concern for public registration and opinion of what they do. There is concern with the precise detail or order of procedure. I have quoted a direct request to the ancestors that the things they left to their descendants will be effective so that other people will speak well of the descendants because of what the ritual performed will enable them to do. They state their belief in the efficacy of the rites, and that men without knowledge of them would be as nothing, ignorant and incapable. They express the idea that the ritual is a source of knowledge of how to do things, learnt from the ancestors, and held in trust by senior men for their descendants. There is a duty to teach it and pass it on. They speak of their pride in their ritual and their trust that by it they will be admired and amaze others; that what they do is not ordinary; that it could not be discovered but only learned; that this knowledge has an origin or first cause; that it is peculiar to the people who practise it. The last extracts show how the symbolism of a particular action is publicly explained, and how men discuss the order of the song performance in terms which assume knowledge of some of its implicit associations. The extracts show the ellipsis that often makes what they say about ritual seem enigmatic. They illustrate how an event in the ritual is given more than one interpretation.

The Gnau do not have a single word for 'ritual'. In the study of ideas in other societies, we look to their words expecting specific terms for concepts. But as I wrote in the beginning of this section, a concept does not necessarily emerge only by being named. The issue is of how words reflect non-linguistic experience, and it is well known not to be simple. The words for snow in an Eskimo language, or the Nuer terms for cattle, are undoubtedly shining examples of how interests and activities may correlate with an elaborate vocabulary. But how precise are these correlations? Can we depend on the lexicon to reveal concepts? In English, there are many words with which to speak of domestic animals giving birth: a hen lays; a cow calves or drops; a horse foals; a sheep lambs; a dog pups or whelps; a pig litters; a sow farrows. And in French, a similar variety: *pouliner, vêler, chevreter, agneler, cochonner, chienner, chatonner, lapiner*. But in Italian, there is just *figliare* for them all (Mounin 1972, p. 163). Is animal husbandry so different in France and Italy? Should a Nuer anthropologist infer from these lexical differences, differences in cultural focus, interest, understanding, technical ability as between people in France and in Italy? A dictionary does not just mirror the ideas in a culture. The wealth of ideas in a book is not exhausted by an inventory of the words it contains. Nor does it follow that something becomes a concept only when it is named. 'Breach for breach: eye for eye; tooth for tooth; as he hath maimed a man, so shall it be rendered to him' (Leviticus 24: 20). The Hebrews had no word for this idea. The Romans called it *talio*. Did the one people therefore have the concept and the other not? Ideas like kinship, sacred and profane, nature and culture, may be important to the people in certain societies, and yet in some of them we find no single words for such ideas. In many cases, the sorts of concept that require more than a single term may be as interesting as (or more interesting than) those which are conveniently labelled and isolated for us by specific words. And ideas may be expressed through actions as well as in words. The English of an earlier age had no word 'taboo', yet the concept was not wholly foreign to them. It is instructive to look as Steiner (1967) did, in his first chapter, at the discovery of taboo in Polynesia. For Captain Cook did not note the word on his first voyage, but he did record actions and behaviours that typified it. 'It is not common for any two to eat together, the better sort hardly ever; and the women never upon any account with the men, but always by themselves. What can be the reason of so unusual a custom, 'tis hard to say, especially as they are a people, in every other instance, fond of Society, and much so of their Women. They were often asked the reason, but they never gave no other answer, but that they did it because it was right, and express'd much dislike at the Custom of Men and Women Eating together of the same Victuals' (Cook 1793, I, p. 91, quoted in Steiner 1967, p. 24).

He did not come across the word on his first voyage, and we must remember that 'taboo' was not a word conspicuous by its use in speech. But on the second voyage, the word 'taboo' was noticed and it was in the journal of that voyage, after Cook's death, that his successor, King, took on himself to explain this word of 'mysterious significance' which he did by laying 'before the reader, the particular instances that fell under our observation of its application and effects'. What followed were the classic passages from which the word 'taboo' became known to Europeans (see Steiner 1967, pp. 23–7). Concepts may sometimes be held, yet expressed in actions far more often and conspicuously than in words. They do not necessarily become concepts only because they are lexicalised. A marked concern with words, and single words at that, figures largely in what some call cognitive anthropology. An exclusive concern with words may blinker us so that we fail to grasp important ideas that are not so easy to identify because they are not conveniently labelled. I think this is the case with the Gnau view of ritual.

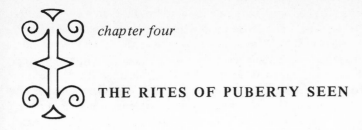

chapter four

THE RITES OF PUBERTY SEEN

The village of Rauit sits at the end of a ridge among sharp-cut foothills and valleys on the inland side of the Torricelli mountain chain. It looks over forest south towards the Sepik river. Four of its hamlets are clumped in one main body at the last high point along the curling ridge. Another hamlet, Animbil, is close to them, but Bi'ip, the remaining one, is a quarter of an hour's walk through sago palms, a bit of forest, gardens, then along a branching ridge beside a cliff edge, away from the main part of the village. The houses of each hamlet are scattered close together higgledy-piggledy, the ground about them sandstone or mudstone with all grass and weeds scraped away. Coconut palms curve up high above the houses and ring right round the hamlets. Their feathery rustling crowns give shade in the village from the sun at noon. Surrounding the central area of bare brown ground and thatched brown houses are many shrubs, hibiscus, small groves of great green-leaved banana plants.

On an ordinary fine day, each hamlet will look deserted from about nine o'clock in the morning to about four in the afternoon. The doors of houses are shut and barred. The two or three grown-ups who have not gone off to the gardens will sit inconspicuous in the shade or under the roof of a day-house, minding babies or snoozing. But on a day when something special happens, the hamlet, not deserted and still seems very different.

The rites of puberty take up a day, and they are staged in the hamlet where the boy or girl lives. Each family has a home space in the hamlet which includes the wife's house and, usually close by, a more or less open-walled day-house (*warkao*), a place to sit, eat, chat, receive visitors, a shelter from the sun or rain. In the early morning on the day, the family of the boy or girl concerned is to be found gathered at the porch or doorway to the mother's house where they are preparing a pot for cooking a special stew in (this stew is called the *wa'agəp*). It will be given to the boy or girl at a later point in the rites. On each occasion I have seen it done, the *wa'agəp* has been cooked in a traditional clay pot, although now many people use an aluminium saucepan or a bamboo tube for everyday cooking. The women of the village have given up making clay pots. The pot is lined with leaves, pieces of smoke-dried meat (*digap beirkatidəm*)

73

are laid in it, and grated coconut is sprinkled over them. The parents contribute some of these pieces of meat and so do people belonging either to their lineage or clan, or else to their hamlet. They come early to give them. As the pot fills up, water from a section of bamboo tied about with coloured cordyline leaves is poured over it. This water for the *wa'agəp* has been collected the day before from one of certain natural water holes or pools and it contains a number of specific substances: it is scented. The lining leaves are bent over to cover the contents of the pot and half a coconut shell placed on top. The mother takes it inside her house to cook.

Meanwhile people are assembling in the hamlet. The visitors drift in casually. Some may bring a few yams or taro or a coconut with them. The visitors are relations of the boy or girl, older sisters or the father's sisters married into another hamlet or village, who come with their families; clan relatives who live in other hamlets, and friends of the parents; but the important ones who should come are the relatives of the mother of the boy or girl.

Most people come dressed as they would be on any day but a few men are noticeable — it is nearly always the older senior men — because they have chosen to stick coloured croton leaves in their armlets, hibiscus flowers or a feather in their hair, a nose-ornament through their septum, or they have put on a shirt, wear a hornbill on their back or carry a decorated hunting bag. The day is early yet and people sit about in open places where the sun will warm them, chat about this and that, and smoke, relaxed, friendly, desultory.

By the time most have arrived, there will be a pile of yams provided by people in the hamlet and visitors. It is the job of the younger men to set to and peel them and cut them up in pieces. Four-gallon kerosene drums black with use, or a row of big green bamboo tubes, are filled with the pieces and put to cook over fires from which the smoke billows up. The older men continue to sit and chat, their talk punctuated by loud demands for an areca nut when one man or another brings one out to chew. The women with the children sit about together in the open rather to one side of the men. While the tubers are cooking, coconuts are husked and two or three of the most senior men sit down to the job of grating them. It has to be the most senior because of rules governing who will be able to eat the grated coconut. When the tubers are done, they are mashed in deep wooden bowls and the grated coconut sprinkled over and mixed into mash. Noisily calling names so no one is forgotten, the men distribute the mash for everyone present to eat.

Men jointly prepare the tubers and coconut mash first, and the women individually in their houses will cook sago jelly with greens or meat later in the afternoon. This pattern is followed at every social gathering or special occasion in the day when visitors come to a hamlet. The more special the occasion or the visitors, the more meat will replace greens to go with sago jelly. If rites are to be performed, they take place some time after the mash has been eaten but before the sago and meat is brought — this sago meal must wait upon completion of the business in hand. These are clear and regular features of Gnau procedure.

I shall begin by taking some extracts from my field notes to bring out certain points about how the rites are now performed. I must warn the reader that just as I did not see or find out every detail of what was done from the first, nor shall he. I wish to leave discussion of the details and full order of events until later.

The first time I saw the rites, they were for a boy called Geryik, whose mother (she was dead) had come from Mandubil. So a party of men from her natal lineage had come from Mandubil with their families to assist and take their part in the rites. I used to write up what I had seen as a connected description just afterwards from jotted notes taken on the spot.

As the sun became oppressive, I went inside the *gamaiyit* (men's house) into the dark brown shadows. A patch of jewelled colours through the doorway and occasionally bodies moving in the light outside. I slept for a while and when I awoke the scraping of coconuts was nearly over and I went outside. We ate the mash of yams with coconut . . . After we had eaten, the men sat down and smoked, ate betel. Some or most of the men from Mandubil moved into the *gamaiyit*. When, after a few minutes, I went inside most were lying down, snoozing. The time was about one o'clock. Geryik was inside the *gamaiyit* standing apart at the end of the house looking undecided, slightly apprehensive, waiting. His father was sitting close by untying a small package which contained leaves and some things which I could not see properly and a white phallocrypt shell (*barwi'it*). Geryik went out to his step-mother's house and I saw that he was shutting the door. He came back and stood waiting at the end of the men's house away from the main entrance. His father came to the end where most of the men were sitting or sleeping. He gave the small package of leaves and the shell to one of the Mandubil men who then went to Geryik and the two of them left quietly through the door at the other end of the house. I noticed no discussion beforehand as to who should go with Geryik: it seemed already decided. I asked whether I could follow them. There was obvious hesitation and reluctance. Someone said they were going to hide. Then Səlaukei (the former *tultul* 'appointed assistant village headman' of Bi'ip) whispered that they were going to *katim kok* and pointed to his penis. In a diversionary way Geryik's father started a digression on how they used to be decorated for initiation. I repeated my question whether I could go, saying if they did not want me to it was all right. No one said yes but instead they began telling me what they had gone off to do. The whole of this conversation between me, Səlaukei and a man from Mandubil was conducted with them and me leaning foward and whispering, no laughter but serious and intent. They would go down to the stream close by and hide from the sight of women. There, his *mami* (in this case his mother's father's younger brother because his *wauwi*, mother's brother, was away working at a plantation) would bleed his penis . . . Throughout our huddled whispered conversation, they said repeatedly that I must not speak loosely of this, that I must never speak of it in front of the women; that I must not write it down in my notebook lest my wife see it and talk to their women; that in the heat of lovemaking I should not tell her. There were a number of little boys listening to us. Even if not all could understand Pidgin, some could, but the men did not seem at all concerned at their overhearing what we were talking about. I said that I had heard of similar practices in other parts of New Guinea. There was enthusiastic assent that this went on all over New Guinea, and that at plantation they had talked to people from other places who had similar practices. They said many times that it was something good, nothing to do with *poisin* (black magic) and behind their reiterations I sensed that they were anxious that I should agree with them, that they thought white people might want to stop them from doing it.

After about twenty minutes Geryik and the man returned. Most of the men in the *gamaiyit* got up and went outside. Betel was brought, doled out. Soon many of the older men were chewing it. At the side of the house towards the rear end in the shadows of a grove of bananas, Geryik was standing, looking slightly self-conscious, no one very close to him, and waiting, his eyes mostly downcast. He was standing naked apart from the new white phallocrypt. If you looked carefully, smears of blood were visible on his forehead and upper arms — no woman was close enough to be able to see this. The women were gathered on the other side of the house by the main door and down in the dip by his step-mother's house. The betel-chewing men came close and were now all dotted about Geryik and among the green shadows of the grove of *lyimaŋgai* bananas, his father with them but not chewing betel. His father laid down beside Geryik a length of the stem of the *lyimaŋgai* banana which was wrapped in dried pandanus leaves and was about two feet long. Dukini and Səlaukei approached Geryik and first spat large blotches of orange-red betel juice on his forehead. Then the others drew close and all in succession spat great blotches of betel juice over him — the blotches fell on his forehead, upper chest, upper arms, thighs, legs, epigastrium, cheeks, and slowly turned brilliant red. There did not seem to be a strict order about this. The later men looked for an unspat area although some seemed to aim at an area carefully, for example, Dukini at the epigastrium, and someone else at the inguinal creases. During the two or three minutes which the spitting took, Səlaukei stood close beside Geryik chanting quietly, sometimes spitting again at him, sometimes blowing. Sometimes Geryik would bend his head slightly to be spat on, or close his eyes as the spit came near his eyes.

When he first stood on coming back after the penis-cutting, he did not look as though he had just been through a painful or disturbing experience. I saw no signs of tears, sweating, agitation or relief. He now stood blotched red all over. Two pieces of cortex from a tree lay on a *limbum* container with a little water in it (someone had asked earlier whether there was some water ready). Dawo from Mandubil picked them up. The cortex was thick and soft, almost cloth-like in texture, and came from a tree called *lu dəglit* which is found in the deep forest. Holding them like platters in his hands, Dawo grasped, pressing with very strong pressure, the thighs of Geryik and began smearing the blotches of betel juice over the skin of the boy. Occasionally he dipped the platters into the water, gradually smearing the betel juice everywhere until his entire body was wet shining red including his face and most of his hair.

This done, there was a pause and from slightly off-stage, abruptly Wanao, his step-mother, rushed across the gathered men, carrying a piece of firewood and a bush knife and stopped in front of Geryik. She touched the firewood to the ground and, calling something out, struck the firewood with a single blow of her knife, and was off back to her house.

After the spitting, a clamour of voices and talking — and it was only at this contrast that I realised how quiet and concentrated people had been until now.

After the spitting Geryik was given a portion of the *wa'agəp* meat from the clay pot to eat and later, with much noise and chatter, the meal of sago and meat was brought, laid out conspicuously, and given out.

I was able to see more of what happens in the rites on later occasions. The rites for a boy called Wowulden followed the traditional pattern more closely, because his father and others felt that they should, as he had had nothing to do with missionaries or mission schools. For him, they tied to his hair the traditional men's headdress, the *waipət*. This was done first and then he was spat with betel and smeared red. I shall quote now from the description of what followed next. (Many names are mentioned in the extract, but I have not tried to identify for the reader who the people are.)

Then they said they must go off to 'wash'. They began getting up to go. On the paths there was talk of placing people at the approaches to stop any women coming. In fact they were only going to the water holes in an open space among the sago palms between the two hamlets of Wimalu and Dagə tasa. Saibuten carried his bow and arrows, others carried the shells, herbs and other things for decorating him [Wowulden]. Tawo, Bilki, Mawikil, Gaita, Sawup, as well as all the Wimalu men and Dabasu, Galwun and Wisuk came. Most of the smaller boys came too but some, for instance the sons of Selpak, Wandi and Wɔkapət, had climbed up into trees. I wondered whether it was to watch or to keep out of the way. Tani, the younger son of Sawup, ran away out of reach, his father telling him off angrily and calling him names, that he was no good.

The men began washing. Wowulden held the bamboo tube of water for Patik to wash. Wowulden did not wash himself (because he had been spat on and the red betel was drying on him). Saibuten made ready the awl-like sharp *kuti* of wallaby bone (for the penis-bleeding), tying scented *dyu'ǝlbi* leaves and *bǝgǝrin* moss and *nalyibʌp* fern on it. Saibuten said that they were not to use razor or bottle on Wowulden but the *kuti* which was the right thing and what their fathers had used.

Wowulden was held in the arms of Patik with his head resting right back on Patik's shoulder, Patik's arms coming around him binding Wowulden's arms bent up across his chest. Patik's leg thrust the body of Wowulden forward so that his pelvis and penis were offered to Saibuten who was to stab him. They were standing slightly downhill. There was a brief flurry as someone thought he saw two girls on the hill. They yelled at them to go; it was a false alarm. Wowulden kept his position, resting back on Patik with his head right back on Patik's shoulder and upraised. Saibuten, bent over the *kuti*, was whispering spells into it. Then he took Wowulden's penis, rolled back the foreskin and bored the *kuti*'s point into the dorsum of the penis just above the glans. It was not rapidly done and he seemed to dig it well in and hold it there. Wowulden's whole body stiffened but held the position: he gave one brief moan. Saibuten withdrew the *kuti* and there were exclamations of approval, congratulation and satisfaction from the older men watching. Wowulden immediately crouched down and held a split length of big bamboo containing water into which blood from his penis flowed for some time.

Tawo (*aorʌpu* — a title given only to great fighters)[1] and Bilki (white-haired) turned to me wreathed in smiles, Tawo bobbing and thumping his foot, slightly turning as he swayed his body downwards, saying it was something wholly good they had done, just as their fathers had done it for them. Bilki, carrying leaves of *nʌlapǝ wimalu* [herbs that were used in war; see Lewis 1975, p. 209], sweating, for the sun at its zenith was very hot — I was soaked in sweat — said to me, 'We are working him well so he will grow up and kill game — we are following our ancestors, their good ways.'

Wowulden was still crouched down and bleeding. Parku stood over him and, taking a splinter of razor blade, stabbed his own penis so that as he stood with Wowulden crouched between his legs, his blood fell onto Wowulden's shoulders and gradually ran, shining in the sun, down his spine. The blood on his shoulders and back was smeared, some smeared on his forehead. Parku's blood was also collected in a piece of banana leaf containing some of the cooked *wa'agǝp*. They took care that no blood fell on the ground.

While this was happening, shouts and cries came from Tiflai (Wowulden's younger brother) who was resisting having his penis stabbed. He was being held by his legs and arms by Wɔkapɔt and others so that he was spread-eagled in mid-air as Saibuten prepared to stab him. But he struggled, wriggled

---

1 *Aorʌpu* is a title of address granted only to men who were quite outstanding killers. There were rarely more than one or two men who merited the title in any village.

and cried so much that despite the exhortations of his father, Sakai, and Wandi shouting that it would help him grow into a man, they eventually let him down without stabbing him.

Other men (Wɔgwei, Gaita, Wandi, Patik, Peikəp — exactly who else I am not sure) then stabbed their own penises and the blood was smeared on sons of Wandi, Sakai, Selpak and Peikəp, and on Tawo's grandson Wɔrmei. Some of the smaller boys were frightened and cried.

All the men present washed after this. Parku carefully washed his penis and gave water to Wowulden to wash his. They put hunting ash (*nawugəp*) on Wowulden's wound. They fastened the white shell *barwi'it* on him for the first time. They ‵carefully poured Wowulden's blood on the ground because there was no stream there. They filled bamboos with water and washed away where the blood was poured many times, and washed the ground where each man had bled for fear that a woman might see the blood or step over it. They rubbed at the ground with their feet to remove all trace. After the bleeding they did not spit Wowulden with betel a second time as they should have; the blood was hard to see against the smeared, now dry, betel from the first spitting.

From now on there was heightened mood of pleasurable excitement, accomplishment and noisy laughter, of talk and assertion over the rightness of what they were doing, that they were doing what their fathers had done for them, that they had been successful hunters and shooters, had defended their village and grown strong. Especially Sawup standing by the water hole, chewing betel, sweating, trembling, who gave a declamatory speech with his snarling, scalded-cat expression, high-pitched voice, repeatedly marking the points in his speech by the bow-drawing gesture pointed right down at the ground, a sinuous twisting rise and a stamp of his left foot followed by the thwack of his hand on his rump as his body straightened up, bouncing at the end of his remarks.

Wowulden stood beside the water hole while his decoration was completed mainly by Galwun and Patik. They gave him the *wardagi* and *daurənda* belts and fastened the shell *woawul* and *saoraŋgəl* round his *waipət* (headdress). But the woven rattan-tube covering with the bird feathers which should hang down from the *waipət* would not fit round it so they left it off. They hung a scented *dəkərwai* leaf round his neck, a shell *watwat* crossed over his chest. More *dəkərwai* was stuck through his armlets. Finally the bound leaves of the *wailtaro, nʌlapə nəmənau*, on long slender stems which they called a *wə'ati* [see pp. 155–7 below] was put into the centre of his *waipət* so that, they said, the *wə'ati* should hang over him and go down into him, that he would shoot pigs and game. The leaf containing the cooked *wa'agəp* meat with the blood was opened. Patik, followed by Wosin and Saibuten, bespelled a morsel of the *wa'agəp*, holding it close to their lips, blowing on it and singing the *nʌnt bulti* (the snake spell) in whispered voice as they pushed the *wa'agəp* skywards to arm's length, their faces raised up to the sky; then in succession turned their backs to Wowulden and gave him the *wa'agəp* with the right hand passed backwards over their shoulders to put it in his mouth. Morsels of *wa'agəp* were given then to the other boys who had been smeared. Some tiny crumbs which fell on the ground were picked up or buried with the toe in the ground to make sure women would not see them or step over them.

Now they were ready to go back to the village. The younger men, Wultu, Gaita, etc. finished combing their hair, others saying, Come on, let's go now. Sawup, in his excited mood, grasped old Mawikil's wrist, urging him, his *wusai* (co-initiate), with his high-pitched voice to come and eat the food which awaited him. Mawikil, making a big show of polite reluctance, was pulled by the wrist, to the laughter and encouragement of the others, the urging of Sawup, along the path to Dagətasa. Sawup, still holding Mawikil's wrist, called and grabbed the wrist of Gaita (Mawikil's grown-up son) and he too, smiling, was led along the path. Calls from many now to go to the village to eat the sago and meat.

Other men went first, then Wowulden in his splendour with the leaves of *nʌlapə* curling gracefully about him and his eyes staring modestly at the ground, other men behind. As they set off, a line of women and girls from Wimalu came along the path carrying food, and Saibuten, in mock anger, drew his bow at them for coming too soon where the men were.

On the way back, Wowulden stopped at a pool to get water to wash his fingers. Sawup advanced to the village calling out to the women and children to run away, get into their houses and hide. Some of the men were humming and whistling Tambin song verses, though not singing properly, as we entered the hamlet. Women in Sawup's direct path made themselves scarce but they moved only to the doorways of their houses or the shelter of a *warkao* (day-house). Murmurs and muted comments from the women as they entered the village.

Wowulden and all the boys who had been smeared went straight into the *gamaiyit* (men's house) away from public eyes. A few men entered it. Tawo stood just inside the doorway of the *gamaiyit* where a bit of light came in. He did the spell *nʌnt wə'ati* for them [see pp. 163—4 below], doing it in exactly the same manner as the *nʌnt bulti*, whispering the spell, blowing it into the *wa'agəp* and pushing, stretching it upwards, then turning to give it over his shoulder. He gave some to most of the boys, including his small grandson Wɔrmei.

The young boys stayed with Wowulden inside the *gamaiyit* until nightfall. The reason for this was that they and, most of all, Wowulden at this time were vulnerable to contamination by women. He was in special danger from a woman stepping over him or his shadow, which would, they said, harm his growth and his ability to hunt. [But he came out to dance that night when there was no risk to his shadow.]

The puberty rites for girls are like the ones for boys in some ways. But girls begin to menstruate in adolescence and a girl's first menstruation should decide the timing of her puberty rites. The following case makes this clear.

Malu was orphaned when young. She was looked after by her father's widowed younger brother Tukri. In fact Tukri had married Malu's mother after his brother's death, though Malu's mother had lived with Səlaukei immediately after her first husband's death, before coming to Tukri. In January 1968 Tukri left to work at a plantation on the coast. In June that year Səlaukei sent him a letter saying that Malu looked ready for her puberty rites. Tukri replied saying they must wait until he returned with his plantation earnings because it would not be right for others to give the puberty payment to her mother's brothers. He himself wanted to carry out her puberty rites. So they agreed to wait.

Malu was clearly pubescent. Partly there was concern about it because of the question of her marriage. Tukri had not fathered any children who had survived. He chose to look after Malu as a daughter, and also a young man called Sabuta as a son. Sabuta's relationship to Tukri was more complicated than Malu's. When Sabuta was still a child, his father too had died and his mother then married Səlaukei. Səlaukei and Tukri belonged to the same lineage. Sabuta's real father belonged to a different clan from them though he had lived in their hamlet. Səlaukei had many children. Tukri decided to bring up Sabuta and pass on half his land to him when he died (the other half was to go to the son Səlaukei had had by Sabuta's mother). Sabuta and Malu were regarded as a 'brother' and 'sister' jointly brought up by Tukri. Sabuta grew up and married Laŋga. Laŋga and Malu shared a house at first when Laŋga came in marriage. With Malu clearly soon to be ready for marriage, Laŋga's relations sent part of a bridewealth payment to make plain their exchange claim on Malu as the future wife of Laŋga's brother. Səlaukei wrote to tell Tukri about this and Tukri replied that this was good but that they must wait for his return to carry out the puberty rites for Malu and then he would send her off in marriage.

Although they had agreed to wait for him, Malu menstruated for the first time on 12 January 1969 and so they felt that they had to carry out her puberty rites. It was thus made clear to me that they must be done if a girl has her menarche.

I have been in the village at the rites for ten girls, and in fact five of the girls had not menstruated at the time they were carried out. Instead the other girls were judged ready for them by the development of their breasts and their stature. The precise timing was partly decided also by the availability of meat: the rites were carried out soon after return from a successful spell of hunting. When girls were thought to be close to the menarche, people would go off to

81

hunt in preparation for the rites. In one case a girl menstruated for the first time but her father delayed her rites for a month while he went to hunt so as to have enough meat for the celebration. But with the onset of her first menstruation, a set of prohibitions came into force immediately and they lasted until the rites were done. These restrictions are ones which the girls consistently stressed when they told me what happened in the puberty rites. They must not eat salt or *nawugəp* (hunting ash) or food cooked with salt. They must not eat coconut, meat or food roasted in the fire. They must not chew areca nut or lime. They must not smoke.

For girls who have not menstruated, the taboos are imposed for a few days before the celebration of the rites. The prohibitions apply strictly until the girl is given some *teltʌg* leaves, which have been specially cooked in a clay pot with *nawugəp* ash on the day of the celebration, to eat. Then the prohibitions are lifted. Before dawn that day, she must get up and wash herself with scented water from a *limbum* container (*rukat*). If she had menstruated, the washing would have taken place at the end of her first menstruation. Men from her family and hamlet prepare the container with scented water the day before the celebration. They go to the bush to collect special herbs, barks, sap and aromatic plants which they crush and mix together with water from a natural pool. The water turns pink because of the sap and juices of the plants. Its scent is strong. The *limbum* contains the crushed plants as well as the water; some of the leaves are brightly coloured. A few orange and yellow paste-apples (*dapati*) are placed on top at either end of the container. The whole effect is pretty and decorative. The container and its contents are called a *wə'ati*.

The girl washes at dawn and perhaps a few times later in the day. People gather for the celebration. Her mother cooks the *wa'agəp* of meat and sprinkled coconut. The girl may help; she is visible around her mother's house, helping with odd jobs, while the men prepare the mash of taro and yams with sprinkled coconut which I described at the beginning of the chapter. However she cannot eat any of this unless the taboos on salt, coconut and meat, etc. have been lifted.

Ideally, the leaves cooked with salt should be ready early in the day and the rite (called *wanu nawugəp* or *wanu teltʌg* 'she eats the hunting ash' or 'she eats the *teltʌg* leaves' — these are leaves of the tree *Gnetum gnemon*) for lifting the restrictions should be done before they come to the part involving spitting her with betel juice. In practice, on the occasions when I noted the lifting of the taboos they were done after the betel-juice spitting. But on the first few occasions I witnessed the rites, I had not grasped the distinctions between the cooked-leaf mixture of *teltʌg nawugəp* and the cooked-meat and coconut mixture called the *wa'agəp*, partly perhaps because the cooked-leaf mixture is given more privately than the other one.

Malu received a bowl with *pitpit* and *teltʌg* leaves cooked with salt. I was specifically told that this was to end her taboos on *nawugəp*, areca nut, smoking, etc. Immediately before Malu ate this, Wani took a long *lyimaŋgai*-banana leaf with three hibiscus flowers stuck in it. He spat two betel-juice blotches on the leaf and called out to Malu's ancestors that they were doing her puberty rites, that she must grow big and well, and he tore the leaf length-wise as he held it over the bowl of *teltʌg*.

During another girl's rites, Silaika's, while they were preparing the *wa'agəp* I heard someone mentioning that they must tear the leaf and I asked when this would be done. Silaika's father said vaguely after they had got the *teltʌg* ready. He also said that they had put some of the taro mash aside for her to wait until after they had torn the leaf. I watched while they were spitting and decorating Silaika and the two other girls who were going through the rites with her on the same day, but I did not notice them tearing the leaf. Two days later I asked Sukadel if he had in fact done it. He said yes, that he had called out to his father's mother, to his dead wife and to his dead wife's mother that he was doing the rites for Silaika. I also asked the girls whether they had had the leaf torn for them, but they said no.

To judge from the way Wani did it, the girls might well have missed noticing it. Malu had already been spat with betel juice and smeared and decorated. There was a gap of about twenty minutes then when people were waiting. Sabuta, her brother, carried out the bowl with *teltʌg* leaves and *pitpit* cooked with *nawugəp*. He also brought the *lyimaŋgai*-banana leaf with the three hibiscus flowers stuck in it and put it down beside the bowl. While the others were chatting to each other and waiting, Wani by himself went over to the bowl, saying to me that he would get on with it so that they could bring the meat and food for the meal. After spitting the blotches on the banana leaf, he placed it over the bowl and tore it. Later he said that he had called to Malu's mother's mother telling her what they were doing, that she should recognise her granddaughter and not give her illness but help her to grow well. After tearing the leaf he put it down, took the bowl off to give it to Malu. I did not see him do it.

The betel-juice spitting is done as it is for boys. For example, Silaika's rites which were done for Silaika together with two other girls of her hamlet, Wɔmni and Warao:

After most people had finished their taro mash, Sukadel (Silaika's father) began saying, Let's get on with the spitting. He went and brought a stalk of areca nuts and gave nuts round to the assembled men who were to do the spitting. He also gave out the betel-pepper catkins to go with it. Quite quickly the three girls assembled under the coconut palms growing by the edge of the ridge. They faced the cliff edge in a line with their backs towards where most people were sitting. The men gathered around them all chewing the betel.

The first blotches were spat onto each girl, then many of the men moved around spitting all the girls. The first spits were roughly over the kidney or loin areas, then others spat legs, back arms or head, gradually making good blotches to cover most of the big surfaces. Ideally the *wauwis* (mother's brothers) should spit first in order from most senior to most junior. There were jokes as I spat Silaika second (So who are you? a senior *wauwi*?). Some horse-play went on during the spitting — some of Bilki's spit sprayed on Samo who was also spitting the same girl, Samo pretended to yell in anger at Bilki, Bilki picked up a stem of banana as though to hit him back; Parku and Wandi joined in mock-fight for a moment; Ramaka kicked Wandi in the pants.

The spitting completed, all put their chewed betel nut into a *rukat* container with water in it placed close by the girls. I saw no one spit on the ground, only onto the girls. Then the betel juice was smeared with cortex platters of *lu dəglit* so that each of the girls was completely covered with the red juice. When they were smeared, water was brought in a bamboo and given to some of the spitters and they took a mouthful and spat it out in a fine spray to either side of the girls. The men called on their ancestors to say what they were doing and that the girls must grow big and well.

The girls stood still with the wet betel juice drying on their bodies. As they stood there, the women ('mothers' and 'sisters') came scurrying round them with strings of coloured trade-store beads to decorate them. They wound the strings round the girls' upper arms and necks. Some strings were tried on one girl, then put on another, I think because they fitted better or one girl did not have enough.

For each girl they brought a shell pubic covering, *timalyi'ep bifaŋ*.[2] I had thought they would not have the *timalyi'ep bifaŋ* put on because I had been told that Rauit had given them up. But they brought them. The sense in which they must mean that they have given them up is that a girl does not get given her own new one at her puberty rites but borrows from a relative. Sila, for example, brought hers for Warao. Sila had been given one of her own when she was decorated. The *timalyi'ep bifaŋ* used to become the possession of the girl, and she would keep it until her first daughter bore a child, when she would have given it to her daughter. So a woman would have her own *timalyi'ep bifaŋ* and, if she was an eldest daughter and had had a child, that of her mother as well.

While the girls were having their decorations put on, Bilki brought out a coconut shell containing the cooked-meat *wa'agəp* with shreds of coconut. Someone said, not yet, wait until their decoration is finished. When it was completed, Bilki broke the meat into shreds and gave a little to each of the

2 *Timalyi'ep bifaŋ* are special pubic aprons made of small bits of white shell shaped in rough crescents and hung in columns on strings which pass from the centre of the waist string belt in front through the small hole at either end of each crescent-shaped bit of shell. The *timalyi'ep bifaŋ* is tied on top of the ordinary *timalyi'ep* apron which each girl wears.

men who had done the spitting. They blew briefly on the meat shreds and murmured words into them and put them into the three girls' mouths, some of them giving them with their backs to the girls, right-armed over their own shoulders. As they were doing this some of the other senior men present were chanting very softly. When this was done, the girls, who until now had stood rather puppet-like waiting for each bit of the rites to be done to them, moved away. The men and people watching, who before had had their attention focussed on what was going on, although there was a lot of noisy horseplay and excited chatter, began moving off or breaking up into groups to sit and chat. One of the girls ran off into her mother's house; some men called out that she should stay outside, not go near the fire in her mother's house.

After the spitting and decoration is done there is a lull while the food for the guests is being got ready. On some of the occasions when I was present, the main organiser beat the *garamut* to let people know it was time for all to bring the meat and sago wrapped ready. The women brought the food. Basically food provided by the celebrant group is given to the visitors from other hamlets within the village and vice versa, though of course visitors from other villages do not bring cooked food with them. Wives bringing the food hand it to their husbands to go and put it down where the food is assembled. The food is laid out as a display before being given out. Everyone is provided for, but with much noisy advice, discussion and care, so that in giving it the rules shall not be broken which govern who may eat the food of specific other men or women. The men eat separately from the women. Each man receives an individual leaf of sago together with some meat. They eat from their own leaves, not calling out for others to come and help them eat as is usual at ordinary meals. Some eat only part of the feast food and put part of the meat aside to take home wrapped up in a leaf.

The women eat more or less communally together with their children. Later, after the food distribution and the meal people sit to chat or snooze and eventually go home.

In the lull either after the spitting or after the meal, the money to be presented to the mother's brothers may be got ready and presented if, and only if, the boy or girl for whom the rites are being done is the eldest child of the couple. However, on some of the occasions I witnessed they did not give this money on the day of the ceremony but afterwards. On no occasion did I see the formal presentation of the big *gabdag* gift of meat and special leaves given to the sister's child by the mother's brothers as it should be on the day of the ceremony for an eldest child. They brought it later on another day.

I now set before the reader a synopsis of the rites of puberty, as the Gnau say they should be done, so that he may refer to it as a guide to procedure when I come to explore, in the following chapters, the detail of what they do.

Day of shining red

Before the day

Years before the day, the mother's brother may decide to rear a pig and reserve that pig for presentation whole, killed and tied to a pole to be carried to the hamlet of the child with the *gabdʌg* gift on the occasion of his sister's first child's rites of puberty.

The child may begin to observe the set of taboos that must be in force by the time of puberty some years before the day of celebration: a first child usually begins observing them earlier than subsequent ones.

With recognition of the evident approach to maturity in the child, plans for the celebration are set in motion. The menarche of the girl will precipitate the celebration. Preparations must be planned in the hamlet of the child and discussed with the child's mother's brothers and matrilateral relatives. The initiative lies with the child's parents. The father and the men of his clan and hamlet must hunt game in the bush in the weeks before the celebration to provide for the feast. In the case of a first child, the mother's brothers must hunt and assemble a great gift of game to give with the *gabdʌg*. This hunting for a presentation to his sister's child is referred to by a special figure of speech, *lilaupən wuna'at*, literally 'they fill up his vital centre'. In return the father must assure himself some time before the celebration of a first child's puberty rites that he can, with the help of his clan relatives and hamlet neighbours, provide the money presentation to be made in return for the *gabdʌg* gift of the mother's brother and his group.

Lagao nəm beirkatidəm 'they taboo dried-out things'. A girl's menarche will decide the time to impose the taboos on *nəm beirkatidəm* (smoking, chewing betel, dried meat, roasted food and coconut). They may be imposed in a formal way with a breadfruit around the girl's big toe. For a boy the restrictions are verbally imposed a few days before the rites. *Lagər wa'agəp* 'they fetch the *wa'agəp*' (special materials). On the day before the rites, vegetable food from the gardens must be collected by women of the child's hamlet. The men must go to the gardens to collect the materials for making the *wə'ati* and *wa'agəp* (these are special materials, mostly plants and herbs, used in the rite and put in the special stew). For a girl's rites, the mother's brother or some substitute for him must bleed his penis and save the blood to give to her the next day, hidden in a betel quid. For a first child, the matrilateral relatives should make the *gabdʌg* gift ready. *Ləbari wə'ati ari* 'they make the *wə'ati* for her'. In the evening at the girl's hamlet, the little barque of scented waters and crushed plants is prepared (it is called her *wə'ati*). The girl may or may not be released from the restrictions on chewing betel that same evening. They go to sleep.

The day itself

At dawn, the girl must go to wash with the *wə'ati* (the scented water specially

86

prepared in the little barque). The guests assemble at the hamlet. For a first child, matrilateral relatives should come with the *gabdʌg* gift. Men cook tubers to be eaten with coconut in a mash. Meanwhile the mother (or a substitute) at her house cooks the *teltʌg–nawugəp* (a mixture containing leaves and salt) and the *wa'agəp* stew in a clay pot.

Ləbal teltʌg–nawugəp 'they give the leaves–salt'. The *teltʌg–nawugəp* is usually given privately to the girl or boy early in the day. If the boy has his headdress put on, the leaves–salt mixture is given to him inside the men's house at the time of placing the basic structure of his headdress. The eating of the *teltʌg–nawugəp* releases the child from restrictions on smoking, chewing betel and eating salt.

Lətauwən waipʌt 'they put on his headdress'. A *lyimʌŋgai*-banana leaf with hibiscus flowers is torn over the *teltʌg–nawugəp* mixture or over the boy as he sits on his *wə'ati* (a banana or plantain stem) to have his headdress placed. Hunting *gəplagəp* (special scrapings of plant and animal materials) are placed in his hair. The *waipət* is not usually made nowadays. It should be done inside the *gamaiyit*. When the first phase of placing it is completed, the boy comes outside. For a first child, married sisters and father's sisters make a presentation to the child which the mother used to tie to the headdress and/or the earlobes of the child. Then the boy is spat with betel juice, and his mother comes forward to strike a piece of wood before him and call on her ancestors.

Laləp ləga 'they go off to wash'. Then, in the case of a boy, comes a sequence of actions done by men in secret away from women and the hamlet. They go to 'wash' (*ləga*) by water. *Lapusəpən ganut* 'they puncture his penis'. The wound is rubbed with *nawugəp* (hunting ash) and his phallocrypt placed in position. *Lagaopən wadən* (*barwi'it*) 'they put on his bamboo (shell) phallocrypt'. *La'ab tambig* 'they strike themselves'. The mother's brother (or a substitute) bleeds over him and gives blood to mix with the *wa'agəp* stew. A girl also receives blood but the giving is dissembled.

Lasual 'they spit them'. Then comes the spitting with betel juice. This is usually done for a boy at the place where he is bled, but he may return to the village to have it done in public, as it is for the girl. The spitting is done by senior men and is accompanied by the chanting of spell verses. The red betel juice is smeared all over the child with special platters and dries on him or her.

Ləbalel wa'agəp 'they give them the *wa'agəp* stew'. The cooked *wa'agəp* is given in a special manner, accompanied by spells. Those who go through the rites together become *wusai* (ritual friends) to each other, by virtue of having sat on the same *wə'ati* stem or having eaten the same *wa'agəp* stew.

Lisarkaki'el 'they decorate them'. After the spitting and *wa'agəp* comes the decoration of the child. If a boy has the *waipət* headdress put on, it is completed and he is given other shell ornaments to wear; then the men return to the hamlet. The boy should enter the *gamaiyit* and receive further hunting *gəplagəp*. The girl is decorated with ornaments of shell or beads and receives her *timalyi'ep bifaŋ*.

Lanu digap—təbəgan 'they eat game—sago jelly'. Game and feast food are laid out for distribution. The hosts and guests eat together. The money presentation for a first child should then be made.

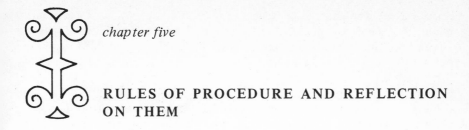

chapter five

RULES OF PROCEDURE AND REFLECTION ON THEM

There is no doubt about whether or not someone has been through the puberty rite. It is done publicly on one day. The boy or girl is singled out, spat bright red all over, and decorated. A person must go through it once in his or her life. It is the first time that he or she must hold the centre of the public stage. During the spitting and decoration, the boy or girl seems bashful; gaze downcast, movement constrained. The others watch and when it is done the chatter breaks out again; there is excited horse-play and declarations of having done it right and well. It is an occasion which needs planning and organisation. Participants must be assembled, and meat, food and money made ready. There is bustle in the village on the day, an agreeable sense of a day set aside from ordinary work; special food, perhaps some extra touch of festive dress; plants and herbs to be found, the scent, the colour, the noise and chat.

First let me say something about those aspects of the rites dependent on the device of the marked stage. They stem from conventions about correct performance and who should take part. These set up a possibility for participation in the rites to be taken as an indicator of status and recognition, and for participation to be symptomatic of someone's sympathies and awareness of his obligations. Particular performances are not only marks of public recognition that some boy or girl has become adolescent, but they also serve to demonstrate and confirm a structure of social relationships set about the boy or girl for whom they are done. In this sense, the rites are clearly addressed to a public made up primarily of those who live in the village. The rites are an important occasion for statement and demonstration of these social relationships which have longer-term implications, and more diffuse ones. They are registered and people may complain about how they have been done.

For instance, Ulibel reached puberty while his mother's brother Sɔwani was away working on a plantation. Nonetheless Ulibel's father went ahead and the rites were done. Sɔwani was indignant on return to find them done without him and therefore cut off Ulibel's hair. Ulibel, by then a burly young man, chose to sit respectfully still for the vengeful haircut. At any performance of the rites there are touches to be observed which bespeak recognition and registration of what is done, who should do it. Note in my earlier descriptions, for example, the letters from Tukri about Malu's rites (p. 81) and the comments as I spat on Silaika: 'So who do you think you are?' (p. 84). People are well able to say who ought to do what during the rites, at least in regard to the main features of participation.

Puberty is one of the marked stages of change in the series of shifts of responsibility and dependence in relations between a couple, their children and the people most closely connected to them. When a marriage is made, the parents of the two spouses should actively arrange it. The brothers of the bride have a say in the choice of bridegroom because he will become their brother-in-law and they will take on some responsibilities for the welfare of their married sister and her children. They take these over after the celebrations for the birth of the couple's first child during which the father of the bride-become-new-mother calls upon her agnatic ancestors to look after her child and wish it well. He announces to them that her brothers will take responsibility for her and her children in the future.

When the first child is about three years old, the mother's brother decides to hold the ceremony to free the child to eat meat, yams and certain other foods. He makes a gift of meat to the child. As at marriage and the first birth, the husband and his group give money (it used to be shell valuables) to the group from which his wife came (Lewis 1975, pp.26–35). The puberty of the first surviving child is the next occasion for a major money and meat exchange. If there were only daughters from the marriage, it would be the last time the mother's brother would be bound to receive payment in respect of children of the marriage. He does not receive any part of bridewealth given for his sister's daughters. But with sons born to his sister, certain duties continue. In the past, his sister's son would have gone through seclusion and initiation in the great Tambin rites. For gifts of meat and what the mother's brother did for him in the rites, the sister's son would present a further major payment of shell valuables at the ending of the Tambin rites. Nowadays the first time a young man goes on contract to work away at a plantation seems to replace the Tambin rites (which are almost abandoned), at least in that when he returns from his long absence at the coast he must make a major payment of the money he has earned to his mother's brother. This payment, like the one that used to be given after the Tambin rites, is made by each sister's son and is not limited only to the first child as were the first childbirth, first meat and yam, and first child's puberty ones.

When the sons of that initial marriage come to marry and the bridewealth for each of their marriages is assembled, the mother's brother and his sons assist them with it. It is the only point in the continuing shifting obligations between the two groups when money is transferred in the opposite direction from the usual one. It points to the interest of the mother's brother in services which the sister's son's wife will provide for him later in the continuing obligations of the sister's son towards the mother's brother and his sons. After his own marriage the sister's son himself, aided by his new wife, should make annual harvest gifts to his mother's brother. He also initiates exchanges with his mother's brother's married sons. The levels of duties are shifting to the next generation. The father passes on what were before his own affinal annual exchange duties to his now married sons, who fulfil them to the man who is at once their father's brother-in-law and their own mother's brother. And they also begin to exchange with that man's sons.

Further payments are made to the mother's brother and his sons when the sister's son's own first child is born, and when this first child has his puberty ceremony; these are token recognitions of the sister's son's continuing debt to them for his well-being shown in his fertility and raising of the child.[1] The last large payments resulting from the original first marriage are at the death of the original sister (the mother of the sister's son) and at the death of the first sister's son. This, the last payment, is organised by the man's surviving brothers or his sons, and is given to the surviving mother's brother's sons or to their sons. The series of obligations is then fulfilled. The children of the cross-cousins may not intermarry but they may in their turn arrange for their children to marry in a way that repeats the original marriage made in the great-grandparental generation of the new couple. This is an ideal marriage (i.e. between FFMBSSD and FFFZSSS).

Such is the bare outline of how one marriage creates obligations between two lineages over four generations. The puberty rites are set in that long-term series. Within the series, events which are accompanied by major payments (bridewealth for the original marriage, the first-born payment, the first child's puberty, death of the original bride, death of the first[2] sister's son) discharge that staged obligation in respect of all the children. But although the payment has already been made, for example, at the first child's puberty, or the first sister's son's death, the matrilateral relatives will take part in the puberty rites or the funerals of subsequent siblings. The relationships of sister's sons with their matrilateral relatives become more individualised after puberty. As the generations succeed, what first appeared as an affinal obligation changes to a matrilateral one. The Gnau speak of the continuity and shift of obligation down the generations as a 'path' opened by the sister's son's father when he begins to make annual harvest gifts (see Lewis 1975, pp. 34–5) to his brother-in-law, and when he makes occasional presents of game to him, a path he is clearing for his son so that, when he comes of age, he will be able to go along it to give game which he has shot to his mother's brother, and, after marriage, his harvest gifts. When a

1 The mother's brothers do not have the same kind of controlling power over the well-being of the sister's son's child as they have over the sister's son.
2 The first of them, that is, to die among those who reached manhood.

91

man considers how to share out his annual harvest gifts, they say, he should think first of his duty to his mother's brother and fulfil that, then of his other obligation to give to his wife's brothers because there will still be time for his sons to remember that later.

With puberty, the boy approaches adult life when he will hunt, marry, go to work at a plantation. The coming individualisation of relationships is shown sometimes in the puberty rites by the exercise of choice and decision in performance of the rites. There may be many brothers and/or either many sisters or many sister's sons. One mother's brother will actually bleed his penis over a particular sister's son and give him blood. Later this act of 'washing' him in his puberty rites may be remembered (see p. 189) as the reason to give him more of the plantation earnings brought back, to choose his sons as the ones with whom the sister's son will enter on exchanges. Given accidents of age, or disparities in sibling numbers or groups, there may have to be some sorting out, pairing off or substitutions and adjustment of relationships to make possible a satisfactory distribution and fulfilment of the duties (Lewis 1975, p. 31). There can be very different kinds of reasons behind departures or variations from the stated rules governing the usual forms of the rites: the absence of men away at plantation; the only mother's brother was too young to act; some men had too many sisters, others had none; relations between brothers-in-law were broken off in some past dispute (see pp. 190–2), etc. But the cause of Tukri's anxiety about the arrangements for Malu's rites, of the vengeful haircut Sɔwani gave Ulibel, is that performance in the rites is noted and may constitute the ground to lay a later claim of obligation or debt. In this sense, taking part in and performing the rites are social acts addressed to other people and because there are conventions, they may refer to or represent intangibles of right, duty and motive which are sometimes complex, diffuse and long-term.

At the level of what people say about their concerns when organising the rites, some attitudes are clear. The mother is the pivotal figure. First comes her concern for the welfare of her children; then comes, though perhaps only in the people's talk, her loyalty to her brothers and their interests. She is pictured as the one carrying the first gifts to her brothers, taking them the first little birds her young son shoots, going to tell them when she thinks the children are ready for the puberty rites, that she is making a great feast ready for them and that they must all come. If her husband should hesitate to give them their due she will remind him, press him to be generous, reprimand him should he think only of his duty to his mother's brothers and not of that towards her brothers. And she urges her arguments in the name of the welfare of her children, for her brothers have power over it, to foster it, control it, and also power to bring sickness and ruin on them.

The first of the ceremonies done in person by the mother's brother is at the stage of development when the sister's child, about three years old, is first allowed to eat meat and a range of other foods. Here the timing of performance should be chosen by the mother's brother. It is done when the toddler has found his feet and can walk well on rough paths; can control his toilet habits; can use the terms for 'mother', 'father' and 'mother's brother' right. The parents or grand-parents of the child may think he is ready and may speak to his mother's brother about it, but it should be he who decides and gives the meat first. The feelings about this run strongest for the first child. I saw a furious row between a woman and her husband's mother because her husband's mother gave some morsels of meat and yams to her first son before the mother's brother had done it officially. When the yelling stopped the woman ran off with the child eighty yards or so up the hill to her brother's hamlet and stayed there with him and her parents for two weeks. The mother's brother chose to give meat many weeks later. In the interval his decision was respected. It was his right to decide.

But in regard to puberty, the onus is different. This is partly because with a girl at menarche her physiology decides the timing. But both the parents of the child and the mother's brother may need to get things ready for the rites. The parents choose the day because it is an occasion on which they must provide a large feast for their guests. They invite their lineage and clan relatives and members of their hamlet, who all assist them with food for the feast, especially the game necessary for this. The wife goes to invite the mother's brothers and their families to come. Great stress is laid on the mother's brothers providing the special gift for the first child, called the *gabdag*. It accompanies the gift of dried game and includes shoots of the *teltati* tree (*Gnetum gnemon*) called *gabargəp*, and leaves called *siwug sirbəg*; it is distinctive to this rite and the rites for the first-born. But the *gabdag* does not in fact have to be given on the day itself. The father of the first child, on the other hand, needs to assemble his lineage and clan beforehand and make sure that he can, with their help, muster the large payment for the mother's brothers, now amounting to 50 kina (equivalent to over £25; see Lewis 1975, p. 33). The setting of the day to do it is thus primarily the decision of the father and his close lineage relatives, for it falls on them and their wives as hosts to have everything ready. The day before it, the father's clan relatives must go to the bush to find the special plants to be used in the rites. The way men speak of how they themselves put on the rites for so-and-so reflects this burden, and they recognise that to do so marks their position as those, for example, who may lay claims later for a share of the bride-wealth that will be given for a girl when she marries. This organisational stress was behind Tukri's written insistence that they wait for him to return before Malu was initiated and the care Səlaukei took to inform him by letter of what was happening lest Tukri think they were trying to usurp his rights. The shared interest of lineage and clan relatives in the welfare of the child is shown in help to provide money for the payment to be made for the first child to the mother's brothers, and also in their help with providing game for the feast.

In the texts about how to do the puberty rites that I obtained early on in my fieldwork, what the speakers mentioned in most detail were these needs to organise: what to get ready, who should do it, who goes to invite whom, the *gabdʌg*, how they should get up early to come, that all must come, that they must assemble generous gifts, that a lot of money would be given.

Points of finer detail about participation emerged later, such as the order of spitting by seniority shown in their comment when I spat Silaika. The two main groups concerned are the lineage and clan relatives of the adolescent, and the matrilateral relatives. The father, after all the organisation and preparation, does not act directly in what is done to his child. Specifically he must not spit on him or her or decorate. He stands aside, sees to his guests, the food and its distribution, and later brings out the money payment wrapped for presentation. If the father should be dead, the duty to organise the rites falls to his surviving brothers or to the eldest 'son' in the sibling generation. For girls especially, but also for fatherless boys, the eldest or elder married brothers in a lineage generation assume responsibilities like those of a father for their rites. They connect this responsibility with the future marriage when they will choose a husband for the girl or find a wife for the boy (they say 'pull' (-*aŋgu-*) a wife).

The mother does two notable things during the rites (apart from her share in the general business of organising and preparing food): first, at her house she cooks in her *malpə* (clay pot)[3] the *wa'agəp* (the special stew — p. 73) which will be given to the adolescent by the mother's brother; second, after her son has been spat on she carries out the act (mentioned on p. 77) of coming forward to strike a piece of firewood with a bush knife or an axe at his feet.[4] As she does this, she calls out to her ancestors that this is her son, and she asks them that no future act of hers may bring him illness, that when she uses her knife or axe to cut things in the gardens and he sits in the village, the knife may not strike him because she holds it, that he may stay well, that she and her husband will present a big payment to her brothers; her ancestors must look well on her son, bring him no harm, no illness.

But she does not do this for her daughters. As there is a difference between what is done for boys and for girls, we may be alerted to consider its implications (and go a little beyond what they say about it overtly). Note that she uses the imagery of metaphor: she strikes with her knife in the gardens; he sits at the village; let him not be struck by her knife; let him not be ill because of what she does. I think it right to hear in this call a note of separation, of future independence, a request marking the end of a kind of dependency which might harm his well-being. Her son is about to enter adult life as a man. On both occasions when I watched this action and appeal, my impression was of the sudden

3 If the actual mother is dead, then the step-mother will cook this. In one case it was the wife of the girl's lineage 'eldest brother' (the *gəmin garut*, the most senior brother) who cooked because the girl's father was a widower.
4 If the mother is dead, a substitute will do this act as Geryik's step-mother did for him (p. 77).

moment of passage of the mother, the blow with the knife on the wood, the boy rising up and moving, as though released. But I neglected to find out if the immobility before was imposed formally.

In contrast she does not do this for her daughters, who continue to be closely associated with her in everyday life until their departure at marriage. After a girl's marriage, the tie with her mother is still thought important. Her mother may advise her about childbirth, may support and influence her, they say, for example, in a decision to stop herself having more children. Her mother is also supposed to have special powers of intercession with her own ancestors to affect her daughter's reproductive life. If her daughter keeps having children who die at birth or just after, she will have a special role in the rite to make her daughter's next child survive. Another sign of the continuing tie in the case of her eldest daughter is the rule that a woman should pass on to her daughter her own *timalyi'ep-bifaŋ* apron when her daughter has borne a child. When the mother's brothers invoke their ancestors in a girl's puberty rite, they call out to her mother's mother, but they do not do this for a boy. It too marks a continuity of ties, as they see them, running between a woman, her daughter and her daughter's daughter.

The passing of puberty changes the roles to be adopted by a girl or boy — but not in the same way for both sexes. The different acts of the mother in the rites indicate this. In fact few rights or duties are immediately changed solely by performance of the puberty rites so far as I know. Neither a boy nor a girl may marry before them. A boy could not wear a phallocrypt unless he had been through them. The puberty rite is the *sine qua non* for the right to wear it. But this visible sign of changed status is no longer the public mark it once was, as boys and young men now wear shorts or *laplaps* (cloth wraps). A collection of stringent food restrictions differing only slightly between boys and girls must be observed after the rites, but their performance does not determine exactly when they are imposed. The father (but it might be another senior man) is supposed to advise the growing child about when to begin observing them. As the restrictions are said to affect the child's well-being and successful growth, they may be imposed quite a long time (for instance four or five years) before he actually goes through the rites. Many people told me that a father would impose them early on and strictly in the case of his eldest child (especially if a boy) but he would be more lax in the case of later children. The reasons behind this involve ideas about how to ensure that children grow and develop well, the first-born first, preserving the right order in development among the siblings; and that raising the first child is hardest because the parents are new to it. A father might see that a particular child is developing poorly and advise him to observe the restrictions early.

One rule applies only after a boy has been through the rites and reflects his changed status. The rule forbids him afterwards to eat from the same leaf of food or the same bowl as his father, who would risk contamination or harm shown by weakening or sickness if he should do so. Sons before the rites may share food from their father's leaf or bowl. The rites also establish a bond between any who may go through them together. Those who sit on the same *wə'ati* (stem of banana) or who eat the same *wa'agəp* stew become *wusai* to each other, having long-lasting duties and rights towards each other, calling each other *wusai* and tabooing each other's personal name. *Wusai* in this strict sense can only become so through sharing puberty rites. They used to be created also by undergoing Tambin initiation together. The term is used more loosely in direct speech to someone to assert friendship and then it draws on the association of the term with a bond established that cannot be denied; it may be used with the connotation 'age-mate'.[5] Otherwise I cannot find specific consequences or changes in right or duty imposed or granted only by the fact of passage through the rites. There is little to put forward that would show that the puberty rites themselves are operative acts which critically set the moment and timing for acquiring some new role, right or status (see Skorupski 1976, p. 93). They are better characterised as rites of demonstration and confirmation.

Mother, father, mother's brother: this is the nucleus of relationships about the boy or girl who goes through the rites. I have indicated that a wider set of lineage and clan relatives of the father and the mother's brother take part in them. The father's sisters and the boy or girl's elder married 'sisters' have a special opportunity to show their relationship during the rites. They give a few shillings that are now collected on a plate together and given to the boy or girl.[6] When shell valuables were current, these shells (*bifat*, a small cowrie shell, or rarely *wilagi*, a large ring, the cut section of *Tridacna* shell) were hung from the pierced earlobes of a girl; for a boy, what the father's sisters gave was hung on the string coming down from the *waipət niŋgi* (the sheath into which his long hair had just been drawn), and what his 'sisters' gave was hung from his earlobes. The valuables were tied on by his mother immediately after the *waipət* had been put on by the men. These gifts of shell or money belong to the boy or girl. It is possible to see this as a claim on future recognition when the boy will hunt successfully and should send them game. It is possible to see the gift of the father's sister and the elder married sister to a girl at puberty as related to a future optional exchange system between married women which I have noted elsewhere (Lewis 1975, pp. 31–2), but in this puberty rite the money flow reverses the pattern that would take place if they were to carry on such exchanges later.

5 In Lewis 1975, p. 40, I mention that *wusai* relationships between men of different villages were transmitted from father to son. I checked on this again on my second visit in 1975 and I was told it was not so. Men might have *wusai* in another village, but only if they had gone to take part in the initiation rites of another village, which occasionally happened; or else they might use the term loosely for someone who was their age peer and had happened to be initiated at almost the same time as themselves, but independently at the other village. The relationships were not transmitted from father to son.
6 I understood that this was done only for a first child's rites.

Rules of procedure and reflection on them

Custom specifies what should be done and by whom in certain circumstances. It fixes some of what would otherwise be arbitrary in social dealings. It calls for recognition of whether the rules apply to you. The fact of ruling may put a significance into what is done which, without it, might not be seen. The rules may be cited as imperatives without conditional clauses to explain the motive, rationale or symbolism that may lie behind them. 'A sister's son must not speak the name of his mother's brother': the rule says what must not be done but leaves the reason why unstated. Yet such rules may be connected with duties and ideals that people feel strongly about. If the rule be flouted, witness the response. As the rule spells out who should do what, so duties and ideals linked to certain relationships are directed into forms of outward conduct that show them. Rules of custom may be linked to belief and morality as practice is to theory. As they are at least clear about some features of the conduct of relations, say, between a mother's brother and a sister's son, so the rights and duties tend to seem crystallised in them. They epitomise what is required and proper. To fulfil them involves at least tacit recognition: the actions may stand for something beyond what is done in simple matter of fact — intangibles of right, duty, sentiment and claim.

In a society without writing or documents, a claim, possibly based on diffuse, complex and long-term expectations, may be acknowledged or registered publicly through participation in a rite or ceremony. The event may provide a point for future reference. Such customary staged events can serve this function as fixed points of focus in a world where daily social interactions flow on, often complex, their significance open to comment by many, sometimes passed over without remark, open to private doubts or misunderstandings. This is a reason for the attention given to some rites, for the devices used to alert the public, the fixing, and ruling; and for the sense in which I would interpret some aspects of the rite as addressed primarily to the public world of social action rather than to individual thought or reflection on its symbolism. The quality of address is not exclusive but it is an aspect whose relative intensity or weight should be taken into account in commenting on the rite. It is a means to identify the genre and character of the rite. In this case, so far, I have tried to bring out, first, its immediate public aspect as a rite of declaration and confirmation about the boy or girl now adolescent, conferring some new rights or duties on the subject, and second, its place in a set of relationships and shifting longer-term claims as a mode for public acknowledgement, demonstration or registration of them.

I have restricted my comments (or tried to) to the rules governing performance, the relationship structure and connected duties. The rules spell out some of the duties and people note whether the requirements are met or not. Their attention is focussed on them because they know what should be done. The specified requirements are taken in part as eminent tokens of the type of attitude and feeling that should prevail generally or more diffusely in the relationship. If the duties by their particular content also indicate some attribute proper to the relationship or desirable in it, even though only a hint or clue, people may be more likely to recognise it because of the attention they pay to the performance of these definite duties.

The direction of association in the mind may run either way. The rule defines a duty linked with a relationship. It may be that the content of the duty is chosen because it is in some way apt as an epitome or index of the desired character of the relationship. I would suppose that such suitability (or the possibility of seeing it) has sometimes been a factor in the choice of object or action that provides the content of the particular duty in a rite or ceremony. There was already something about the object or action in question that prompted people in the past to choose to use it so; and this aptness helped to fix and preserve the practice. On the other hand, to fix some object or action strictly to one situation or frame of action may lead people to transfer the ideas they have about the situation to the object or action: and by a conditioning of ideas people come to associate those ideas with the object or action as though they belong to it intrinsically. If someone is strongly urged to do a particular act or avoid it, but he is not told why, he may be tempted to use whatever knowledge he has available to him that seems relevant to put some sense into the requirement. He will pick on things that fit and neglect what does not. The fixed ruling, imperative but unexplained, may provoke some individuals to speculate about a reason for it, to reflect on the relevant relationship, or the object or action, and think out a connection. This sort of response must vary greatly with individuals and their personal experience. The answers that an anthropologist may get to many of his questions about the meaning of things done in rites will often reflect this individual variation in speculative thought or the lack of it, as well as the variation that stems from age, sex, doctrines established or esoteric, and the other ways in which knowledge and ideas are controlled and passed on in a particular society.

I hope the texts and commentaries above (pp. 48–70) provide some insight into the style of learning in Gnau ritual situations. There is little of the school about them, no set periods of instruction. Learning is a matter more of practice and experience, of chance remarks which explain or interpret, individual views, and less a body of ideas and doctrines consistently and purposefully taught. As some of the objects and actions of the puberty rites recur or reappear in rites at other stages of the life cycle so a person's experience of them alters and his views about their meanings may change, and they may change too when he takes part in them, first as witness, later as participant, collector of the herbs or materials to be used, or as organiser for someone else's passage rather than as the subject for whom it is done.

Formal rules may make a range of experience connected with certain things or views common to the general run of people, and make for some consistency of understanding. Consider the content of some of the duties, idioms and rules connected with the relationship between the mother's brother and the sister's son as though you knew nothing about the attitudes or sentiments to be desired or expected of them towards each other. Look to the collection of idioms, metaphors and customs which follows now, for clues to discover them. Then remember that most of these examples are known to everyone who is Gnau from an early age and that, for example, the prohibitions to be described are constantly in force.

(1) The evening star (*gə'uwan*), they say, climbs first into the sky and then goes before the moon (*gə'unit*) to pull it along its path: the evening star is *wauwi* (mother's brother) to the moon, who is *mauwin* (sister's son).

(2) The sulphur-crested cockatoo (*igambati*), they say, first excavates the holes in trees in which nest other parrots, like the eclectus parrot (*məlangəti*): the cockatoo is *wauwi*, the eclectus parrot is *mauwin*.

(3) I was on a hunt in thick forest. I heard the beater's whooping to indicate that a pig was running, then the thwack of a hand on a thigh to mark a bow shot, grunts of agony from the pig, and a man's tremendous ululated cry. The man was sister's son: it was his shot that killed the pig in forest on the land of his mother's brother; therefore he cried this out: 'Lightning comes down the great tree to strike you dead, [pig]. Is it good lightning? No, terrible in power.' The form is either 'Lightning comes down a great tree' (they name one of a few kinds of conspicuously tall trees) or 'Lightning comes down to a pool' to strike dead on the mother's brother's land. The power like lightning comes down a great tree or to the pool.

(4) A further metaphor heard in use: a young man had asked for help with his bridewealth in a way that the man asked thought would have been appropriate if he had been *wauwi* to the young man; but he was not. As comment on this, what someone literally said was: 'A banana plant but one in the bush, but if instead a *lyimaŋgai* banana (of the village), yes, you plant it in your ashes; but this banana, one belonging in the bush.' To explain the metaphor: only certain kinds of banana, among them the *lyimaŋgai*, are planted inside the hamlets, and the people who plant them bring and put ashes from their house fires on the ground where they plant them to make the ground fertile and the plant grow well. Bananas planted in bush gardens are not fertilised like this. The metaphor assimilates the sister's son to the *lyimaŋgai* banana planted in the village in ashes from the house fire. The young man in question — he was a banana belonging to the bush garden.

(5) The *mauwin* (sister's son) cannot eat the *lyimaŋgai* banana nor any banana planted in ashes at his mother's brother's hamlet. He can eat bananas from other hamlets, or bananas from his mother's brother's bush. The metaphor I quoted above assimilated the sister's son to the *lyimaŋgai* banana.

(6) The sister's son must not eat such a banana. Nor may he eat any bird, bat, snake or lizard, or furred animal, that nests, has its home, or lives, in a hole, if it was killed by anyone on the land of his *wauwi*. I saw many instances of the

care people took to find out where such food was killed, and who killed it, before they ate. One day, I asked someone to come with me to the bush. He refused, he said his *wauwi* had asked him to stay in the village, because he was going to cut down a tree on his land in which he had seen a hole where bats were roosting. He wanted his sister's sons to stay in the village while he cut down the tree lest — and this was what the sister's son explained to me — the bats should fly from the hole when he cut down the tree and escape him.

(7) The sister's son should not look in holes or fissures on the land of his mother's brother. I remember most clearly the sudden screeching reproach of a mother who caught sight of her son (about thirteen years old) about to poke a stick into the hole from which the main post of her brother's men's house had just been removed. They were destroying the old house. All the sister's sons had come to this; they announced their presence, gathered to watch but not to do anything of the cutting or breaking up of the house, which would be, they said, as though to cut and break their *wauwi*. At the meal which celebrated the completion of this work, the sister's sons abstained and ate nothing. The Gnau now bury the dead and do not smoke and dry the body on a platform as they did before. The sister's son must not come close to dig the hole in which to bury his mother's brother, nor look into it; nor must he throw earth to cover the body over; nor may he eat the meal which celebrates the end of the mourning dietary restrictions and is part of the rites by which they send off the dead man's spirit, his mother's brother.

(8) The sister's son should not eat betel-pepper catkins (*wa'albi*) grown on his *wauwi*'s land. The betel pepper is a vine that climbs on trees for support.

(9) Nor should he eat lime (*ta'ap*) of his *wauwi*, which, apart from lime now brought in from the coast, is made from a small mollusc found in streams and pools.

(10) In each hamlet, men plant (or used to) particular wild aroid herbs which are used in rituals for fighting. The kinds of aroid differ with the clans and are particular to them. If a mother's brother should find one of these aroids which he planted in the ground of his own hamlet, broken or shrivelled without cause, he should take this as an omen of danger to his sister's son and go to warn the men of his sister's son's hamlet not to let his *mauwin* leave the village, saying, 'A wild aroid of my hamlet is broken for no reason there: one of your axes, a good axehead, will be pulled out', meaning one of your men (a good axe: my sister's son) is in danger.

The chief analogies in these images are the plant which grows up from the earth, the creature which shelters in a hole, the banana plant nourished by ashes, the moon led by the evening star. In each case the stress of the analogy or metaphor is on the first term, to which the sister's son is assimilated, and on the benefit he receives. There are not clear images for the *wauwi* except as the star, unless you choose to take him as the earth, or the hole, but I think the accent is rather on the benefit he provides (supporting growth, support for the vine, shelter, nourishment, showing a path). Certainly ideas of benefit, of indebtedness to the *wauwi*, of help in growth, nourishment and the idea of shelter are quite clearly associated with the relationship between sister's son and mother's brother. The only plural form for the kinship term *wauwi* is interesting: its form is quite unrelated to that of its singular and can be given another meaning. The plural form is *wigǝt adji*, or more briefly *wigǝt*, and *wigǝt* means 'home', 'place', 'hamlet', 'village': *wigǝt adji* means 'your home'.

Right and duty in the relationship of *wauwi* to *mauwin*

Where one's *wauwi* lives is not one's home. During childhood and after his marriage, a man lives in the hamlet of his father. This is where he builds his wife's house. He sleeps in the men's house where his father slept or sleeps. He does not garden on his *wauwi*'s land; neither does his mother inherit any of it (except in special circumstances). The rule is that when a woman goes in marriage to her husband, she retains only one keepsake which is hers at her brother's hamlet, a coconut palm planted for her by her father. When she dies, it reverts to the children of her brothers who may call the palm after her. Her son's house and hamlet is that of his father; his land and trees, the magical knowledge he gradually acquires for gardening and hunting should all come to him from his father and men of his own clan, not from his *wauwi*.

But his *wauwi*, in other ways, has much to do for him. What he does is seen at once both as right and duty, if right is taken to suggest something desirable and worth preserving, while duty implies something burdensome and constraining. Here there is a question of balance and correlation. A right is usually correlated with a duty. Broadly speaking, in this relationship the *wauwi* has rights and the *mauwin* has duties. The debt is asymmetrical. The *mauwin*'s mother was taken from the home of her birth beside her brother when she married. Her son belongs in her husband's home. The asymmetry is to be found in many features of the relationship between mother's brother and his sister's son, and most sharply in the ideas of how a *wauwi* may kill his *mauwin* by magical techniques which are special to the relationship. The *mauwin* cannot counter these; and he has no similar or comparable power to deal death to his *wauwi*. He must not speak his name but call him *wauwi*; even when his *wauwi* is dead, even if the *wauwi* died in childhood before the *mauwin* was born; even should the name be in some song, having no reference to the person of his *wauwi*, he still may not sing the sound. But the *wauwi* calls him freely by his name. And should the *mauwin* speak his *wauwi*'s name, it is not his *wauwi* who will suffer but himself. These are their assertions.

Given a broad asymmetry of right and duty in the relationship, there is still the balance of right and duty to consider in details of the relationship. And as one looks at the details, it becomes much harder to decide whether the stipulated action is felt to be a right or a duty. The compound of attraction and constraint is characteristic of moral sentiments (Ginsberg 1961, ch. 7). The attraction of what is ideally good also involves the ideal in its other aspect of that which ought to be, 'ought' implying both the duty and the difficulty, for ideals may go beyond what it is easy to attain. The *wauwi* has the right (or should I rather say the duty and the responsibility?) to foster the growth and health of his sister's son. As a man might put his house-fire ashes in the ground so the *lyimʌŋgai* plant may grow well, so a *wauwi* hunts game and gives meat to his sister's son. It is not that the father provides no meat for his children but that there is a special virtue or benefit in what the *wauwi* gives. If they grow into fine up-standing young men, they are a credit to him. The finery of the *wauwi*'s dress will come from them; the plumes of birds of paradise in his headdress, the horn-bill at his back, the torque of pig tusks round his neck, the trophies on his hunting bag, his belt of cassowary quills – if he can wear these things and say, My sister's son killed and gave me them, it is good. Not only is his sister's son a good and dutiful *mauwin*, but it is also good that he has become such a man because his *wauwi* hunted well, and gave him meat to grow him, and gave him the ability through health, strength and steadfastness to hunt and kill. There is certainly an aspect of repayment in the giving of these things, though they are the finery of dress rather than valuables in the sense that shells (*miŋgəp*) rep-resented wealth. And the *wauwi* also hangs up on a line in his men's house or at his garden house the skulls of pigs and the breast bones of cassowaries which his *mauwin* has shot, and they show off the prowess of his sister's son. These things are given to the *wauwi* as his due, even though he does not teach his *mauwin*, or perform on him, the rites which are most closely connected with achievement in hunting and killing: these rites and knowledge are transmitted within the clan, that is, within the father's clan to which a young man belongs.

The point which I am trying to disentangle, perhaps seeing a subtlety beyond the warrant of my evidence, is this; if the trophies were given to repay the benefit of hunting magic, they should be given to the killer's father and to other men within his clan; if they were given to repay the benefit of health, growth, strength, steadfastness, they should be given to the *wauwi*. In practice, men can and do wear trophies that they have shot themselves, or that their sons and grandsons have shot, as well as those their *mauwins* have presented to them. But it is best to be able to say that this which I wear my *mauwin* gave me. If you ask what is the rule for giving plumes of paradise, boars' tusks, cassowary quills, you are told, 'You should give them to your *wauwi*.' But in practice there are alternatives; it is a matter of some freedom of choice, of recognition, sentiment and responsibility, in complex interplay. To give to the *wauwi* is both right and good, and the reasons for his satisfaction are complex.

On the part of the *wauwi* is it a right or duty to control and foster the growth of his sister's son? To find much game is hard. To give a great amount, such as is given with ostentation at certain stages of the life of the sister's son, is demanding. This game to benefit his *mauwin*'s growth, as ashes do the *lyimaŋgai*, is given *beirkatida*, that is, 'smoked and dried'. If, as he should later, the *mauwin* gives a meat present to his *wauwi*, he gives him meat *subagda* ('wet' or 'fresh'): it may be cooked or raw, but it should not be smoked and dried.

The stages I referred to when the *wauwi* makes a special gift to his sister's son are first at the ceremony to free the child to eat meat when the child is about three years old, and secondly at the puberty rites. The great meat presentation for the first child is accompanied by the gift of certain customary things. They are called *gabdʌg* and include items which point to the aspect of the relationship which I am emphasising here. The first item is of parts of the *tulip* or *saior* tree (in Gnau *teltati*; the tree is *Gnetum gnemon*) whose leaves are a usual component of Gnau diet. The parts given are the new sprouting shoots of the tree, and they have a special name (*gabargəp*). The second item is made up of broad leaves called *siwug sirbəg*. They resemble those of the wild plantain, which commonly serve as wrappers or platters, but these leaves grow fast and straight up from the ground on a strong thick stalk. The people note them for the rapid vigour of their growth. A third item is coconuts. I should remind you of the mother's coconut palm at her natal hamlet, the long life of the palm, and the point that coconuts are only planted in the village, never in the bush.

These things which are given in the large presentations of *gabdʌg* are also given in smaller private presentations between families. These take place every year. They involve exchanges, and the *mauwin* also gives things to his *wauwi* each year, but the items he gives are different (see Lewis 1975, p. 35). Both *wauwi* and *mauwin* give each other meat and vegetable foods, but the kinds of food that go in each direction are different. The asymmetry that I mentioned before is again apparent.

In these important rites for stages of the social and physical maturation of the *mauwin*, the *wauwi* should perform a decisive part. But they can be done, and sometimes are, without him. The Gnau attribute to the *wauwi* a power to bring disaster to his sister's son who either himself, or through his parents, fails to respect the *wauwi*'s rights. In the main rituals for the stages of development, what the *wauwi* should do is laid down explicitly, but the rationale or reason for his doing it is not so clear or even necessarily stated. In keeping with a general view that success in hunting and killing, health and strength are desirable in a man, that this is a great part of virtue in a man (a view that recalls the Roman concept of virtue as strength and the ability to achieve a set and freely chosen end by exercise of will), whatever special benefit may come to the sister's son through performance of the ritual, the benefit is also said to include that general one of health and strength and success in hunting.

The movable or optional rites, the ones that are done only when some particular act has been accomplished or is to be accomplished, rather than the grand set of events of the life cycle, are thus by choice and setting linked more clearly

103

to a specific and limited aim. The control and benefit for growth that can be exercised by the *wauwi* stands out in the rite called *litau waniwani* which is done, if necessary, at some time between puberty and the third and grandest ritual occasion — initiation in Tambin. *Litau waniwani* is done by the *wauwi* for a boy or young man who is too small or sickly-looking for his age. After special preparations the *wauwi* applies red-hot stones to his sister's son's *wuna'at* (vital centre). A number of men had scars on their fronts just below the breastbone as a result of this ministration.

As part of this general theme of concern for his *mauwin*'s welfare, I have mentioned shelter and steadfastness. Steadfastness is a benefit from the *wauwi*. When killing went on before white men stopped it, boys were brought to an enemy who had just been killed to stick a spear in the body or shoot an arrow into it — it was a kind of accustoming. On the first occasion that a boy did this, his *wauwi* was called to come with his shield and cover him with it and sit on the shield placed on top of the boy laid flat on the ground, so that in years to come, the boy grown up would stand firm before a charging man or pig and not loose his arrow too soon, nor turn to run.

As for shelter (the bats in the hole), there is an expectation that a sister's child, chided beyond bearing by his family or confronted by a determined father bringing him (her) an unwelcome spouse, will turn for escape to his (her) *wauwi* and with him find haven. It is easier to note this expectation than to point to a symbolic action for the feeling about shelter. In the initiation rites of Tambin, the initiand was repeatedly beaten with nettles. This was done at certain points by men of his clan and then the *wauwi* might by custom interpose his own body to cover his *mauwin*'s and receive the stings, for, they say, the *wauwi* would feel sympathy for his *mauwin*'s pain and would try to shield him.

In this account of the relationship between mother's brother and sister's son, its duties and its idioms, I have used the customary content of the duties as though to discover for you expressed symbolically some of the sentiments expected of those who stand in that relationship to each other. Alternatively I might have begun with sentiment and feeling and tried to show you what was involved by description of observed behaviour, by records of what they said to each other and of what they answered to me about what they felt. To do that well would demand the skill and sensitivity both to observe it and to write it down without distortion. With art it might be conveyed more briefly, but without that gift I would have to try to give so full an account of what I heard and saw that, by the patient accumulation of details, of gesture, words, situation, character, time, place, you could discern and recognise the sentiments for yourself and judge the truth of what they said about their feelings. After long reports, the situations differing and multiplying, I might manage to present enough for you to see some of the patterns of feeling involved and their different forms and strengths. Your interpretations of these would approach a match to those appreciated by the people themselves, if I were a good enough witness. They would approach this match because they would be based on the same kind of evidence and experience as the people have, but you would have it only second hand, only in words, and much less of it. Instead I have concentrated your attention on certain idioms, certain customs and duties. I hoped it might be the quicker and clearer and easier way to tell something about the sentiments; also such evidence might less provoke your uncertainty about how much I put in by selection, my judgement of character and my bias. I have tried to use Gnau idioms and customs to show you more quickly and plainly the sentiments that they expect between a mother's brother and his sister's son, provoking perhaps less uncertainty about my selection of scenes from daily life. And I think that there is a parallel to note in the role of the idioms and customs in the society itself. Because they are formal or conventional, they direct people's attention to them, or at least give them pause to consider whether the requirements have been met or not. In that pause, it is possible that some people, at least, may consider at times why the rule should have been set, why it should be apt, and as they do so they may perhaps discover, or see more plainly, something of the desired content of the relationship; at the least they may think about the relationship, 'ungating' their thought to speculate about it and its requirements.

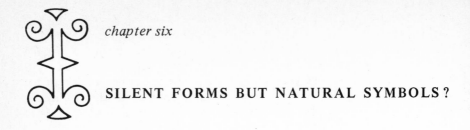

chapter six

SILENT FORMS BUT NATURAL SYMBOLS?

I quoted some Gnau idioms, metaphors and symbolic actions in the last chapter: the moon and the evening star; the *lyimaŋgai* banana planted in ashes; the bats in the hole and the sister's son sitting in the village (pp. 99–101). Gnau people do sometimes use metaphor and do sometimes understand the relationships involved in symbolic action and have the power to comment on them and explain them. The observation, which I stress, cuts this way: I have seen the act of penis-bleeding in the puberty rites. I may be tempted to interpret it as a symbolic menarche, but Gnau men said to me that they had not thought of it like that. By what right or argument shall I maintain that it is symbolic menarche even though they disagree? That it is a 'natural symbol', and they are silent about it? Is it symbolic in itself? Only to me? Or to them also, though somehow unadmitted, hidden from their conscious minds? This is the question with which I began.

If we think of drawing a parallel between the girl's menarche and the boy's penis-bleeding, we should consider first the grounds for comparing the girl's rites with the boy's and for seeing them as equivalent. Are the rites identical and bleeding the only thing that differentiates them? Do elements of the puberty rites recur in rites that mark the passing of later stages in the individual's life, and, if so, do these elements differentiate men from women, or identify them? Are such recurrent elements isolated differently for men and women, or are they the same, suggesting or representing continuities or discontinuities of theme, or themes distinctive to one sex but not the other? I face this issue of equivalence now as first requiring an answer before I embark on the discussion of the act of bleeding.

Sometimes the same naming is used for the rites of boys and girls. The Gnau may refer to either boys' or girls' rites by the word *lisarkaki'el* 'they decorate them', although, as I noted on page 57, there are other naming phrases which differentiate the rites for boys from those for girls.

The same rites can be shared by boys and girls. In some of my descriptions, the rites were done for one person, in others for more than one. The ones I witnessed in which two or three people went through them together involved

106

either only boys or only girls. But it is permissible for both boys and girls to have them on the same day. *Latelel bigəp lagapa wutəba* 'they initiate them and do it on one day'. Some people had had it done like that. Then the initiates called each other *wusai* (ritual friend; co-initiate) and tabooed each other's personal names irrespective of sex.

I have mentioned already (p. 93) that special exchanges take place between the parents and the mother's brothers on the first occasion a child of the couple undergoes the rites. Normally the eldest child is the first to go through them and the major formal exchanges are said to discharge the exchange obligations associated with puberty rites for all the children of that couple. If a daughter is eldest then the exchanges at her puberty rites cover the obligations for her younger siblings irrespective of sex, and the same is true if a boy is first.

The identification of the rites for both boys and girls by one word, the equivalence of *wusai* status, the singleness of the major exchange payment (at the puberty rites for the eldest of the siblings irrespective of sex), all indicate that the Gnau see the rites for boys and girls as the same.

These aspects are easy to specify, so I put them first. But I should also indicate sameness in the actions which take place in the rites, which requires more care to identify. The observer notes that at puberty something special is done for both sexes. Do they distinguish puberty as a point or a phase of development common to both sexes? Menarche, the first menstruation, is a natural event and potentially a decisive one, a point. There is a day on which it happens. But for a boy nothing so clearly marks a moment of change in the progress of growing up. The Gnau have various phrases for indicating stages in the process of growing up and growing old. No phrase perhaps exactly matches the concepts we have of puberty or adolescence. But they do pay attention to size, stature and the appearance of secondary sexual characteristics. They say they look for these signs to decide when to do the rites: in boys, for stature, genital development, pubic and axillary hair; in girls, they note stature, breast development and menstruation.[1]

For example, in the myth of the python there is an episode in which the myth Python transforms the children of a village by magic. Their parents, who are absent, come back to find their children suddenly grown up. Here is part of the myth told by Kantyi: 'The Python washed them, spat them, bespelled

---

1 Puberty is late in this area. Wark and Malcolm (1969) found that the menarche occurred at 17.8 years in the girls near Lumi, on average. I estimated that most Gnau children have their puberty rites when they are between 16 and 18 years old. The census records at Rauit began in 1952 and were incomplete at first, so it is hard to be sure of ages. None of the ten girls with puberty rites in 1968–9 was younger than 16 years old to judge by the census records. Of these ten girls, one was 16 years old, five were 17 and four were over 17 at the time of their rites. Of the ten, all but two had reached maturity stage 5 of Tanner's breast-development rating (Tanner 1955). Gnau people regard the upstanding breasts of nubile girls as immature although they have reached maturity stage 5 of Tanner's standards. In many cases, the breasts then droop even though the young women may not have borne and nursed children.

them, they grew adult [*lil latiyi latiyi matibawul* 'they grew up, grew up adult']
– the girls their breasts jutted forth on them [*galagdel bimaŋgəp məwuməmel*
'the vulvaed ones' breasts sat and sat on them'], the boys bearing their penises
and scrotums [*ganuŋgdel litoawa ganuŋ wɔsyibəg* 'the penised ones carried
penises, scrotums'] – they were grown up, big. The parents came back and saw
them. "Duk!" they cried. "Our children! But they have grown up! We must
kill our Python for the boys' rites [*ala mitauwel garug waipəg* 'so that we may
put on their hair male headdresses'], for initiating the girls [*mitelel bigəp*,
literally 'we may cut their arms', i.e. 'we may make them beautiful; see p. 57].'''

The Gnau regard pendant breasts as fully mature ones. In this sense the
puberty rites are set at the approach, and not at the achievement, of maturity.
Likewise for a boy, the Gnau do not expect beard growth to have begun by the
time of his puberty rites. Formerly the prolonged Tambin seclusion and the full
assumption of male headdress was supposed to fit roughly with the time a young
man's beard grew: by this time he might have fathered two children.

They recognise adolescence as a phase of growth. The girl's menarche is not
paralleled by some discrete natural event in male development. The menarche,
ideally, signals when the girl should have the rites done. Half the girls I saw who
had them done had not in fact menstruated. The menarche is not a rigid requirement of their timing. As with boys, if there are a number of girls who look ripe
for them, they go through them together. They plan in advance so as to get
enough food ready for the celebration. They also like to be able to do them for
more than one child at a time so that the boys or girls will have *wusai* (ritual
friends) of their own sex. But this is not essential. Both boys and girls may, as
in some of the examples I have described, have the rites done individually.
They are puberty rites rather than initiation rites in the sense of the distinctions
made by Allen (1967).[2] The rites are concerned with individual development.
This is most clearly indicated by their precipitation when a girl has her menarche.
But similarly they may be performed for a lone boy too, because the boy has
clearly reached the necessary stage. The rites mark out the approach of maturity.

Of all public rites along the course of people's lives, the rites of puberty are
the only major publicly feted events which all people must undergo personally
– except for those done after death. The rites of birth are public only for the
first child of a couple: the major public rite of marriage is the celebration of
this birth – not all couples have children. There are of course rites which most
people take part in at some time in their lives, but of the personal rites the
others are not such public celebrations. Certainly the individual focus, that the
rites must be done for each and every individual, that they require public

---

2 Initiation rites are held at set intervals for a number of candidates simultaneously.
 Puberty rites are performed separately for each individual at the appropriate moment
 in development. The types are clear at either pole and the Gnau would seem to lie closer
 to the puberty-rite pole than the other one. The issue is primarily whether the individual
 has reached a stage of development appropriate to having them done.

observance, marks puberty in a way that only death can match among the Gnau. They must be done.

I tried to convey by description what the rites were like to see. As I said, I have not given all their details. To make clear the extent of sameness and difference now, it is necessary to begin to go into the detail of what is done. For example, I wrote that girls are forbidden to smoke, chew betel or eat coconut or smoke-dried meat or food roasted in the fire, from the moment that their first menstrual period begins (or for a few days before the day of celebrating the rites if they have not had a period) until they are given the special cooked leaves with hunting ash (*nawugəp*) – *teltɑg–nawugəp*. In fact, boys are also forbidden the same things for a week or so before their rites. They too eat *teltɑg–nawugəp* early on the day of their rites to free them from the restrictions. But I took a much longer time to find this out. The girls and women (as well as men) who told me on a number of different occasions about how the rites for girls were done always mentioned this aspect of their rites. It stood out in their accounts, and I saw it done too. With boys, I never noticed it being done. It was only because I asked about each detail that I knew about, to find whether it was so for both sexes that I found out. I think there is more to the differing stress here than just poor observation on my part. I think that it conveys an aspect of their relative attitudes to the rites, and it should be taken into account in the analysis. In a different rite, the one for the birth of a first child, a very similar set of taboos are imposed on both the mother and the father of the newborn child. Both men and women made it sound a taxing and memorable feature of these rites. Is there the germ here of something which may explain the stress differing between boys and girls in regard to the taboos in the puberty rites? I shall take it up later (in chapter 8). I cite the instance of the first-birth rites to show that, while the taboos are salient to both sexes in the first-birth rites, they are so only for girls at puberty. Men differ from women in the attention paid to the same set of restrictions which occur both in puberty and in first-birth rites.

A second example lies in a concealed parallel: the giving of penile blood by the mother's brother (or someone else in place of him) to the sister's daughter. Here there is intended secrecy. A boy will see the bleeding done. He even crouches between the legs of his mother's brother so the blood drips down on him before the smearing on his body. But a girl receives penile blood unwittingly. I was never able to see for sure that it was done. I knew only because I was told so. The penile blood let the day before is concealed in the betel quid prepared and chewed by the mother's brother to spit the girl. Thus he transfers his blood to her undetectably.

At one level they do the same thing for both boys and girls – they must transfer penile blood from the mother's brother to the sister's child – but by a subterfuge for the girl because men wish to keep their secrets. What women may know about the rites, both for boys and for girls, differs from what men know. The difference in this second example rests on intended deception. In the first, the response of the actors to the same thing (the set of restrictions) is differently weighted, perhaps by reason of the balance of significance between that and other things (e.g. painful bleeding or not) which happen in the rites. What answer is given to the question of sameness or difference in the rites will depend on the precise question (whole rite, specific action, reason for doing it), the perspective chosen (men's or women's, organisers' of the rites or adolescent subjects'). Some parts of the rites are done unobtrusively or privately (witness the uncertainty I mentioned on p. 83 about whether or not a *lyimaŋgai*-banana leaf was torn); other parts are obvious to everyone (to be spat wet bright red).

The rites for both sexes are similar in these respects: the age to undergo them; their being done on one day; the general pattern of participation in them – the parents, family and hamlet neighbours, the mother's brothers – men organise them; the restriction on betel, coconuts, etc.; the *wa'agəp* stew of meat sprinkled with coconut; the spitting with betel juice; the transfer of mother's brother's penile blood; the decoration; the exchanges of food and money; the one main reason for doing them – that the adolescent entering maturity may grow well. These things are common to both sexes.

The main differences between them are: girls menstruate; men do certain things and keep them secret or private from women: the boy used to (and may still) have his hair fastened in the male headdress inside the men's house; the boy is bled from his penis outside the hamlet; the boy has a phallocrypt put on, the girl her pubic apron of shells, the *timalyi'ep bifaŋ*; the mother has to do something in the boy's rites which she does not do for a girl; the mother's mother is singled out in the invocation for a girl but not for a boy.

In many features the rites for boys and girls are similar. The approaching maturity of both sexes is given public recognition. One may choose to point out what is evident, viz. that girls lose blood from their genitals for the first time in puberty and boys do not do so spontaneously, though men contrive to make them do something like it. But I think it would be distorted to go on to say that we should interpret the rites for boys as a reflection of men's envy of women's menstrual power or that men seek to prove by their rites that they can match the 'natural' powers or experience of women by contrived 'cultural' means. To interpret the act of penis-bleeding in that way requires isolation which excludes all the things done on the same day which are also done for girls, and leave only the blood flowing, the genitals and the first time as elements for interpretation. If nothing at all were done at puberty for girls and only penis-bleeding for boys, it might be argued that the difference or opposition – spontaneous : contrived (nature : culture) – was more evident, since there would be little else to attend to. Even then the interpretation chooses to select some features of the act and neglect others – for example the pain inflicted, the operator who

110

pierces the boy and their relationship, the secrecy. What the anthropologist's eye selects — genital bleeding for the first time— and interprets as an imitation of the menarche is not seen by the Gnau in the same way. The interpretation is denied. How exact must imitation be for the interpretation to gain acceptance when the anthropologist infers it and the actors do not state it, indeed deny it? Is a stabbing of the penis above the glans with a bone awl close enough?

Other forms for bleeding boys in puberty or initiation rites are found in New Guinea — for example bleeding in puberty from the penile urethra (Arapesh: Mead 1970, p. 399), from the nose (Eastern Highlands: Berndt 1965, p. 91), from the tongue or gums (Wogeo: Hogbin 1970, p. 117; Kwoma: Whiting 1941, p. 66; Iatmul: Bateson 1958, p. 131), from the back (Iatmul: Bateson 1958, p. 77). The list is not exhaustive. The details of the method of bleeding from the penis differ (twirling twigs in the urethra, scraping with nettles, stabbing with an awl). The Iatmul, who do not bleed the penis,[3] make cutting and scarring the back a cruel part of initiation to manhood, as Bateson's photographs in *Naven* make clear. At what point does one begin to be uncertain when it is the observer left to decide about imitation or mimicry on the sole evidence of his eyes? Is urethral bleeding closest, stabbing the penis less close; the mouth or the tongue a surrogate for the vulva, the nose for the penis; but the back unacceptable?

With this question before us, I will now face the problems of accepting an interpretation of the act of penis-bleeding as a male 'first menstruation' in defiance of the Gnau view. By using the word 'interpretation' I perhaps evade stating exactly what I think I am doing. I agree that I must not suppose or suggest that this is what the Gnau say about it. It is not a 'meaning' they attach to the action and can put in words. Even if the action was at some former time planned to communicate that meaning, it is now lost to the reflective minds or intellects of the people I talked to who carry on the practice. They do not recall it or point it out. If by a symbol we mean something standing for something else, we cannot say that penis-bleeding stands for menstruation or the menarche in Gnau minds. The idea of a symbol entails the idea of reference to something else, the image referring to some actual or imaginary reality (a motif in the outer world or the inner mental world of the thinker) which is different from it. If a distinction is not made between the two, it becomes impossible to speak of one thing being the symbol of something else, because it is not: they are both forms of the same thing — either alternatives or substitutes — for the class is extensive enough to include them both.

In the case of Wogeo, where the link between penile bleeding and menstruation is clear, Hogbin (1970, pp. 88, 102n) reports that the people of Wogeo apply their word for 'menstruating' to both men and women. They define and

3 I have not found a report that the Iatmul do so, though the practice is so widespread in the Sepik that my statement may need to be corrected.

class the event by its function, neglecting whether it is natural or artificial. They say that the function of menstruation is to remove dangerous fluids acquired from the opposite sex in intercourse; men do not do this naturally so they substitute an artificial act. If swabbing the arm before giving an injection were shown to make no difference to the frequency of subsequent infection at the injection site, we would have the same ground to call swabbing the arm a symbolic act that we have for calling Wogeo penis-bleeding one — both would be based on mistaken ideas about how to avoid a risk to health; both would 'express' something about theories of the cause of illness, one concerning the danger of germs, the other the danger of sexual fluids. There might be no reason to call penis-bleeding a symbolic act — it might not stand for something else; it might be just a means to an end. The Wogeo might do it with a conscious purpose, as we swab the arm. If penis-bleeding were called 'symbolic' then so would menstruation be for the people of Wogeo.

To see it as symbolic depends on our choosing to classify penile bleeding apart from menstrual bleeding. The idea we have of menstrual bleeding is that it can be applied correctly only to something which happens to women. This is an essential attribute, an intension, of our definition or understanding of menstruation; real or true menstruation can only happen to women. Therefore male bleeding must be apparent menstruation, symbolic or mimic menstruation. This is so because we have chosen to classify in that way. According to Hogbin, the people of Wogeo have not chosen to make 'spontaneous', 'natural', 'womanly' essential to their definition. Their concept of 'menstruating' differs from ours — men and women both 'really' menstruate. Men do not menstruate symbolically, they menstruate. If I say I went to London, then just because you walked and I went by car, you would not feel that because you went naturally and I went artificially that I went symbolically. The concept of going (in 'went') does not bother about this distinction. If I choose nonetheless to report that Wogeo men 'symbolically' or 'metaphorically' menstruate, I must accept that I have imposed my own categories on what they do. I tell you about my categories, not theirs. And you may prefer what I tell you to what the Wogeo say because my categories correspond with yours and those of the Wogeo do not.

If symbolism involves the notion of one something standing for or representing something else, it must depend on a particular classification that separates the one thing from the something else it represents. It rests on an intellectual perception of the boundaries of the categories. To say of some other people that they symbolise x by y must therefore require a knowledge on their part that x and y are not the same. This involves awareness. The same arguments apply to 'metaphor' when it is used by anthropologists in relation to the ideas, words or actions of other people. The people must recognise distinctions between two concepts for one to be used *metaphorically* of the other by them.

A symbol of something is not the same as the thing itself. A metaphor is only a metaphor — the sea of my troubles would not support the lives of fishes, nor could fishing boats bob upon it. For the individual to see that what he uses is a metaphor or a symbol, he must see at some level of consciousness that one is after all merely a picture, the other the land in front of him; one an image of the god, the other the god itself. One may be the best way for him to figure what he has in mind but nonetheless it is not truly or exactly what he has in mind. He may have but an inkling of it and the image be the best way for him to figure that inkling for you — the inkling might be obscure or mysterious, but he would recognise that the figure he used or produced in his effort to apprehend or convey what that inkling really was or might be was something different from the thing itself.

I have tried to stress that there should be an intellectual component in the recognition of symbol or metaphor, that it depends on classification and the boundaries of categories. Of course usages that are initially metaphoric may lead to changes of meaning or innovations. The example of the shift of meaning in the Latin word for 'mask' (*persona*) is a good one (Mauss 1938; Ogden and Richards 1923, pp. 129–30). The meaning of the word was extended and eventually changed from that of 'mask' to 'person'. As 'person' became an accepted meaning of *persona*, that use was no longer metaphoric. This is one way in which metaphor may lead to change of meaning, blur and then dissolve a metaphoric sense.

But there is another major aspect to the instability of perceiving something as symbol or metaphor. This aspect involves emotion as well as the intellect. The stress I have first given to the intellect requires correction. The problem I have in mind lies with the fallacy of misplaced concreteness and superstition: it comes within the magical field of symbol and metaphor. The relationships we have to those things we assert or affirm can be most various — from unshakeable faith, strong conviction, agreement, consent, through cool neutrality that sees it might be so, to uncertainty, half-doubt and then its willing suspension, and at last to a mere wish to think so and a measure of voluntary delusion. The implications or the consequences of what one asserts or affirms may differ in how they matter for the conduct of one's life. What is said in one situation may be casual and have no direct bearing on what one is doing or will do then, but the same words used in another situation may bear very directly on one's choice of action. The later situation or context may demand, excite or imply quite different degrees of emotional commitment to what one asserts or affirms. The passions evoked by the real experiences of life — desire, hate, misery, joy — may submerge or blur that distinction between appearance and reality on which the intellectual recognition of a symbol as a symbol depends. When hate or desire so swamps a man that he no longer sees his act as symbolic — when he sees the idol not as symbol but as the god itself — we start to think of superstition. He mistakes the symbol which is concrete for the transcendent reality which he had tried to grasp better and figure forth by it. The element of conscious make-believe is lost. The recognition of the difference between the image and reality, the distance and the half-doubt, may vanish in the desire to accomplish something. The difference may be suspended before the will to believe in the truth or efficacy of what he asserts, the desire for something to happen, the hate seeking outlet in vengeance. In one situation or frame of mind and emotion, the distinction, which in another is readily admitted, disappears or blurs. In the discussion of the Gnau magic by which a mother's brother is said to be able to kill his sister's son (chapter 9) I will try to show more exactly and with particular examples what I mean by this interplay of intellect and emotion in the perception of symbols.

Part of the sense of a strange or magical quality in effective symbols seems to me to lie in the ability they have to produce dissonance between the intellectual awareness of their make-believe, conventional or factitious character, and the appeal they may also make to the emotions through corresponding to, or getting close to, or touching, something truly wanted or needed. People may vacillate between the pull of the intellect and the pull of emotion. The balance between the two pulls may alter greatly in different situations — sometimes the symbol will seem to be the thing itself.

Some anthropologists discuss and interpret symbols as things purely of the intellect, to be analysed in terms of logic and categories, as structures of the mind, abstracted from attitude, motivation and emotion. If this approach is followed for fear of trespassing into psychology, it makes a strange distinction between intellect and emotion as subjects for psychology. If the approach is followed because of an assumption that matters of reasoning and intellect are social and appropriate to anthropology in ways that emotions and feeling are not because they are supposed to be instinctual or animal, then the grounds for the separation are grotesquely naive (Fletcher 1971, sect. 3). To leave out the emotional side of social behaviour because it is difficult to study, to record, to analyse, or because the anthropologist feels incompetent, may be more honest as reasons for leaving it out, but they are hardly justified if the aim is to interpret and understand social behaviour — in this case people's ritual behaviour.

I entered into these problems with the question of how close must the imitation be for the anthropologist to assert his interpretation of penis-bleeding as a sort of male menarche (or menstruation) in the face of the Gnau saying it is not. If he speaks of it as symbolic menstruation, either he implies that real menstruation must be distinguished from apparent menstruation in terms of his own categories of classification, or he implies that the Gnau make this distinction at some level of awareness. But the Gnau do not state what he states, so he must imply that we can know what they are conscious of from other evidence than their words, which deny it. Otherwise the common senses of symbol and metaphor are lost in the obscurity of presumed unconscious knowledge and we become confused.

A herring gull sits on its clutch of eggs. You remove an egg from its nest and put beside the nest a painted piece of wood which is quite like the egg in shape and to touch. The gull will retrieve it and sit on it (Tinbergen 1953b, pp. 144–59). The gull will neither affirm nor deny that it is sitting on an imitation egg or a symbolic egg. Should the anthropologist on the grounds of his own classification say it is a symbolic egg? It sounds like nonsense to suggest that it is a symbolic egg for the gull. But it is not so to suggest that it serves the gull as substitute for an egg. To the broody gull, the round object placed in that situation close to its depleted nest will release a response – it retrieves the round object and sits on it. The object serves as an egg for the broody gull. To say it substitutes for an egg derives from observation of its use or function; to say it symbolises an egg is to make a bizarre inference about the herring gull's intellect.

The assumption possibly made by the anthropologist confronting Gnau penis-bleeding is that some elements in the action – bleeding, genital and first time – are so clear as equivalents for the menarche that his interpretation cannot be denied despite what the Gnau say. He assumes this because he judges that these elements resemble those of the menarche, and because he supposes that all human beings respond to certain natural aspects of their experience of the human body in like ways, though presumably at a level differing from the superficial one of what they speak about. The human body is our common frame and the modalities of sensation are common to us all, and so are some aspects of experience of the body's functioning. The hypothesis rests on an assumption of 'natural symbols' to which we all must respond: the response is supposed to be intuitive and innate. Gombrich (1960, chs. III, XI; 1963, pp. 56–9) examines whether we are justified in making this assumption when we try to understand works of art.

The issue here is primarily one of stimulus and response – the release of a response rather than understanding in the sense of intellectual awareness and differentiation. Biologists investigating animal responses have shown that efficacy in releasing such responses does not depend necessarily on how closely the object's external form is imitated but on imitation of certain privileged or relevant aspects. The male stickleback which Tinbergen studied did not respond much to a naturalistic dummy fish unless it was painted red below, but caricature dummies with plenty of red aroused violent reaction. Indeed, there were cases when dummies aroused more reaction than the real thing. Sticklebacks in the aquarium even postured when they saw, through the window, red mail vans going past on the road (1953a, pp. 65–6). The herring gull would choose a painted wooden egg twice the size or eight times the volume of its real egg in preference to one of normal size: it made frantic efforts to sit on it without falling off (Tinbergen 1953b, p. 158). The release of a response depends on certain relevant or privileged aspects in a configuration – the closeness of imitation of some external form is not a sure guide.

It seems likely that human beings do respond to certain configurations of biological significance with special readiness. The pattern of the human face and the two eyes looking might be the best example. But our readiness to see a face in the moon, or on the wings of a butterfly, in a pattern of leaves or on a crumbling wall, varies with our mood and our thoughts. To the broody gull with a depleted nest, a round piece of wood will release the response, but in another season of the year or away from the nest it will not. To the famished wolf, the rutting stallion, the timid deer, a mere hint of what it hungers for, lusts after or fears may suffice to evoke a response, and so it is with man too. The response depends on mental set, arousal and alertness, the situation or context, not solely on 'objective' external aspects of the stimulus. The closeness of imitation is not a sure guide to response.

Leonardo said of the blot of paint on a crumbling wall 'You may see whatever you desire to seek in it.' We have the ability to project things we are familiar with, like faces, onto vaguely similar shapes, but whether we do so, and what we see, will alter with our expectations. We differ in our preoccupations, our moods, the state of our desires, in our readiness to see something or to see a resemblance. Rorschach devised the ink-blot test for diagnosis. He thought his subjects revealed things about themselves by their interpretative projections in response to the blots. Might not the anthropologist be revealing himself and his preoccupations rather than the Gnau's when he tells us that the Gnau penis-bleeding is a kind of male menstruation when the Gnau do not see it so?

The efficacy of substitutes or symbols lies in their ability to release a response, and this depends on a combination of their intrinsic attributes, the context in which they are set and the power of expectation (the mental set, arousal and readiness to respond) on the part of the animal or person who perceives them. This view of efficacy may lead us to question whether our search to understand ritual activities in terms of symbol, metaphor and communication is directed right. To the extent that we seek to find imitations of nature or symbols of other things, the communication of meanings, may we not misconceive the nature of ritual?

I began discussing ritual by pointing out that what was clear in ritual was knowing how to do it rather than knowing about what it meant. I would argue, following Gombrich (1960, ch. III), that in ritual too, as in art, making comes before matching, that creating or doing comes before imitating. The traditional view of representation, as imitation of external forms, involves a degree of intellectual abstraction which may come after that other sense of representation as the finding of things which will serve as substitutes. Objects, actions and images may represent in the sense of serving as substitutes rather than by imitating the external form of something else. The piece of wood may serve the gull as a substitute for an egg; the baby's thumb, as substitute for the mother's breast; the idol, as substitute for a god; the wax dummy, as substitute for the person whom the sorcerer desires to harm. The question of reference may be quite independent of the degree of differentiation of the image or how life-like it is.

116

The common factor between the object or the action and its substitute or symbol is function rather than form. The baby may suck its thumb when it cannot suck the breast. If the thumb is said to represent the breast, the representation depends on its ability to meet the minimum requirements of function rather than on formal similarity of external form. Gombrich (1963) takes the hobby horse as the exemplar for his argument. The simplest hobby horse does not represent a horse because it calls up to the child's imagination by description or portrayal an idea or concept of a horse. It may be just a stick to ride on. The common factor is that it is ridable. To turn the stick into a hobby horse, the stick must have a form just possible to ride, and the child must want to ride. Then the stick may serve as substitute, as focus for his fantasy. The child creates his substitute out of the materials to hand; the greater his wish to ride, the fewer may be the features that will do for a horse. What is important is that it will function as a substitute and will serve as focus for his fantasy: communication need not come in at all. Having found his stick, he may look around for things to use to make it more effective and life-like; he may attach some rope to the head of the broom for reins, some buttons for eyes. He proceeds to differentiate and make his hobby horse more like a horse, more clear as a horse. Substitution may precede portrayal, creation may precede communication, making may precede matching.

I have tried to show reasons for objecting to an interpretation of penis-bleeding as a kind of male menarche when the Gnau do not say it is. The wish to focus discussion on a specific example of interpretation has led me to present the argument in a way which perhaps reverses its development. Though I have taken a specific example, I believe the arguments may apply to some other examples of the anthropological interpretation of ritual. I shall summarise a few main points.

To presume that ritual is essentially a form of communication prejudges what is to be found out. The presumption leads to a search for meanings when the actors in the situation do not name them. The emphasis on communication can lead to a contrived intellectualisation of ritual in which the conviction that it is to be understood by means of a linguistic model distorts observation, and provokes such ingenuity in detection that the actors are told what they mean when they do not know it. Sometimes the interpretation may provide much insight into why or how the actions done or the objects used are effective in their context or situation, and may help to explain the choice of them. However, the insight is translated into over-intellectualised terms and/or into the terminology of linguistics, by using the terms in ways that stretch their accepted meaning, or their meaning to the linguist, beyond recognition (Mounin 1970, pp. 11—86, 199—214). The meanings of metaphor, symbol, code, message are so changed and confused that the difference between the actor meaning these things knowingly, with understanding, and his supposedly meaning them though he cannot recognise what, is lost.

If people want to say something, why do they not just say it? If people do ritual, it is because ritual can also do something different from saying it or something more than just that. It may be that it is difficult to phrase or formulate something they wish to say — the actor lacks the words for what he feels or senses obscurely, or he can express it better, more powerfully, by action and object (as Dr Johnson kicked the stone to refute Bishop Berkeley's argument). But it is not just this possibility of saying something better or managing to express it at all that accounts for ritual. It accords with experience and what people say to point first to the practical side of ritual, that people have established ways to do it. It is primarily action — a way of doing, making, creating, showing, expressing, arousing — a complex form of stimulus to which people respond. Things done in ritual also have the power to arouse or to release, to serve as substitutes, as focuses for fantasy: they meet needs and stem from motivations. By seeing the objects or actions as substitutes that will make do perhaps for a god, for an enemy, for a horse, for a breast in that situation, we do not have to exclude emotion and feeling, we do not have to traduce the usual meanings of metaphor or symbol, nor do we have to suppose that the actor necessarily bothers with the distinction of appearance from reality.

There is a current of correspondence running between some of the points I have raised. With the herring gull and the egg we are quite content to speak only of the piece of wood serving as a substitute: the stimulus which releases the response. We have no wish to apply the terms 'symbol' and 'metaphor' — likewise with the baby who sucks his thumb in place of the breast. With the child and his hobby horse we might begin to worry about whether we should speak of it as a symbolic or metaphoric horse or just as substitute for a horse. It serves because it is ridable. The child does not worry himself with this question — it is a kind of horse to him because he can ride it. He extends the class of horse to include it. But if we asked the child, 'Is that a real horse or just a make-believe or play horse?' he would probably tell us, 'Of course it's not a real horse.' Piaget (1932, pp.19—56) observed that the child believes for himself what he wants to. From the ages of two to four years the child does not ask whether his game symbols are true or not. Although he can recognise that they are not true for others, he does not try to convince his adult entourage; the satisfactions he derives from his game symbols carry their own convictions — a subjective truth. He does not make or use his hobby horse to communicate something about his idea of horses. To ask the child whether his horse is really a horse or a symbolic horse is to ask a question he does not bother with in his play. We ask him to consider what kind of horse he has and match it against his grasp of our concepts. What he is doing is playing, not thinking about concepts or communicating. To interpret his actions as an attempt to match his concept of a horse would be to go against common sense. The approach which searches in rites only for symbol and metaphor, and for communicated meanings, seems to me to involve a parallel mistake about the nature of ritual. It falsely intellectualises what it is trying to understand. As with the child's hobby horse we may pose irrelevant questions about whether the actors see what they are doing as symbolic or metaphoric, and find that they answer both yes and no. Ritual may indeed seek to convey, through symbol and metaphor, particular ideas: that is, or may be, part of what it does and how it produces its effects, but it is only part, not all.

The uncertainty we note as to when something is or is not a symbol, the frequent instability of decisions on this, the instability of what words mean, their extension and change in meaning, reflects the kinds of problems some philosophers have posed in trying to unravel the meaning of meaning, even as it applies to words (see Taylor 1970, chs. 10—14). They sometimes also take a functional view that a 'Word has a meaning only in the sense that it has a use and a word's use is clearly not a further thing. It is a characteristic of utterances of the word itself — of the manner of its employment' (ibid. p. 183).[4] 'From the point of view of this theory of meaning, no clear distinction can be drawn between metaphorical and non-metaphorical uses of words. From this it might be concluded that one should say of all language that it is metaphorical. To do so would be a mistake, for such a conclusion would deprive the word "metaphorical" of a specific sense, hence deprive that conclusion of any content' (ibid. p. 170). A metaphor is held to be an extended use of a word. To speak of the extended use of a word implies being able to speak of a non-extended or central use. The central use conforms to some definition or to some notion of what is essential to a thing described by the word. The extended use occurs when some of the essential properties are lacking, or when certain conflicting properties are present. The notion of metaphor depends then on definition, or the notion of a central use, and unless a word can be consciously characterised by such essential properties (not all words can) we cannot speak of metaphor in its normal sense; without the notion of a word's central use, the idea of extended use makes no sense. A definition of a central use is established by convention (this may change); the act of recognising or knowing a metaphor (as distinct from responding to it) depends on conscious reference to that convention or definition, and awareness of it. Metaphors, symbols and signs are slippery things; they may shift from one category or another (see Gombrich 1960, pp. 83—4).

If we reject the interpretation of penis-bleeding as imitation of the external

4 But Gellner (1970, pp. 143—4) convincingly points out that 'concepts and beliefs do not exist in isolation in texts or in individual minds but in the life of men and societies. The activities and institutions in the context of which a word or a phrase or a set of phrases is used must be known before that word or phrase can be understood.' He takes issue specifically with Wittgenstein's view that the meaning is its use. The use of some word may depend on its lack of meaning, its ambiguity, its possession of wholly different and incompatible meanings in different contexts, and on the fact that it gives the impression of possessing a consistent meaning throughout.

form of natural womanly menstruation, we might still consider whether the Gnau seek by penis-bleeding to fulfil some function that they also attribute to menstruation or the menarche. If they were to attribute the same function to both, then we might have grounds for agreeing to their correspondence, for seeing penile bleeding as a substitute for the menarche or menstruation. I consider this in the next chapter.

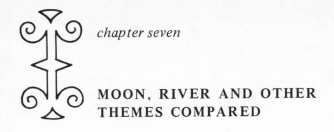

chapter seven

MOON, RIVER AND OTHER
THEMES COMPARED

Questioning the Gnau on menstruation led me to conclude that they were undecided and uncertain about its function. What people find curious, demanding or worth investigation, what they probe or search to understand, does vary. Not every man or woman is equally born a natural philosopher; the want to understand is unevenly distributed, the questions framed for differing purposes, the tug of interest and need set by various circumstance. About a thousand people, men, women and children, speak Gnau as their native language. The range of their social intercourse with others round them was limited before the imposition of peace. They bear a culture which is distinctive to them. It occurred to me often to wonder how the encyclopaedia of Gnau knowledge must have varied in each generation according to the chance bestowal of genius, bad memory, curiosity, inattention and pedagogic zeal, when in each generation so small a number of people bore the total load of knowledge for teaching to their children. And from this to wonder whether there might be, in the diversification of knowledge, in the depth, complexity and coherence of answers to most varied questions, differences between cultures which stemmed from the scale of the society, from sheer weight or lack of numbers, so that any given piece of knowledge, each particular connection seen, was statistically less or more likely to be lost as it depended for its transmission on one man or many. That many know some things because those things are deemed important by necessity to life, by attachment to some centrally established doctrine or some action regularly performed, reflects selective social needs and interests in particular societies, but there will be many other insights perhaps seen at one time by some among them, but then lost or half lost fortuitously by the generations that succeeded them. In the present, some domains of knowledge are clear, well set out, systematic and coherent; others are not so, and bits and pieces are brought in answer. A faithful picture should record the difference between the well-shaped forms and the fragments, the difference sensed in forthright easy answers, compared with puzzlement, speculative bits and pieces uncertainly brought forward. To the degree that the Gnau do not seem to hold a sure or dominant idea or dogma about the function of menstruation, it becomes impossible to say whether or not they consider penis-bleeding to serve that function.

They say the cause of the menarche is the moon which strikes the girl. The phrase *gə'unit wa'ab* 'the moon strikes her' is the common and conventional way to say that a girl has had her first menstrual period. I asked them what they meant by this. One man answered that he supposed the moon, like a man, somehow copulated with her, another that the moon heated (*wəgə'aiya*) the girl's *wuna'at* (vital, thinking centre; see Lewis 1975, pp. 208—14) and so the blood flowed: others just repeated that they were moon-struck and speculated no further. At some times of the year when we walked along a stream, I remarked the boulders in its course which were spattered by small dark crimson blotches like the puke or excrement, though flat like lichen, of small birds that had eaten crimson berries. What were they? They said, 'The moon drips its blood' (*gə'unit wəwə'ata gaŋgi ari*). Did the moon then menstruate? No,[1] nor were the blotches apparently a subject of their curiosity or special interest. If pressed to say, they said the moon was like a man, not a woman[2] — for example, the man who thought the moon copulated with the girl to cause her menarche; and the moon is called sister's son (*mauwin*) of the evening star, its mother's brother. I have heard women tease the children hopping from boulder to boulder over the drops of moon-blood that they would menstruate.

Yet in answer to my question why, exactly, the moon was connected with menstruation, others referred to or told me a myth which perplexed me. I could not see, nor could they say, how it had anything to do with menstruation. What it told about was how the moon was put into the sky and gave men its light so that they could hunt for phalangers by night. That is its significance for them, and no one who has experienced the difference between the darkness of night in the forest with no moon, and night there when moonlight gently floods the trees, can miss it.

In brief the myth tells of a woman who caught the moon in the river with her fishing net. She hid it in her house under a pile of firewood to cook and eat it later. She called it a turtle (*baglut*). But first she had to work to get enough sago ready. While it was hid there, each day she barred her house and each evening she would not let her husband in but set his food for him to eat outside, always outside. He wondered why. So in the day, while she was out, he peered through a crack in the wall and saw the light under the firewood. He called his brothers in secret to come while she was gone next day. They entered and stole her moon and, singing, pushed it with a pole of joined bamboo high and higher up into the sky. A tiny mouse[3] helped them when they could not push it higher,

---

1 But one fifteen-year-old boy said of the blotches, 'That's the moon menstruating' (*gə'unit wap gaŋgap*).
2 The Abelam in the Middle Sepik make the moon feminine and an exception to the general rule that all inanimate objects are masculine (Kaberry 1941, p. 242).
3 A marsupial mouse, like a dormouse to look at, that makes its nest of moss.

until at last the moon stuck fast to the sky. The woman at her work looked down at the red-leached sago washings in the *limbum* vat and saw the moon reflected. Desperate, she rushed back. She found her loss, cursed her husband and chased him, furious.

The men hunted by night now and killed the phalangers. They hunted and hunted. Always they gave what they killed to the woman. Always, until at last her teeth were worn down and her jaws ached and then she said, 'My grand-children, I was cross over my loss. I took all you hunted. From now on you may eat the phalangers.' She made it up with them, called them friends, and laughed with them.

If determined to find something in the myth, we see that it links woman, moon and river; that the woman keeps her husband out of her house when she has the moon (her moon) there; that she sees the moon reflected on the red surface of her sago washings (*wɔlyibati*). But no one Gnau pointed these things out to me or saw them as significant in the story, and the woman feeds her husband while she has the moon with her, which no menstruant Gnau woman would ever do. Indeed the woman in the story is an old woman.

One thing is clear about menstruation: it has something to do with the moon, to the Gnau as to so many other peoples. And yet the Gnau put some uncertainty into the very lunar cycle of menstruation. Most women declare that they do not menstruate every month; most say they go two months between periods or sometimes longer. They recommend that those who menstruate every month (which some do) should take certain herbs[4] as they do for those whose blood loss is heavy, which they dislike. They use no pad to absorb the loss but sit near or in the house – they say they let the blood soak into the ground. For most the loss is scanty, lasting only a day. Girls marry within a year or two of their menarche and anovular cycles are common in adolescence, and many women are nursing their babies or pregnant for the greater part of their reproductive lives – thus adolescence, then pregnancy and lactation may make the monthly character of menstruation less apparent. Infrequent sporadic menstruation and scanty blood-loss conserve blood and would protect from anaemia, and most adult women in this area probably have low haemoglobin levels. Irregular menstruation and amenorrhoea have been noted before among women in various parts of the world (see Ellis 1936, p. 89, Abbie 1960) and associated with undernutrition (Le Roy Ladurie (1974) discusses in detail the historical and comparative evidence for this). I would accept what Gnau women say about the

---

4 My wife was shown fruits and bark of a tree (*lu gaŋgasa* 'red' or 'blood tree') and also the stalk of a herb. Some women said they also ate a red button-toadstool. Some ate the bark with cooked dry sago, others in a betel nut, others with coconut; some said they ate herbs every month on the evening the new moon appeared, some that they took them after a heavy loss, some that they never took them, some that they took them every five or six months. I doubt that the herbs work pharmacologically, for the ways they take them are so various, but I do not know.

sporadic irregular nature of their periods and note that even so they make a link between the moon and menstrual bleeding.

The moon provides a reason why a girl first menstruates, but another occasional answer that I heard tells why women as a sex are subject to this bleeding. Briefest of all the Gnau myths I learned, each time I heard it from men they grinned about it as though it was just a story which they did not really believe and found rather funny.

First it was men who menstruated by peeing blood and the women had beards. One man took a piece of firewood and, with his finger, smeared it with his menstrual blood. He called his wife, told her to make a fire with the firewood. She did. Since then, women have menstruated and men have beards.

The story will serve to introduce the theme of the antithesis between men and women. The story makes one point: that men might menstruate had they not tricked women into it. They are both creatures of one kind (*matildel* 'human beings') but they are different and divided by sex into *galagdel* 'the vulvaed ones' and *ganuŋgdel* 'the penised ones', into *ləgibəg* 'the men' and *bawul* 'the women'. In what respects does this obvious difference of sex matter in relationships between them? How far do the Gnau see menstruation as the mark of womanhood and the blood that seeps out as essence of the difference between the sexes, having properties of danger, value or virtue in relationships between them?

Their answers do betray certain attitudes to menstrual blood. It may be tempting to characterise the quality of relations between the sexes as opposed or antagonistic, but the relations are rarely so simple or single as to be described by only one informing quality. Different and opposed, hostile and dangerous, but also co-operative and complementary, with mutual and shared interests — the relationships have many aspects. Sex is both genital and an attribute of the whole person. The difference of sex accedes to full significance after puberty when it flowers in sexual activity and reproduction. The Gnau say that menstrual blood is dangerous for men, but small boys and girls may play around their menstruating mother, sleep in the house with her, eat food she has prepared. If the danger of menstrual blood be taken to show 'sex antagonism' then we must note that it matters for the man but not the boy. On the other hand, many social distinctions or discriminations between the sexes seen in work, gesture, right and duty go with gender as an attribute of the whole person rather than with sex in the genital or active sense.

A menstruating woman is dangerous to men: the danger is of any woman's menstrual blood to any man; a sister's or a daughter's blood is not less harmful than a wife's or an enemy's wife's blood. Variously they say menstrual blood could cause a man to die, fall ill or fail to find game in hunting. They do not say exactly how, except of failure in hunting, of which some said that 'The blood would flow down over his eyes' to hide game from him.[5] Therefore a woman

5 This explanation resembles the reason which men of Ligawum (Laeko, a nearby village)

menstruating will not cook food for her husband or other men. She stays in or near her house; she does not leave the village. Husbands and wives sleep in different houses anyway. At the end of her menstrual period, she goes to bathe. To menstruate is to be in a 'bad' condition: in Gnau they say *li wɔla* 'she is bad' i.e. ill, indisposed) or *li wɔla, wap gɑŋgap*, literally 'she is bad, she stays with bloods'. The word *wɔla* has a range of meanings including 'bad' 'ill' and 'dangerous' (see also Lewis 1975, p. 130). But a woman is also vulnerable while she menstruates. She stays in the village because if she were to go in the forest, her blood might drip on the vines, leaves and plants used by men in ritual (*lu lambɔt*; see p. 48), the sun might burn down upon the drips and 'take the blood' (*wigɔr gɑŋgi*) and both these things would harm her ability to bear children (childbearing and menstruation are linked). She is at risk from the spirits associated with water pools, with sago (usually the spirit Panu'ɔt), and with natural pools[6] and marshes in the forest (the spirits are called generically *malɔt*). They are likely to strike her, supposedly in her genitals, if she goes near the water while menstruating.

Contact with a woman menstruating could ruin some of the rites men do and the materials they use in them, because she is 'cold' (*magi*) and men doing rites and the things they use must be 'hot' (*lɔwiti*). Women are not 'cold' all the time; rather it is a matter of degree – the 'cold' ones,[7] so they say, are women who 'menstruate, who copulate, who are pregnant'. But the women are also vulnerable to the substances men use in rites; to men who have done 'hot' things, killed much game or men. There are many activities of men – such as planting yams, organised hunting, doing hunting rites – from which women are debarred because their presence would ruin the success of the enterprise, and also because the women might suffer harm. In every organised activity from which women

give to explain why on marriage a husband must ceremonially cut his wife's pubic covering off and throw it in a river, after which she must go naked.

6 In the myth of Lamu-Wɔlpawei, the two sisters Dimuwi and Damuwi trick their husband Wɔlpawei by simulating menstruation as they travel on a journey and they use their fears about the spirits of some forest pools as a reason for not going on: 'She got some red fruits of the tree *na'apɔgi*, crushed them and brought them and rubbed them on her *timalyi'ep* [pubic apron], on her groins and thighs. She spoke (to her husband) saying, I am bad, menstruating. He said, I have got my bone dagger, let us go on now. Then the elder sister said, But here she is, menstruating. If we go on those pools of yours that we have heard about, the ones on our path, they will strike us. No, we will stay and wait here (until her period is ended) then we will come to join you.'

7 An incident of one clan myth links cold and menstruation and makes cold the cause: 'Weiyapan went and watched. She saw her husband dancing. She went and linked her arm through his and now the two danced together. The dance went on. A great wind and rain came; the wind came; the wind blew, clouds thundered and rain fell. Wiyan asked the strangers, saying, Hey! All of you sheltering in that house. Look! that house over there is empty. Can I go with my wife to shelter there? The others answered, No, there are too many in this village. There is no room for you. He asked again and again they refused. So Wiyan took his shield which he had carried as he danced, and he held it over himself and his wife. The cold blew and went through them. And his wife "had blood", she menstruated. She touched her vulva and she rubbed his face with her hand and the blood was white like pus.'

125

are specifically debarred, the activity is accompanied or associated with ritual. There is a distinction between the two kinds of reasons for debarring persons from being present. When the reason is that the ritual would be harmed, the persons debarred are women during the period of their active sexual lives (this is phrased as women who copulate, who are pregnant, who menstruate), but when the reason is that people would be harmed by the ritual, children, women, or men in certain relationships may be the persons excluded.

The antithesis which stands out is between the sexual nature of women and the conditions for ritual success. It is phrased as one between 'cold' and 'hot'. These are relative qualities linked to sexual function. The female quality of 'cold' varies during a woman's life as it does with her monthly periods.

A complex of notions (about hot and cold, wild forest plants and pools, dangerous women and dangerous rites, moon and river, male and female) is found widely throughout the Sepik but assorted in different ways. A clearer picture of the relative stresses given by the Gnau to certain of these features may appear through comparison of what they do and say with what is done and said by some of the other Sepik people who have been written about.

In comparison with other Sepik peoples, the Gnau do not show much concern about menstrual pollution, despite what they say about its dangers. Gnau women do not have to withdraw to special menstrual huts during their periods as do Abelam women (Kaberry 1941, p. 361) and Mountain Arapesh women (Mead 1970, pp. 420–1); they merely stay in the village to avoid spirits of the forest and pools. The Mountain Arapesh also fear spirits they call *marsalai* in Pidgin (ibid. p. 248) but they take the ideas further. 'There is no feeling that the *marsalai* is a friend of man and an enemy of women, but rather he stands for an extreme danger point on one side of the line, just as the menstruating woman represents the extreme danger point on the other hand' (ibid. p. 250). 'A man who sees a *marsalai* knows that he has been sorcerised and is doomed to die. He then turns, for safety, to a menstruating woman, to the extreme expression of the power antithetical to that of the *marsalai*. He goes to a menstruating woman – his wife, mother, sister, or his brother's wife – any menstruating woman will do. She either gives him a drink of water in which leaves stained with menstrual blood have been soaked or she massages his chest or beats him upon the chest with her closed fist' (ibid, pp. 249–50). This use of menstrual blood as though to counter one power by its polar opposite is not matched by any similar Gnau idea or practice; contact with a menstruating woman would add to, not counteract, the disastrous effects of spirit-caused illness.

Rites like magic and sorcery – and spirits – are sometimes described by the Gnau as 'hot'. The places at which ritual is performed and the men who take part in it assimilate the heat which is dangerous for women and children. The simile of fire and heat for power is a vivid one. By contrast, places where no ritual is done are relatively 'cold' but, more specifically, places where women gather, and especially their houses where they sleep and cook, are said to be 'cold' because they are liable to contamination by menstrual or parturient blood and by women's faeces and urine. Again the Mountain Arapesh share this idea but formulate it more explicitly: 'The women further inland have to keep the adolescence taboos too long and they are too cold. If we marry one of them we must keep the taboos or later the coldness of the women will be fast to our skins and we won't be able to find game or to grow yams well . . . Our own women are not so cold. If they menstruate and menstruate two or three times, we can sleep with them, while further inland they (boys whose betrothed wives have menstruated) must taboo meat, cold water, plant yams and hunt for a year or more. When our betrothed wives have menstruated two or three times we try them. But if our yams fail, if our hunting fails, then we go and rid ourselves of the coldness of this woman, we purify ourselves with bark and leaves in the bush, and set the woman afar off, we speak of her as a sister or a mother' (Mead quoting in translation a Mountain Arapesh man — 1970, pp. 419—20). The Abelam say that female blood is cold and male blood hot (Kaberry 1941, pp. 245, 355); Mead writes that the 'Arapesh conceive of women as cold and men as hot' (1970, p. 248 n28) and that the 'heat of sex contact is believed to be very great and very dangerous. Unless both partners can exorcise it from their bodies, the woman will not bear children and grow and cook taro, the man will not be able to hunt game and grow yams' (p. 256). But the people of Wogeo associate coldness with illness, with 'contact with the sacred and those who have been in contact with the ritually unclean' (Hogbin 1970, pp. 83—4). They also associate coldness with spirits (ibid. p. 81), both men and women may be cold; they both menstruate. The quality of coldness in women seems to be associated both by Arapesh and Gnau with menstruation rather than with sexual intercourse, which is a hot activity.

It seemed to me that for the Gnau this sexual heat was little more than a fact of observation — people sweat when they make love, so they speak euphemistically of sweating and heat to refer to sexual intercourse. Sweat mingled in the act can be used for sorcery just as semen can, and in the moment of death by such sorcery a man bursts into sweat, so they say, revealing by what means he dies. Though a man and woman may put themselves into each other's power by the sexual act, the Gnau do not harp upon this danger. They do not talk of stolen sexual leavings used in sorcery by others, as do the Abelam (Forge 1970b, p. 262). The Gnau wash their bodies clean of sweat and sexual fluids after intercourse because, so some say, they would not like to risk licking sexual matter from their hands when they ate for fear of illness. This is a casual view rather than a dogmatic warning of conspicuous danger. Unlike the Arapesh (Mead 1970, p. 256) the Gnau do not rid themselves of the danger of first intercourse by careful ritual measures and penis-bleeding, nor does the dangerous heat of sexual love occupy much place in their explanations or conversations. The Arapesh (ibid. pp. 250–2) and Abelam (Forge 1970b, pp. 261–2) make much of the hazards of love for men, of strange women who lure men into copulation so that they can kill them by sorcery. The Gnau pay only fitful regard to such ideas of women's sorcery through sex – they think of men as sexually aggressive. Men sometimes say with rude laughter that if they met a strange woman trespassing on their land, they would knock her down and rape her. In various tales, the man who has been tricked or angered by some woman, even an old hag, rapes her to revenge himself.

The people differ in where they put the stress – on the dangers of sexual intercourse, or on women as such and their blood. The Wogeo say that penis-bleeding and menstruation have similar purposes: both are to remove sexual contamination by the opposite sex, women lose it by the monthly period, men by penis-bleeding (Hogbin 1970, pp. 87–91). The Abelam also stress that penis-bleeding rids them of sexual contamination. They are taught about the danger of sexual contact with women for long yams and sacred things in general. 'Abelam have very strongly held beliefs about the dangers of sex to sacred activities. Although the dangers are expressed in terms of vulvas, it is not women as such who are dangerous, but the sex act and the aroused vulva; thus for six months while the long yams are growing, a man observing a sex taboo will happily take food from his wife, but should she have committed adultery the food will contaminate him and hence his long yams' (Forge 1970a, pp. 267–7). In the Arapesh ceremony to exorcise the dangerous heat of sexual intercourse the man rids himself of it by penis-bleeding (cutting), the woman by urinating on a coconut tree (Mead 1970, p. 256).

The Gnau do not say that penis-bleeding or menstruation serves to remove contamination by opposite sexual matter, but they recognise that sexual intercourse carries with it some risks. For example, a very sick man (but not a sick woman) ought not be touched or carried by men tainted by recent sexual intercourse. The risk of worsening illness is powerful but imprecise; it resembles the ideas which make such a sick man fearful and agitated if many women gather round and press too close about him. When men plant their yam and taro gardens,[8] when they cover up the *yammami* plants, when they set traps, they should not have sexual intercourse for about a day before or afterwards, else the success of what they do would be harmed. These are male activities. A man returning from plantations is not free to have sexual intercourse until after a feast to remove restrictions on this and certain foods, lest as a result he shoot no game or fall ill. Men who undergo rituals for hunting success, men who sleep

8 The Gnau also say that menstrual blood would ruin the yams if a woman menstruating came into the garden. I was told that men used to bleed onto their yams before they planted them but that they have given up this practice since contact with whiteskins. When they bled on the yams they planted, they would themselves eat none of their own yams; nowadays they can.

in the men's house during major rites should not cohabit with their wives until the dangerous heat of these rites has cooled. In the case of hunting rites it is a matter of waiting a day or two; in the case of major rites and the Lyigʌt ritual which followed killing a person, the final ceremonies involve rites of purification with penis-bleeding after which a man may re-enter his wife's house and have sexual intercourse with her. The danger is to the wife from the heat transmissible to her by her husband which might provoke her illness and draw the spirit's attention to her.

It is clear that among these various peoples penis-bleeding may serve as a means of purification or of removal of some dangerous quality, either that associated with sacred things or defilement by the opposite sex. Women menstruate and seclude themselves. When the period ends, they wash or otherwise make themselves free from the menstrual blood to resume normal life (Arapesh at the end of the menarche have the *walawahine* meal and moon taboos (Mead 1970, pp. 416–22); Abelam, post-menstrual restriction (Kaberry 1941, p. 361); Wogeo, fasting after the menstrual period (Hogbin 1970, p. 89); Gnau, washing). The Arapesh, like the Gnau, use 'washing' as a euphemism for penis-bleeding (Mead 1970, p. 256n41): the Gnau men literally wash before the penis-bleeding; Gnau women wash after menstruation to wash away all traces of contaminating blood. Gnau men bleed themselves at the very end of major rites which they have performed in the men's house. They go to the river, bathe and bleed themselves so that, free of ritual heat, they may again enter their wives' houses, play with their small children, have sexual congress with their wives. Women bleed, then bathe; men bathe, then bleed.

Where penis-bleeding is said to be a way to rid a man of pollution by women (e.g. Abelam, Wogeo) it is practised before undertaking important and hazardous enterprises (e.g. Abelam before entering sacred gardens (Forge 1965, p. 281); Wogeo before a war raid, trading expeditions, making a sail for a canoe or a net to catch pigs (Hogbin 1970, p. 91)). The Gnau practise it after, not before, contact with sacred things to protect women and their born or unborn children.

In some ways menstruant women resemble the sick: the Gnau regard them as *wɔla* — bad/ill/dangerous — and vulnerable. But they are not spoken of as sick (*nɔyigɔg*; see Lewis 1975, p. 146). They alter their behaviour as do sick people, until the flow has ended, when they go to wash. The blood they lose is spoken of as bad (*wɔla*) for men. Although the Gnau consider that 'bad' blood may accumulate in illness, as at a swelling or a bruise or in the throbbing of an ache, and that it is good to cut the skin surface to let it out (Lewis 1975, p. 202), they do not, when asked directly, agree that menstruation serves this purpose of letting bad blood out so as to be cleared of its harmful effects in the body — it is not stale or dried or dead blood that is lost, nor blood contaminated by food impurities. The blood is not seen as intrinsically 'bad' but as bad for men. If pursued, as I pursued them, with questions, they observe that women

129

menstruate because the moon has struck them, they may tell the funny story about men having once menstruated, they may observe that women stop menstruating when they become pregnant.[9] The woman's blood is thought to become the placenta and lochia (see p. 176 below).

They do not say spontaneously or explicitly that menstruation is a way to remove harmful impurity in blood. But this is what they say penis-bleeding does for boys at puberty and for men in certain circumstances. They bleed the penis (the common phrase for this when men speak among themselves is *na'ab tambit* 'he strikes himself') to draw off the bad, dried (*taŋgi* 'tough') blood so that it goes from him, so he will be well. The boy who does not grow well, who is thin, dirty, dry, unsweating and often ill, has blood that has 'died' (*wag*), gone dry (*wɔr beirkati*). The man who is often ill, dirty, dry, must bleed his penis to rid himself of bad blood, he must strike himself, release the blood so that he will stand up and get well (*nyitiyi nyipəl tambit* 'he will stand up and change himself'). When ill, he is heavy; he strikes himself so that he will stand up, feel light. Such ideas of releasing bad blood which impedes growth and health are shared by the Kwoma (Whiting 1941, pp. 63–4, 82, 211), the Arapesh (Mead 1970, pp. 252–9), the Wogeo (Hogbin 1970, p. 91) and the Abelam (Kaberry 1941, p. 361). But the Gnau do not consider that menstruation provides this release of bad blood for women. The Arapesh on the other hand, like the Wogeo, do (Mead 1970, pp. 258–9). Blood-letting by the men and menstruation both release bad blood. Some of the acts associated with menstrual or post-parturition seclusion are called by the Arapesh the women's *tamberan* in Pidgin, as purificatory penis-bleeding is called the men's *tamberan*. 'Male blood letting especially from the urethra (the only form which occurs in purification, but does not occur in the letting of blood to feed the sick) is equated with menstruation and the discharge of a dangerous and undesirable quality; again urination in the male is equated with menstruation in the woman; still again, urination in the woman is equated with purificatory blood letting in the man' (Mead 1970, p. 259). There is, she writes, a constant interchange of symbolism.

The menarche should set the timing of a girl's puberty rites, but the Gnau do not make it a rigid requirement. As with boys, they often perform the rites simultaneously for a few girls of roughly appropriate age. Among Arapesh, Abelam, Kwoma and Wogeo, the analogous rites are set by each girl's first menstruation. Arapesh girls are taught to accelerate their growth by thrusting a roll of nettles in and out of the vagina and this menstrual usage is called the women's *tamberan*; they call the secret method of dyeing women's skirts, done

---

9 To be exact, they say that if a woman's periods stop, she may become pregnant (*wuna'am ta'ati* 'with foetus') but not that she is necessarily pregnant, since the woman is declared pregnant only when she shows the signs of change in her breasts and belly. The husband must first help to make the foetus by sexual intercourse during the time she has no menstrual periods – her periods may have ceased but the foetus is not there yet. The wife notices that her periods have stopped and she says to herself, *Gap gʌŋgap bədənau, dəgasa dəg yina'am ta'ati* 'I have stopped menstruating, I think I will be with foetus'.

during menstrual seclusion and the seclusion following childbirth, also the women's *tamberan*. These are in 'pallid imitation of the men's secret ceremonial' (Mead 1970, p. 258). Nearly all the peoples in this area scarify girls in adolescence. These scarifications are done in rites which, in some cases, seem to correspond to the puberty or initiation rites for boys or young men. The Arapesh girl is scarified by her mother's brother on the back of the shoulder and on the buttocks on the third or fourth day of her first menstruation (ibid. p. 417). The Abelam girl is scarified on the belly at her first menstruation by her father's sister or mother as she is held by her mother's brother, and the scarification is followed by rites with ceremonial secret from men and accompanied by trans-vestite pantomime (Kaberry 1941, p. 361; Forge 1970a, p. 274). The Kwoma girl is scarified on the belly at some time before marriage. According to Whiting, she enters adolescence with the ceremony held at her menarche, and adolescence ends when she is scarified (1941, pp. 211, 9, 40), and Hayes reports that the girl is led to believe by men that they give her the power to conceive and bear children by scarification, though the women are by no means convinced of this (1973, p. 133).

Gnau girls are also scarified and men are excluded from this ceremony. They say that the pattern of scars deeply cut on one buttock, or rarely both buttocks, should be done before the menarche, although most of the girls who were done while I stayed in the village had passed their menarche. Senior women make the cuts with bamboo as the girls are held over a river boulder. Silt and *dambug*, the powder pushed up in termite colonies, is rubbed into the cut. Again there is a connection with the river,[10] but the women denied that the ceremony had to do with menstruation and always maintained that the scars were purely decorative. Both women and men (and one small boy who had seen it done) said that there was nothing more to the scar-cutting than beautification, no secret female ceremonies.

But detail runs away with us — I shall not go deeper now into the forest of Sepik ethnography. As almost each and every point is revealed in one particular society, then sought for in the other societies, we find resemblances and differences in precise timing, assembly of elements, reasons for the actions, links and setting. It would be possible to trace correspondences in many details (tongue- and gum-bleeding; scratching oneself; smoking, betel, coconut and meat taboos; methods of bleeding by incision; nettle-scraping, twig-twirling in the urethra; the occasions for penis-bleeding; the correspondences of the taboos for menstru-ation and childbirth; the relationships of initiator and initiated, bleeder and bled, scarifier and scarified; acts connected with the great toe; bamboo

10 The streams and rivers are the places where the women go to fish with nets on day excursions in little parties full of carefree chat and the sun flickering on the water. Men do not accompany them. Women also fish at night with bamboo flares and nets and often then go in parties unaccompanied by men.

phallocrypts; bleeding into water; bleeding and the creation of 'blood' or ritual friends or kin; spitting or anointing red). The exhaustive pursuit of all these details would be indeed exhausting. Some of the points could not be settled, as the writers have had different questions or themes in mind. Not all write with equal detail on each point (for example, Bateson is silent on what the Iatmul do or say about most of these issues). None matches the ethnographic detail of Margaret Mead's reports on the Mountain Arapesh.

But it is striking to find how many of the elements are there when looked for, even though the societies are scattered so widely in the vast area of the Sepik district. It is not as though we looked at neighbouring societies; the ones chosen are chosen only because anthropologists have happened to study them. They are a haphazard selection of a few from among two hundred (Laycock 1973) different language groups in the Sepik area. Comparison reveals how details of practice persistently recur yet in disparate fashion, suggesting perhaps a certain fickleness in rites as they are transmitted, no doubt with borrowing, over generations, subject to changes in the assembly of elements, consistent in general form but with some freedom of attachment to a meaning. What most surprises me in these comparisons is the recurrence of apparently minor or inconspicuous detail which one is less tempted to labour to explain (e.g. taboos on coconut, smoking, scratching oneself, actions towards the woman's great toe). The anthropologist who reads one meaning into an action when the people concerned do not see it in that way may be able to find that the meaning he had deduced is indeed explicitly recognised by some other people of a different culture in the area. If this should seem to confirm his interpretation, then the method which is putative and imputative veers towards suggesting that the meanings of the actions are intrinsic to the actions themselves, rather than being meanings which exist for the people concerned. Whether the people see the meaning or not becomes disconnected from the answer as to what *the* meaning *is*. Thus distinctions between cultures tend to dissolve: questions about why one culture should choose to emphasise or interpret an aspect not similarly seen by people of another culture will disappear with uniform interpretation.

It is clear from what I have said that the Gnau are troubled by ideas of danger from menstrual blood, and more generally from mature women in their courses. I will maintain (pp. 167, 180–2) that penis-bleeding carries heavy significance by virtue of its place as a special secret of men's rites, which they all share and keep from women. The context is required for an interpretation: penis-bleeding could be isolated from its more diffuse context, and by mistaking that context we could put emphasis on penis rather than bleeding, look for expression of something about the sexes or sex rather than something about the blood, or growth or ritual heat. The problem phrased more abstractly is to get classifier and modifier right: is Don Quixote a comic novel with tragic overtones, or a tragic novel with comic aspects (Gombrich 1963, p. 66)? By comparison we come to see that what is opposed is the sacred, part secret, life of men and

132

ordinary domestic life; that there is a balance to be protected between the dangers in women for the successful outcome of what men do in rites and the need to preserve women and their children from the assimilated hot danger intrinsic to the powers involved in ritual activities. The emphasis on risk in sexual contact is less than in some other Sepik societies; penis-bleeding is an act in part of responsibility for the well-being of the person as a whole and his growth, in part of responsibility for the well-being of his dependants and those he has contact with. Different emphases are found elsewhere in the Sepik. Wogeo men and women bleed; then they both must go into retirement, keep prohibitions for a time — both bleed to remove defilement by the other sex; the issued blood is polluting. Abelam men bleed before they take part in sacred activities because bleeding is intended to remove the defilement of sexual intercourse with women. Gnau men bleed after sacred activities to protect their women and children. The Wogeo and Abelam link the need to bleed with the dangers of genital sex. But Gnau bleeding is linked with manhood and participation in rites which men control, with attributes of the whole person, rather than with sex in the limited genital sense. I have selected some aspects of bleeding for discussion here, but there are others — indeed the main themes which dominate in their explanations: these I discuss in the next chapter.

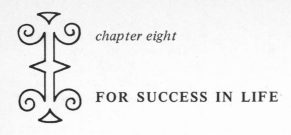

chapter eight

FOR SUCCESS IN LIFE

This may be a difficult chapter. It is a commentary on the detail of what the Gnau do in the rites of puberty. I am concerned with the responses and understanding of ordinary Gnau people and not solely those most expert or articulate about them. Their responses vary and the meanings that they find for what they do change with age and experience. Their style of ritual is not one that leads to conspicuously explicit or fixed interpretations.

One dominant theme informs the meaning given to the rites: the rites are done for the growth and successful development of the individual. Various clusters of associated ideas are set about this theme. In the first part of the chapter I shall explore some reasons for the variations in the people's responses and comments on the meaning of the rites. I seek to show how these responses depend both on their knowledge of things outside the situation of the ritual performance, and on attributes intrinsic to the conduct and patterning of the rites. I distinguish responses dependent on connection within the ritual performance itself from ones extrinsic to it. Certain motifs in the puberty rites recur in other rites. By recurring they point to connections between the rites. Responses to the motifs change with experience of them. The understanding of why they are done and of what they mean is revised, changed and expanded in the light of later knowledge and experience. Men and women do not necessarily attach the same meaning to a particular motif, nor do the young have the same experience as the old to draw on.

The dominant theme of growth and development is one that alters its character as the balance of attention is given more to achievement and success as main aspects of development of the individual in maturity. The stress on success in marriage, domestic life, having children replaces the emphasis on growth as such. For men the stress also differs because of values they attach to success in hunting and killing. The puberty rites have a future, causative mood.

In the organisation of my comments on the detail, I shall therefore begin with the theme of growth and those senses of development which apply to both sexes. I shall then move on to those senses which diverge to distinguish men from women, and come last to that side of the ritual life which is set apart for men and excludes women.

The Gnau understanding of life and development involves various clusters of associated ideas. For the process of human growth to maturity and then senescence, they have ideas of drying out and toughening, which also refer to or are drawn from the plant world. I shall concentrate on one motif to do with dried foods to show how the motif which appears in the puberty rites recurs in other rites, points to them, and is responded to differently by men and women. Other motifs are linked to it to reinforce the pattern. The idea of stage, progress in achievement and ordered sequence is very clear in prohibitions and rules to do with food. I shall examine these food taboos to show how food provides a distinctive medium conveying a wide range or spectrum of associations that they may draw on. But the way in which the rules are observed and transmitted leaves room for variation in understanding: it does not establish a system of meanings fixed and explicit. The links or associations that they use in interpretation may run in various directions: the qualities of the food may lead to a reason for the rule, or the rule may suggest a quality in the food. The notion of growth to a state of wholeness but inexperience is then connected with their view of progressive achievement in maturity, and with the values set on success in domestic life and public life. These differ for men and women: special duties and responsibilities are linked with the sphere of men's ritual life from which women are excluded. The secret of penis-bleeding is part of this sphere and is linked with the values set on hunting and killing as well as the notion of wholeness, experience that toughens but in the end wears out. Blood provides a focus for the imagery of identity and kinship and the conditions for well-being. Men share responsibility for the correct performance of the rites for the sake of the whole community and their juniors: a responsibility received from the ancestors and watched over by them. The rites derive part of their meaning from their understanding of spirit power and they are addressed to the ancestors as well as to their fellow men.

The dominant theme is growth and development. The chief ideas have to do with many subjects: wetness and drying out, freshness or newness, wholeness, progress and experience which toughens; identity and a stock diminished by use and transmission; the life cycle of generation, reproduction, domestic life, the control of public life, and responsibilities exercised by men, the values they set on hunting and killing, the bonding power of secrecy. These ideas are clustered round images associated with the plant world, animal foods and human blood. I shall discuss how the Gnau interweave the images connected with plants, food and blood as these appear in relation to the sequence that begins with growth, the first shared, but then progressively diverging, stresses that bear on men and women in the course of their lives and experience. My aim is to show what is condensed by the rite of puberty which every individual must undergo. Study of

135

what is done leads into these issues as soon as the attention is concentrated on the detail in an effort to interpret it. An understanding of the rite does not come solely from what is given within it, for much of the detail of what is done points to the future and outside the situation of its performance. I hope that my account will not misrepresent, through disproportion of stress, what I learnt from the Gnau.

Two senses to life

At the outset, as I think to go beyond some of their interpretations, I remember two experiences of amazement. They were cautionary experiences: on both occasions something that I had taken for granted, without a thought to question, stood suddenly revealed to me as wrong. The second of these experiences belongs to a later point in my account, but the first happened this way.

Six years after my first stay with the Gnau, I was standing in the house where we had lived before, and very high in the tree beside it the butcherbird[1] (*tawurgin*) began again to sing — loud, liquid, lovely, swooping notes. I happened to say to Sabuta who stood beside me:

'It's come back, the *tawurgin* is singing.'

Sabuta: 'Yes, it always comes to sing in that tree. It goes off when it sees a whiteskin, or someone with a shotgun. It is frightened of being shot. It goes down to the bush at Lɔgau. That bird is no fool, it knows, it has good sense . . . It always comes to that tree. Even long ago, the ancestors used to call it a good *tawurgin* because it announced the dawn and that was in the time before they had chickens.[2] They did not have cockerels to tell them then. That bird has been coming to sing there for generations, on and on and on.' He must have seen something from my face. 'Well, birds don't die, do they?'

I: 'What do you think?'

Sabuta: 'The same thing. Wild animals, that is. Same as birds . . . Well they would die if they had no food, or if someone shot them. Village pigs and dogs, yes, they grow old and die. Dogs go grey on the muzzle, when they get old. But wild animals, birds, don't. Nor snakes, they change their skins, they go on living . . . Butterflies die but that is because their wings get wrecked . . . I have seen dead lizards though, and they change their skins . . . Trees, palms, they're different, they grow, they dry up, wither, they die.'

Over the next few days, I asked many people individually what they thought. The answers of some were similar to Sabuta's. Others said animals and birds did die, except for the wild pigs and the cassowaries which went on living, although if men should all die, they would die with them too. Those who answered like

---

1 The butcherbird is *Cracticus cassicus*
2 Chickens were not known to their early ancestors, they say, but when they first came is unknown. The word for chicken (*tuwuti*) seems to me as good a Gnau word as any other, and there is a special term for the tail feather of a cockerel, *radut* (the feather is given to someone as a homicide ornament if he was fourth to shoot the man).

that, I think, drew on an association between wild pigs and men in contrast to domestic pigs. What may lie behind it is an established explanation about the spirit Taklei causing epidemic death, especially death to domestic pigs by anthrax, which die so that men and wild pigs may go free (see Lewis 1975, pp. 81–2, and 1977, p. 230). Still others said animals and birds died; of course they did, they had found them dead in the forest. My *tawurgin* was the son and grandson of the previous ones who had sung there before. Some answered the question straight out without hesitation and these unhesitating answers went both ways; others thought first before they answered and did not seem so sure of what they said. The view that trees, palms and plants have a life span, that they grow and toughen, dry out, wither, and in the end die, was held by all; it was a clear view which a number of those unsure about birds and animals mentioned in contrast to their uncertainty about the moving creatures.

I treasure the feeling of discovery I had then for three reasons. Firstly, I had presumed that something was as obvious to them as to me and I was wrong. Yet I had lived with them more than two years without finding out so great a difference in the answers we would give to that question. Secondly had you asked me before whether I thought a particular people might have no fixed or sure answer to the question, I would have supposed it most unlikely. 'Do birds and animals die?' does not seem a question that would be left unsettled in the general knowledge provided in some culture. Two years passed until chance revealed it to me. Thirdly, the contrast between plants and animals which some people stressed led me to make clearer a distinction I was half aware of. For human beings one aspect of being alive is consciousness, being able to move, purpose guiding action;[3] the other aspect of life lies in its contrast to death, a life as a passage of time, a span with a beginning and an end. Animals and birds can certainly move, act and choose to act; they have intentions and awareness. The Gnau are clear on this. Whether animals have a conscious understanding (*wuna'at*) like that of men and know things in the way that men know things is a question the Gnau answer more variously and after reflection, sometimes with subtle distinctions depending on different observations of the behaviour of wild and domestic animals; and they differentiate among the orders of the animal kingdom. But the capacity to move and to will to act attests to life. Men and beasts are alike in this respect but plants and trees are not. Man also has life in the other sense of a span with a beginning and an end, growth and decline. For this sense, the Gnau turn with more certainty to the plant world to find a parallel to human life rather than to the animal world.

Plants which grow and die in a season, and trees or palms fixed to the place where they were planted once by some known ancestor, stand witness to the

3 Questions of medical practice and ethics have been raised over defining death with respect to people who show no signs of cerebral activity but are kept alive by artificial respirators and tube feeding. Consider also the vulgar metaphor of 'vegetable' used to describe them or their state.

sequence of growth, decline and mortality more clearly than wild animals or birds. Gnau men and women see some wild creature, it moves, is gone, and who can tell the next time whether it is the same one or another like it? Some say these creatures all must die, some say not, others are not sure.

Growth and maturity

Gnau people turn to plants and trees to help them understand some aspects of human development, and the process of growth and decline through a life. The puberty rites are intended to make young people develop into well-grown adults: the Gnau state this clearly. When asked why they do them, the answer which dominates whatever more or else they may say about the rites is that they do them *kə lil lyitiyi, lyitiyi wuyil* 'so that they [boy or girl] may grow up, grow up well'. The word they use, *lyitiyi* (root *-tiyi-*), means 'get up' or 'stand up'. It refers to human growth or action, but it is not often used of plant growth, for which there are other verbs. People grow slowly to maturity, to a peak in which they are fully, though but newly, made. This peak is not reached until some time after puberty. The Gnau speak of the person as becoming whole, *nəmblin*, entire; but the word also carries the sense of new, inexperienced and untried (see Lewis 1975, pp. 138–9). This peak reached, the person then is tried, tested by experience, toughened, begins to be used up, and ages on a downward path towards senescence. Some of the imagery they use to understand this curve of growth which waxes and then wanes is vegetable.

The young plant is soft, sappy, full of water, growing. The mature plant toughens. Maturing involves a drying out which goes on with ageing so that old trees become dry ones. Toughening with age, they increase in resistance, but in the end the drying out must lead to death. The newly whole young man or woman is still untried, not tough. Toughness will come with experience. He or she must be careful in doing new things − that is a recurring theme of caution towards new experience.

The Gnau divide things people plant for food into *nəm taŋgim* 'tough things' and *nəm talyim* 'soft things'. Crops that must be replanted each year are *nəm talyim* and if the use of land is granted temporarily, these are the only things that should be planted there. Should the temporary user plant *nəm taŋgim*, tough things that once planted may live for many years and go on bearing, the man who let him use the land would have acknowledged cause for anger because such things 'pull' (*metə'aiy*) the land, pre-empt its use and may be pointed to in retrospect to give substance to a claim over the land. *Nəm taŋgim* is the stressed member of the pair, sometimes having the sense of things planted by forebears.

Things that are *talyim* are soft. The word *talyi* is used by itself to mean 'green coconut', the drinking one full of water but no meat; when the milk dries out into the meat and the water has reduced, it becomes a proper coconut, *wə'at*.

In fact the adjective *təlubi* means more precisely 'fresh', 'full of sap and water' in respect of plants generally, but *talyi*, which means 'soft' (as a baby's hair, for example, is soft), carries the association of wetness in the contrast between *nəm taŋgim* and *nəm talyim*.

The process of ripening in fruit is similar: unripe (*namum*) fruit is full of water (*wɔr subat* 'is watery'), but as the sun dries it out, it becomes ripe (*ləwu*). I was surprised by the frequent application of the Pidgin phrase *em i-no mau, i-gat wara iet* 'it isn't ripe, it is still watery' to some hard, slightly astringent fruit like unripe bananas, green pawpaws or unripe tubers. Equally I was surprised by how they explained to me in Pidgin the sense of the Gnau verb *naragəl*: *em i-drai pinis* 'he is dried out'. This verb is used to describe the state of maturity when someone is fully grown. Expanding on their explanation they would say *naragəl* means that he is fully grown, big, strong, his beard hair is growing properly and he has hair on his chest, his arms and legs feel hard and muscled, not soft (*talyi*). This stage is not reached until some time after puberty and the people they would point out as examples of those who had reached this stage were young married men. The verb is also used to describe a corresponding maturity in young women. The change in their breasts from jutting out to drooping down is remarked on instead of beard and chest hair.

In maturity, the process of being hardened by experience and ageing continues until a man reaches the stage which they distinguish by the phrase *nauwərun nəsupat*. The sense of the idiom is harder to grasp. The Pidgin translation they gave me was *em i-drai pinis, bikpela pinis, hap-lapun hap-yangpela* 'he is dried out; fully grown; half-old, half-young'. They pointed to men in their fifties as examples. The equivalent stage in a woman is referred to as *wəwag wɔr siwug* 'she hangs down like leaves' — it refers to her breasts flapping thin as leaves. The figure of speech used for men has two verbs: *nauwərun*, which on its own means 'to crush', 'crumple' or 'roll' (e.g. to roll a cigarette between the palms, to crush and crumple herbs used in ritual which releases their scent), and *nəsupat*, which on its own means[4] 'to get rid of' as applied to scraping off dirt, wiping off a smear, coughing up phlegm clear, squeezing hard, rubbing something into the ground. The idiomatic conjunction of these two verbs provides the intransitive phrase *nauwərun nəsupat*, which concerns us here (the male direct-pronoun marker at the end of the first verb refers to the man of whom it is spoken): the phrase has the sense of maturity toughened by experience — a stage of development. The phrase is also used transitively to refer to a man who likes disputes and fights, engages in them cleverly and wins, someone who is hard and effective, who crushes resistance, e.g. *nauwəru nəsupatagao* 'he keeps on getting into disputes with us and squashing us'.

Drying out and toughening permeate their general understanding of a number

---

4 I associate the verb chiefly with throwing a spinning top when they press the top between the palms very hard to throw it spinning fast away from them.

of processes of development and change. The action of the sun ripens plants, dries out mud; smoke and fire dry out meat, tobacco. The newborn child in its first days of life should be held over a fire, or in the sun, by the mother until it sweats; this is to toughen its skin. The newly constructed men's house must be seared by fire (see pp. 41, 68 above). Fresh meat is full of water (*wɔr subat*): it is classed among *nəm subagdəm* ('fresh things' or 'watery things') in contrast to smoke-dried meat which is *beirkatidəm* 'dried-out'. And this classification into *subagdəm* versus *beirkatidəm* is used as the guiding principle behind some of the rules about food during the puberty rites, during Tambin initiation, during the rites surrounding the first birth of a child and the infancy of a child. The things forbidden as *nəm beirkatidəm* 'dried-out things' are tobacco, betel nut, salt (either the traditional ash or real salt now introduced), coconut, smoked meat of any sort, tubers or vegetables of any kind if cooked by direct roasting in a fire. All these things tend to be forbidden *en bloc* as like things. In contrast, vegetables that are boiled in water without salt, meat that is fresh and boiled in water are *subagdəm* 'fresh' or 'watery' and permissible for the period when the *nəm beirkatidəm* are forbidden. In the puberty rites, the dried things are forbidden to boys and girls for a short time before the day on which the rites are done (it is usually for less than a week, but it may be for up to a month). If the girl has her first period, they must be imposed immediately; a boy is told to observe them in preparation for the day. Release from the restriction comes on the day by the act of eating *teltɑg–nawugəp* (leaves and ash salt) or, as it is also called, eating *subag–nawugəp* (water and ash salt) (see p. 82). As I have mentioned, girls stress this restrictive aspect of the rites and boys do not. Why should this be so?

This question rests on my impression of a differing stress in their comments, coupled with what I was able to observe. I think I recorded a difference impartially, but there are various elements of chance and uncertainty in whether I have got the observation right (who answered my questions, how they were put and so on), and perhaps legitimate doubt about whether the question really deserves the attention I propose to give it. I think the possible answer will exemplify a number of issues in the interpretation of other people's responses to rites and their symbols. I have chosen to put the question at an early point in this development of my comments on symbolism within the rites. I have asked the reader to accept initially a view of growth and decline as a process conceived partly by analogy with plants. The heterogeneous items of Gnau knowledge and idiom which I presented above to introduce the idea come from their common knowledge and language and are not specially relevant to the puberty rites. The items do not define by themselves the idea of the process or the analogy: they are a cluster of associated items. The people state no other aim or meaning for the rites and what they do in them more clearly or more often than the aim of achieving successful growth.

Commentary and interpretation

The main features of the process of growth are common knowledge in the culture. Their relevance to what is done in a rite to promote growth may be left implicit: there is no special reason to repeat what everyone knows. The anthropologist cannot assume that his readers share the same background understanding. Part, then, of his commentary must make the unfamiliar knowledge plain. He had to learn about it himself. He must spell out ideas or associations that are obvious or open to them to draw on. If the anthropologist and his readers share the assumptions of the people he describes, he will feel less need to spell out what is implicit or latent for discovery in the rites — for example, the Gnau idea that food is necessary and important for growth. So he runs a risk of upsetting the balance of his commentary by overstressing the unfamiliar when he translates implicit ideas or associations into discursive and explicit language. A commentary should not read ideas into the rites when they are not there. The structure of imagery may provide tacit evidence for them. The proportioning of emphasis in the commentary should bear a rough analogy to the proportioning of emphasis in the rites. This requires a sense of tact which may be disturbed by the need to push a point of interpretation when it is implicit but unfamiliar and the point is pushed too far.

When the Gnau say that they do the rites so that the boy or girl will grow up well, they set the dominant and general theme or frame for understanding them. The thematic mood or aspect is future, causative and conditional. Understanding the phrase must entail knowledge of what growth is and its process, the criteria of success, and the values involved in assessing human development and achievement. We shall see that these are not identical for men and women. The phrase is simple and clear: its general meaning shines right through the rites, but it is not easily confined. Knowledge of the growth of plants, the various kinds of food and their virtues and dangers; maturity, marrying, having children, success in hunting, size and strength, experience and ability — these provide a complex of ideas which all play a part in the eventual meaning that might be given at length to define and elaborate what growing up well implies to the Gnau. These meanings come from the common flow of thought about development and growth, and various streams of ideas contribute to that flow.

The Gnau do not have a style of ritual marked by didactic explanations of the symbolism of what they do. What is done without necessary explanation is open to comment or reflection chiefly in the light of what is common knowledge. Some special knowledge is restricted by sex, age or other criteria. Restriction relates primarily to the spells and secret names, to certain actions. Experience may throw a different light on what is done, particularly when a man learns more about the preparation and collection of herbs and materials to be used in the rites. Experience may also throw a different light on what is done because the older person has seen the event repeated on other occasions from different perspectives, or because he or she may have seen the same actions performed, or the same materials used, in rites for situations which are different (i.e. not for puberty). As the things are done without fixing by instruction what they mean, the individual who is provoked to think about them will draw on his general knowledge and experience to find associations which make sense of them. He is likely to do this guided by the dominant theme, which is so clearly set. That theme has many strands and potential implications. It is not obscure, but the abilities of individuals to see the relations of details to it vary: it is a matter of observation that the meaning Gnau people ascribe to some details of ritual actions differ. In this sense, if the ritual actions are symbolic, they are polysemous.

A degree of consensus about some items may be reached because everyone shares the relevant knowledge and experience. A degree of consensus might also be achieved because that meaning or interpretation can hardly be missed once one has seen the rites done. A meaning may be implicit in the straight-forward sense that people do not ordinarily state or comment on what they think it is: if seen, the meaning is left unspoken. But there is a second aspect to implicit meaning which is harder to identify. It has to do with the direction of association in symbolism.

Inward and outward association

A symbol may stand for something else in the sense of pointing outwards to external reality: it indicates it by description or imitation. It points to things outside the place, situation and the time of the performance. It documents something in the existing world or provides an impression of some external reality which is already known — for example, the common use of images of death and rebirth, or crossing thresholds, in *rites de passage*. The representation may be left implicit because the description or imitation is so clear. This, for example, is the case with the symbolism of death and rebirth in the Tambin rites of initiation among the Gnau: most people can, if asked appropriately, recognise and state a theme in them as a representation of death, or as a sequence of actions reminding them of what happens because of death. Frye speaks of this aspect of symbolism as centrifugal; the attention is directed outwards and keeps going outside the present actions or things seen, to what they may refer to, the associations or memories they evoke (1971, pp. 73–83). He contrasts it with an aspect of symbolism which is centripetal. The direction of attention is inward, towards the part which that element plays as a unit in the (ritual) structure. The element 'is not primarily a symbol "of" anything, for in this aspect it does not represent, but connects' (p. 73). The attention is inward because it is directed to the context in which the element is placed and to the aspect of its meaning which cannot be told apart from the context. Frye writes

142

about literary construction and criticism. Both centrifugal and centripetal aspects may be involved in the understanding of a piece of writing, but the weight of emphasis varies in different kinds of writing.

In descriptive or assertive writing the final direction is outward. Here the verbal structure is intended to represent things external to it, and it is valued in terms of the accuracy with which it does represent them. Correspondence between phenomenon and verbal sign is truth; lack of it falsehood . . . In all literary verbal structure, the final direction of meaning is inwards. In literature the standards of outward meaning are secondary, for literary works do not pretend to describe or assert, and hence are not true or false. Literary meaning may best be described, perhaps, as hypothetical, and a hypothetical or assumed relation to the external world is part of what is usually meant by the word 'imaginative'. In literature, questions of fact or truth are subordinated to the primary literary aim of producing a structure of words for its own sake, and the sign values of symbols are subordinated to their importance as a structure of interconnected motifs . . . The reason for producing the literary structure is apparently that the inward meaning, the self-contained verbal pattern is the field of the responses connected with pleasure, beauty and interest . . . The fact that interest is most easily aroused by such a pattern is familiar to every handler of words. (p. 74)

The creative, imaginative element in literary structures leads to their classification as fiction, fable, myth, with the secondary sense of untruth and lying. The controlling aim of descriptive accuracy is absent. What entertains is prior to what instructs. In assertive verbal structures the priority is reversed. 'The proportion between the sense of being pleasantly entertained and the sense of being instructed, or awakened to reality will vary in different forms of literature' (Frye 1971, p. 75). The question of truth and falsehood in relation to ritual may be similar. It may contain propositions or assertions which depend not on being descriptively true to the outside world but on conforming to a set of hypothetical postulates belonging to that ritual context. The understanding of these postulates depends on considering the creation itself which in this case is a rite, or the ritual system as a whole, but in the literary case might be a play, a poem or a work of fiction. In such a case, the meaning or the part of it which is intrinsic is discoverable only through attention to the work itself. Its recognition depends on accepting the hypothetical or special nature of the work which one seeks to understand or to which one responds, and looking within it. It depends on recognition of the convention which applies to the work; someone 'who quarrels with the postulates, who dislikes Hamlet because he does not believe that there are ghosts or that people speak in pentameters' (ibid. p. 76) radically mistakes the convention, the contract between the writer and his audience: he is someone who cannot distinguish fiction from fact. Rather similarly, in discussing the relation between ordinary propositions in everyday life and symbolic statement in ritual, Sperber proposes a general view of symbolism as statement 'within inverted commas' (Sperber 1974, pp. 120–2); and Bloch maintains, in a closely reasoned analysis of the formality of language and movement in ritual, that the ordinary propositional content of language is denied within ritual by its very formality. To the degree that the words and actions are rigidly imposed, they 'drift out of meaning' and lose their potential propositional force to gain instead a social and emotional force called illo-cutionary. The fixity imposes sequence rather than meaning to the units in ritual, for they must follow in order regardless of what they might mean in situations of ordinary life, or of how they might relate to experience in the real world outside the ritual context. They are isolated from the need to correspond by logic or truth with understanding of an everyday sort. Statement is frozen and detached from those possibilities of choosing what to say and how to say it which are essential to normal communication. The effect of this formalisation is to increase the ambiguity or uncertainty of what meaning to ascribe to that which is said or done in ritual, and there is a resulting gain in emotional and illocutionary force. The disconnection between religious statement and the real world is produced by the mode of communication of ritual (Bloch 1974).

I have tried to show that the Gnau do recognise the special nature of ritual action, that it does not necessarily stand in an ordinary relation to everyday reality, nor to the discovery and verification of facts about the outside world (see pp. 48–57 above, esp. p. 53). The commas are inverted around ritual state-ments in part by the alerting and arousing devices of formal ruling, fixity, noise, colour and scent: the framing devices. But I would remind you that these are variable and relative aspects which may be more or less stressed; just as direction towards inward meaning (centripetal) or towards descriptions of external phenomena or assertions about them (centrifugal) are not attributes which exclude each other: symbols as well as rites may provide leads of varying intensity in both directions.

By the contrast of inward (or intrinsic) meaning and outward (or externally directed) meaning, we distinguish one direction of association and understanding (that looks within a whole or unity to see patterns and interrelations between the elements of which it is made up) from the other direction which goes outside the present context to draw upon a wide knowledge of the world and other things. As Carlyle wrote, 'Of symbols, however, I remark further, that they have both an extrinsic and intrinsic value; oftenest the former only . . . Another matter it is, however, when your Symbol has intrinsic meaning, and is of itself *fit* that men should unite round it' (1831, book III, ch. 3).

Pattern and motif

One of the reasons for the difficulty anyone faces in trying to put the meaning of a rite (or a poem or a painting for that matter) into discursive language, or into other words, stems from the inward-pointing aspects of its meaning and the particularity of the media used; it underlies the heresy of paraphrase. The effect of the rite or some part of it comes from the choice of the particular elements and their specific arrangement in the context of that work, the interlocking arrangement and connections between elements within it. The meaning is context-dependent, dependent on the pattern set up and fixed within the rites. Torn or isolated from that context and without the surrounding relationships of the pattern, the element by itself may have no particular meaning or quite different ones. Pattern and relationship are basic to the structuralist method of approach to detecting intrinsic meaning.[5] The example of the bride's white dress and the gain in significance that may come from linking it and setting it in contrast to the widow's black one (Leach 1976, p. 58) makes the point about pattern within a set clearly. It also draws attention to the possibility that particular elements in one rite may change, gain or alter their significance when they come to be placed within a wider frame of ritual action, the wider unit that may be a whole ritual system, whose different parts are staged at long intervals of time from the point of view of the individual for whom they are done.

I hesitated about using the words 'meaning' and 'significance' in some of the above paragraphs. Pattern and relationships within a structure give rise to a 'field of responses connected with pleasure, beauty and interest'. The patterns or rhythm created by repetition, by contrasts of activity v. passivity, tension v. relaxation, pain v. pleasure, recurrences of like actions, like restrictions, noise v. silence, crowding v. isolation, outside v. inside, etc., have effects on the participants, which may lie (though not exclusively) in the field of emotional and aesthetic response. Such responses may arouse or submerge interest and attention and so affect the intellectual responses given to particular parts of what is done. Awareness of significance is coloured by the seriousness, excitement, agitation, boredom or exhaustion which someone experiences when he is caught up in the action. Intellectual meanings, which are implicit and may be relatively clear or relatively ambiguous, derive differential weighting from such responses. The eventual perception of their significances results from a complex of emotional, aesthetic and intellectual influences which may be hard to disarticulate and give grounds for in discursive language; it is hard to explain why

5 Some structuralist analyses seem (at least to me) to imply that *the* meaning found is intrinsically and objectively present. The myth or rite (or whatever it is that is taken for analysis) contains that meaning self-evidently, irrespective of whether or not anyone else has spoken of it before, or written it down, in the case, say, of the myth of Oedipus, or some parts of the Bible. The history of interpretation of the Bible must surely be the most eloquent testimony of all to man's unending ingenuity in finding meanings. But for the fact that it is no human construction, the same argument might allow one to assert that the lammergeier, wings outstretched against the sunset (p. 18 above), was in itself portending war, that the meaning was intrinsic to the bird and the scarlet cloud-rack. So have many men at different times and places seen the meanings of an omen, read the flight of birds or the pattern in stones, or bones thrown, thinking truth to be revealed by a pattern, a coded truth, a meaning waiting there implicit, silent. Denying that the designs are God's and assuming the construction to be human, the structuralist would seem then to imply that the meaning he alone perhaps has made explicit by statement of it, recovers some lost intention of men dead now to set that meaning there. Or else that all men or many men have known that meaning without being able to say

one knows from the experience that this part matters more or less than that part, or why this part is conspicuously linked to something else; because that knowledge comes from feeling and response as well as reason.'Le cœur a ses raisons que la raison ne connaît point.' The emotional and aesthetic colouring affects the intensity of significance.

Imagery within the rites of puberty draws on various clusters of associated ideas which contribute to the meaning of growing up well. Certain motifs in the imagery recur frequently and the repetition within a limited range gives a distinctive tone to the rite. Repetition of an item which points to an association, say, with plant growth also has a rhythmical or patterning effect. The motif may point outwards in the further sense of connecting the rites of puberty with other rites, not for puberty, in which the element recurs and which contribute to the overall meaning that element may come to have within the ritual system considered as a whole.

I started this digression with a question about the response the Gnau make to the rule forbidding *nəm beirkatidəm* 'dried things' in the puberty rites. I remember one answer which struck me at the time as one specifically conveying a sense of response to the pattern quality, or meaning inward, in the rites. I had asked Tuawei, a highly able married man, who was often perceptive in finding reasons for doing things, why coconuts should be forbidden. The answer he made was that they were forbidden because if we did not forbid them first, what could we give when we came to the time for decorating them? Restriction is imposed so that afterwards there can come release.

Food as a ritual medium

Food is in general a powerfully effective medium to use for giving the sense of sequence, succession and pattern in ritual, and also in everyday life (e.g. consider the convivial pattern imposed on the day in every society by mealtimes). All men work and hunger for food, it sustains life and growth: it is essential. Rules about its use may touch the person to whom they apply so as to bind him to awareness of an aspect of his identity: he carries the constraint with him all the time that the rule applies. And almost any day or at any place if the food is there and can be eaten, although not by him, it thereby asks him either to accept that identity and what goes with it; or to deny it, betray it and eat. An invisible constraint, a burden without material weight, is set on him and it goes with him wherever he goes, he cannot discard it (Fortes (1966b) has presented this argu-

in words what it was they knew. The view that a meaning may be independent of men being able to perceive it, or that there is an ideal right answer about that meaning, single and discoverable from the data themselves, seems to me bizarre and false. If the search for a single meaning were abandoned, and responses rather than meanings considered, then I think the power of some of these analyses may be saved to give insight into choice, aptness and the reasons why such constructions endure and are valued by the people to whom they belong.

ment clearly). What gives such rules their power is the knowledge that it might be eaten, that others may eat the food and do do so, but not me because I am who I am now. If no one thinks of eating it, because no one thinks of it as food, as almost no one English thinks of eating squirrels or bats, then no rules about it are needed. The question 'Why don't we eat squirrels or bats?' to us seems only a bit less stupid than the question 'Why don't we eat grass or string?' But to people who eat bats, such as the Gnau, the question 'All right, well why don't you eat bats in your country?' (a question which quite rightly I have had to answer when I pestered them in the same way) is a reasonable one. Restriction derives its force from its contraries, permission and possibility.

For the Gnau few foods are neutral, just food and always food to all persons. Nearly all have valencies which make their use right or wrong for certain kinds of person or for persons in particular relationships or for persons in particular situations. The valencies are created by many different pulls of association: that this kind of food is forbidden to nearly everyone except for those few in the village so old as to seem near death, whereas these others are free to nearly everyone always, except, say, to a man when first returned from the plantations, or this is the only kind of yam he cannot eat yet; that animal is always edible except if it comes from the land of his mother's brother; those birds are always edible except if his sons or younger brothers have shot them; no salt today because he covered up *yammami* yesterday; these are the only kinds of bananas he can eat now that he is sick; that bird only when he knew all hunting magic; this one not for young people to eat lest they leave their spouse, become adulterers; not this lizard because he knows the spell for that magic; this grub delicious but almost only eaten at a feast; that gourd so rarely found in the forest, never tasted; these fruits only eaten in the dry season; this taste quite unlike any other; that always eaten raw; this mostly eaten in the gardens; that should not be eaten after dark; this not to be eaten with cassowary flesh, etc., etc. The associations go inwards and outwards, the weighting of direction this way and that, sometimes to the rules themselves, or the person, the place, the relationships, the time, some conspicuous idea about it, the food itself, its commonness or rarity, its taste, quality, how obtained, how cooked, how served.

This makes their food considered as a whole range seem something like a colour spectrum or musical scale, from which particular colours or notes may be picked, placed in different patterns to evoke responses which depend on a welter of past and present associations as well as on patterns and relationships that are created by the choices made in the particular situation.

One theme running through a whole range of food rules is that of sequence. It occurs first in the rules which progressively make various classes of food free to the infant or child to eat after it passes some chosen and conspicuous stage of development (see Lewis 1975, p. 91); secondly in the restrictions imposed with maturity, which are to be lifted later on passing through a sequence of achievements; thirdly in the order in which some kinds of animals and birds

147

are supposed to open the paths of game and are therefore forbidden to men until they achieve certain hunting successes; fourthly in the inverse relation between two orders where as one set of things becomes forbidden through development or achievement, members of the other set gradually become free to be eaten. The rules depend on recognition of the kind of food and the development of the person. Two separate ordered sequences are linked together in the case of hunting achievement and the special order of animals and birds that open the game paths. In the case of child development, the sense of sequence perhaps passes by association from the human case, where it is clear and ineluctable, to the classes of food bound by convention to an order of change in the child.

The restrictions on *nəm beirkatidəm*

The things which are classed together as *nəm beirkatidəm* and forbidden before the day of the rites of puberty have something of the character of a motif in music. Restriction of the same things *en bloc* comes into force for a short period in the rites of puberty and for longer periods in both the Tambin rites of initiation and the rites surrounding the birth of a first child, and again, but for shorter periods, with subsequent children. There are restrictions on some of the included items in other situations, depending on who planted them, who carried them, etc., but these are not a restriction on a class of things *en bloc*. That is what isolates the *nəm beirkatidəm* as a motif repeated in these *rites de passage*, and a motif that points to a connection between them. In the puberty rites the restriction lasts usually for only a few days; in the case of a girl, it should be imposed on her immediately she lets someone know that she has menstruated for the first time. Ideally this is done in a curious way: a senior man in her hamlet or clan should be called to her, a breadfruit (*gənaŋgət*)[6] should be baked and then he should break it in half hot and, placing her great toe between the two halves, he should bend her sandwiched toe sharply downwards so as to make it crack. A boy is merely told to observe the taboo.

I was told no reason for the curious act with the breadfruit except that it was the proper custom. On the occasion of the first birth to a couple, *nəm beirkatidəm* are restricted from delivery of the child until the celebrations and the feast, when the pollution of birth which confined the mother and child to her house and kept the husband from holding his child or touching his wife or entering her house is washed away: this may not be for up to six weeks after

6 G*ənaŋgət*: this word refers to (1) the whole class of breadfruit trees; (2) the variety which is first among them; it has the broadest leaves, is first to ripen, and only the seeds (chestnut-like in size and taste and texture), not the pulp, are eaten; (3) specifically, the seeds within the fruit; (4) kidney. The other main kind of breadfruit tree is called *ginati*, a word which also means 'heart'. As the *gənaŋgət* trees bear for only a few months of the year (see Lewis 1975, p. 54), the inauguration of the restriction on a girl at menarche cannot always be done in this way.

the birth. The moment of delivery of the child is the moment when the cord is cut.[7] As soon as it is cut, the placental end is tied around the mother's great toe lest, so they say, it go back into her belly and the placenta not be expelled. Women give birth in a squatting position and I saw that the cord was indeed tied round the toe in those few cases in which I was asked to assist delivery. But when I called to their notice the link I saw provided by the great toe sandwiched at menarche between the *gənaŋgət* breadfruit halves and, at childbirth, with the umbilical cord tied round it — a link which to me made the act at menarche seem to point towards childbirth — they showed no spark of agreement. I was prepared to go further and see a resemblance between the seeds in the breadfruit and future children in the belly, but again they said they did not think of it like that.

The restriction on *nəm beirkatidəm* after childbirth is drawn out for weeks but at puberty it lasts only a few days. In the formal ending of these restrictions for childbirth, the act to release the couple to smoke and chew betel is done on the evening before the acts releasing other things, which come the next day, when *teltʌg—nawugəp* (leaves and ash salt) and then the *wa'agəp* stew are eaten (cf. pp. 82—5 for the puberty rites, where these are usually bunched together on the same day). On completion of the rites for the first birth, the marriage is established. The bridewealth, given but put away at marriage, is not distributed until the birth confirms it; then, together with the payment for this first birth, both are shared out (see Lewis 1975, p. 30).

The point of these remarks is to show that the pattern of what is done in the puberty rites in a short time is repeated at childbirth, but stretched out over a longer time. The motifs recur and connect the two. From the point of view of a girl, marriage and having children are what perhaps stand out before all other things as those in which she should hope for success and an ideal outcome. The rites to celebrate her first child's birth are longer and more magnificent than any other of the *rites de passage* she must undergo;[8] their timing is set by the birth which is conspicuously her achievement. The general theme in puberty rites is that the girl shall grow up well, and they are patterned formally so as to prefigure or rehearse in concentrated form what will recur in rites at a climax and testing point in her life's achievement, when she first bears a child. It is, I think, perhaps because the restrictions on *nəm beirkatidəm*, on smoking and chewing betel, provide a link to the chief rites which mark an achievement and success in her life that one finds that girls give a greater stress to them than do boys when they talk about what they have to do in the puberty rites.

From the point of view of a boy, however, the situation is different. His

7 The act is significant because if a mother did not wish to keep the child, she would not cut the cord. In cases of attempted infanticide that I was told about, another woman sometimes came forward to cut the cord to save the child, thereby taking responsibility for it and laying claim to it.

8 The marriage, in the sense of the time or moment when she comes first to live with her husband at his hamlet, is not publicly celebrated (see Lewis 1975, pp. 29—30).

attention in the puberty rites is deflected from the *nəm-beirkatidəm* restriction by other things that happen in them, especially the penis-bleeding and (if it is done) the first making of his man's headdress. Attention is partly a matter of balance and weighting. When, as a young married man, his wife bears their first child, then his attention gravitates towards the *nəm-beirkatidəm* restriction. In this setting these are the rules which weigh on him as actor more heavily, for there is a relative lack of other conspicuously fixed things he has to do during that time. Thus by association the restriction comes to be most eminently a thing attached to the rites for a new birth. By the age of puberty, both girls and boys know well these main aspects of ritual pattern in their culture and this seems to me part of the reason for the differential stress given by boys and girls to what they have to do in the puberty rites, despite the fact that both observe the same restrictions on *nəm beirkatidəm*.

I have chosen to examine this restriction in isolation because I hoped to make these points of interpretation clearer by so doing. In the rites themselves other linked motifs underscore and reinforce the parallel. With regard to the girl: the *wə'ati* (p. 82) is one of them. Her *wə'ati* is the water scented by the screwed-up herbs and leaves, reds and greens, placed in a container of *rukat*-palm flower-spathe, folded in the shape of a little boat with a yellow *dapati* paste-apple skewered at each end on a sprig of crimson cordyline leaves, the whole so decorative and pretty. Her clan relatives (the men) make it in the evening at the village when they return from collecting the herbs and leaves on the day before her rites of puberty. And she must rise early in the morning to wash with it, to wash at the end of her first menstruation, repeating it to purify herself. Just after this, she is given the *teltʌg–nawugəp* which ends the restriction on *nəm beirkatidəm*. In the rites to purify mother and child from the contaminating blood loss of birth, the same decorative little barque of scented herbs and waters recurs, made this time by her husband's father and clan relatives assisted by her father. But the pattern is stretched out. The *wə'ati* to purify the mother and child is prepared six or eight days before the celebration of the rites and during this time she must wash with it many times so that, purified, she comes to the day for eating the *teltʌg–nawugəp* and release from the restrictions on *nəm beirkatidəm*. Her *wə'ati* in the rites of puberty points forward to the rite for first birth, just as the *nəm beirkatidəm* do.

These aspects of pattern, the repetition of motifs, a limited range of chosen elements, placing and balance in relation to other elements, are used to evoke responses and connect them within the setting of rites in a way comparable, I think with some contrivances of art analysed by Gombrich and Frye (see pp. 28–32, 142–6 above). It may be hard to define our response to a work of art precisely and give reasons for the ideas and feelings that occur to us before it. We may find part answers but they seem more or less inadequate: exactness in identifying what it means and why commonly eludes us. Nor are the evoked associations fixed and the same for all who see it.

I have focussed on the differential response of boys and girls to this extent because I thought it showed the point and what may lie behind that sort of inarticulate response. I have purposely not said much about Gnau answers to direct questions about the meaning of the actions. These answers themselves show how open the motif is to differing interpretations. Answers vary with the individual asked and the way the question is framed. Many answers to a question about *nəm beirkatidəm* which did not refer to a particular rite were of the sort 'It is our custom'; if referred to puberty, then 'It is to make them grow well'; if referred to the first-birth rites, the most common reply giving a particular reason was that if the mother or father broke the rule, the baby would cry a lot in childhood and be annoying, and others said, 'We do it so the baby will be well and won't get sick or thin.'

But an approach by way of the Tambin rites led most men who were asked to put another line of interpretation more clearly. The Tambin rites of initiation are the grandest and perhaps most complex of all their rites. They entailed the long seclusion of young men in the men's house. The rites were inaugurated by formal acts and preparations a year or two before the complex phase of seclusion began. The young men to be initiated were then confined inside the men's house, I was told, for four to six months. During that time they were not allowed any of the *nəm beirkatidəm* and were forbidden to light fires and to sleep near them, but had to sleep cold with their heads resting on the special *wə'ati* of Tambin (see p. 156 below). In the day they were expected to wash frequently in cold water, to rub themselves with nettles dipped in cold water, and afterwards to rub their skins with the black paint (*gablit*) made of soot from burning the creeper *lambət gablit*. They were fed with fresh game from the frequent hunts by senior men to provide them with abundant meat. The meat was boiled, always and only *subagdəm*. Vegetables were always boiled but without salt. As the months went by, the bones of the meat were hung on a vine-rope around the men's house as a tally of the passing days and months. This continued until they performed a series of special acts which led up to releasing them from the *nəm-beirkatidəm* restrictions by eating *teltɑg–nawugəp* and the *wa'agəp* stew, and their emergence from confinement magnificently decorated, to a final dance and feasting. Again the same pattern and motifs as in the rites for puberty and for the first birth, but stretched out this time even longer and greatly complicated by many special acts set into the pattern.

Growth and the condition of blood

During the confinement they said that they were fed great quantities of meat to make them grow fast and big. It had to be *subagdəm*, boiled fresh meat. They rubbed their bodies with nettles which made their skin itch and pimples swell up on them, the skin felt hot, they could feel the skin growing fat and

151

filled-out. They had to avoid fires which would dry them out prematurely. They had to stay confined in the house lest, by going in the forest, their blood was drawn out from them by *lu-lambət*, the forest herbs, barks and vines used in hunting magic, lest the sun burn down upon the *lu-lambət* with the blood and dry up their own blood inside them (cf. the similar statement with regard to women's blood during menstrual confinement – p. 125 above). How many times, whenever on this subject, my ears have resounded to their boasts that their fathers and the men before them were twice as big as men are now because they kept these Tambin rites and did them often. The men I saw now were puny half-men compared to their fathers, who had stood tall as the main posts of the house, their thighs like tree trunks, great muscled calves on them, their chests broad as two shields set side by side, their backs like the door of a house.

Such good growth depends on the condition of the blood. The blood should move (*wəgatəm*, literally 'follow after') throughout the body. Stagnant blood is blood that dies (*wag*), goes tough (*taŋgi*), dries out (*wir beirkati*). As a man ages, his blood dries out and stills and dies and this is shown by his dry, wrinkled, darkening (*wɔr tamalyiwug* 'becomes soot-like') skin in old age. The bad condition of the blood in a sick man may similarly be shown by his thinness, his dirty, dark, unsweating skin. Signs like these (dryness, dirtiness) in the young indicate that they will not grow well. Such a boy ought to drink water often, he must sweat and keep washing, wash frequently to improve the condition of his blood; the boy who sweats a lot and keeps washing will grow well. Clean water on the skin helps to improve the condition of the blood. So the young men must wash regularly and often. Old people may excuse themselves from washing on the grounds that they are old; it does not matter for them, but for young people it is necessary so that the blood will stay (*wigət*). The blood in a person is a stock which can be depleted by loss from wounds, by blood-sucking creatures like leeches and mosquitoes. They hate them and say that a man attacked by mosquitoes in large numbers repeatedly would age prematurely, his skin would darken, go dry and wrinkled. And a child too would suffer in his growth if his parents were too harsh and struck him in anger too often, for they might bruise him, damaging his blood, making it bad (*wɔla*), making it die (*wag*). Above all they should not strike the child's head, a special point of growth.

On the other hand, the man who works and sweats and who washes often keeps his blood in good condition. His skin shines. If he sits still his blood is quiet (*wɔl bərin*) but when he hurries and works hard his blood will go fluid (*wir subat*, literally 'will be water') and will flow about in him (*wigatəmən*). Sweating is a good sign: dry, dirty skin a bad one. The father who sees his son with dirty skin will urge and order him to wash. Sweat (*məltagəp*) exuded in exertion by senior men may be rubbed on babies, boys or young men to help their growth,[9] just as they say blood from senior men rubbed on the body

9 I noted this especially at the time when men, having danced the heavy masked *tumbuan* figure of Malyi, came out from under it in a heavy sweat.

will aid it to grow well. In reverse, the sweat and dirt of a baby's body, or soiling by its urine or stools, is avoided by young men who dislike having to nurse young babies for fear of contamination by this sweat and body dirt and harm to their own growth. I have seen responses of extreme disgust and anger in young men inadvertently soiled by a baby. I have heard heated instruction called out that one small boy must not carry his younger brother like that because he would be contaminated by his brother's body dirt and his growth would be spoiled. The pattern of views about sweating and its effect on other people's growth follows the pattern for blood. Blood, like sweat, is like water. The penis blood used in rites is often spoken of euphemistically as the man's 'water' (*subat arən*). The sap of a tree is its 'water' (*subat*). The rubbing of blood on the boy's skin in puberty rites is spoken of (euphemistically) as 'washing' (*ləga*) him.

The composition of the *wə'ati* and the *wa'agəp*

Sap, sap flowing, freshness, watery things (*nəm subagdəm*), washing, blood, blood flowing, sweat, water, cleanliness, shining skin form a cluster of associations with the process of growth and filling out in contrast to drying out, toughening, maturing, ageing, withering, depletion, dying, *nəm beirkatidəm*, smoke, salt, ash, fire roasting, dirt. The associations with plant growth are liable to be more clearly apparent to men than women, and especially to older men. The reason is that they collect the herbs and plants necessary for preparing the *wə'ati* and *wa'agəp*. Some of the components are common knowledge but others put in the water are not. Everyone can identify by sight the yellow or orange *dapati* paste-apples, the crimson cordylines (*dauwalyi wɔda* or *dauwalyi wə'ati*); they can smell the scent of the crushed leaves of *nilapə* (a species of ginger), *dyu'əlbi* and *nʌlapə dəkərwai* (an aroid). These are used for decoration or for preparation in almost any rite or ceremony: they mark an occasion by their colour and scent. But what goes into the special pinkish water contained in the bamboo tube (see p. 74) which is used to mix with the *wə'ati* and the *wa'agəp* cannot be guessed. It must be learnt by taking part in the collection and preparation. Young married men are asked to help with this a few years after their own puberty when the rites for a 'brother' or 'sister' in their hamlet provide an appropriate occasion. Then they are directed about what to get. They must collect cortex from the trees *lu gaŋgun, gəbut* and *wuyi* for boys, because these trees have a lot of sap (*subat* — literally 'water'). The cortex is beaten and pounded and washed into the water. *Lu gaŋgun* is also said to be appropriate because its leaves sting as nettles do. For girls, the trees are *lu nəpəlit, dəglit* and *wuyi*, likewise full of sap to be pounded out. Of *lu nəpəlit*, they said that they used it so that milk would come into a girl's breasts when she had a child.[10]

10 I was not told that it had a milky sap, and there are a number of other trees and shrubs *not* used which do have conspicuously thick white sap.

Lu dəglit is the forest tree that also provides the platters of thick cortex used to smear the betel juice over the boy or girl after he or she has been spat on (see p. 77). They stress that the tree grows very thick and well. One Gnau phrasing they used to mean 'the tree grows well' was this, a metaphor with a curious bi-directional quality of association (which incidentally can be found in the views I reported about sweating and washing, as in a number of their other statements linking two phenomena): *li wɔgai maŋgəp wuyim* 'it [the tree] gets good calf muscles'. The sap of these trees is pounded out and put in the water to be used to promote growth, as they also use sweat and the blood of men. This is my comment, not a translation of their direct statement.

They must collect and prepare tiny scrapings of the following plants to put in the water. All these tiny scrapings come from growing points in the plants. From bananas they take scrapings from inside the tip of new off-shoots; from pandanus screw pines they take them from the sprouting points of new leaves; from the breadfruit from just under the rind of a new fruit. The kind of pandanus used for girls is *təlyigi wanəmbəti*, an inedible forest-growing kind that grows big; for boys *təlyigi lə'at lugi'in*, which means 'long-boned pandanus', because it grows so tall. The inclusion of *gənaŋgət*-breadfruit scrapings in the *wə'ati* is the reason for the rule forbidding someone to eat *gənaŋgət* for six months or a year after the puberty rite. It is the only rule of a short duration set like this. Banana plants are huge fast-growing herbs. They like to use the kind called *təpir*, an inedible wild plantain which provides a type image for conspicuously fast growth; the idiom to identify a really well-grown son, daughter, dog or pig is *nəŋganin təpir, niŋgi, bati* or *bəlu'ət təpir*. The most commonly used material for the *wə'ati* on which the boy sits (see p. 96) is a section of the off-shoot (*mɑmbla'at*) stem of *təpir*, bound round with dried *təlyigi*-pandanus leaves. But it may be made of an edible banana stem, one of the other kinds of banana from which they take scrapings to put in the water. These as a group are some-times called 'the bananas of the ancestors' (*təbawug beiya mami marigəl*); the varieties are *lyimɑŋgai, gelkitu, sutəwal, wagər* and sometimes *meiwasi*. The first four of these are strongly associated with taboos on eating them until late in life, and with the myth known as 'the Pig turned them mad' (*Bəlu'ət wambərəriyel*), in which a spirit, ambiguously Pig and/or Dog, chased a woman to Rauit on the night that Tambin was first ever sung there. The spirit was killed by the woman and her parents, using these bananas as though they were tusks, and the spirit's death turned some of the people singing to stone (their stone bodies lie in the village still) and made others crazed so that they ran about dispersing from the village. Thus ended the first settlement in the ancient past of the place now called Rauit. In answer to questions about the use of these bananas in the *wə'ati*, men said the bananas are really the Pig's tusks. I learnt in connection with this from some men that the wild plantains *təpir* and *gaowati* (which some say can also be used for the *wə'ati*) have grown from or grow from wild pig's (but not the Pig's) tusks. A younger man told me that *siwug sirbəg* also grew from wild pig's tusks: *siwug sirbəg* scrapings are included in the *wə'ati* water too. Other men did not confirm that this herb grew from tusks. It is one example of a different answer recorded because I asked individually about isolated items. The common view about *siwug sirbəg* (see p. 103) is that they grow very fast and this is the reason for their use in the *wə'ati* as well as their role in the *gabdʌg* when they are given with the *teltʌg gabargəp* (new shoots of the *saior* tree).

The above scrapings added to the *wə'ati* are conspicuously associated with fast or big growth and are all taken from growing points (cf. the head of the child which must not be hit — p. 152). It is rather as though essences of different growth-promoting factors were being collected to add to the water. The bananas also provide a clear association to a myth and village ancestors, and a point to observe, to which I will return, is that in the rite the children receive minute particles of a food or substance that is to be taboo to them for a long time thereafter.

I come last to the pieces of *wə'ati* which are put into the water. These are bits of the flower or leaf from special flowers that usually grow epiphytically on palms or trees: they are collected from the trunks of sago palms or in pandanus groves, although some come from other trees. A few, I thought, were orchids. The Gnau do not have names for these apart from *wə'ati* 'flower', *wa'agəp* 'flowers'. To learn to identify the right ones, you have to see them. Knowledge of the right *wə'ati* for different purposes is, I think, apparently most esoteric: to a greater extent than with the other items, it may depend on one man saying 'I know that this is the right one because I am sure it is the same as the one I was shown before by X'. The other older men then gather round to look and see if they agree about it. About the flowers I was told no more than that they help growth.

There would seem to be a contrast in Gnau interest in trees compared with flowers, the contrast between strong interest and near-indifference. I recorded without great effort over three hundred particular names for trees, palms and shrubs, but I was unable to record more than three particular names for kinds of flower: flowers were either *wə'ati* or *tapəlut* (the hibiscus flower, and also any big bell-shaped flower, for example, a blue convolvulus) or *tʌglabəg* (a pink succulent flower conspicuous on forest paths).[11] They had many more distinctive names for kinds of leaf than they had for kinds of flower. Yet the word which means 'flower' generically is the word they use for two kinds of thing of special power that they prepare in rites.

I can find no satisfactory equivalents in English to translate the meaning of the terms when used for these two kinds of thing. First, *wa'agəp* (the plural form) is used for cooked substances (they are usually like a thick soup or stew in consistency) which are prepared in rites and eaten. They must contain certain

11 The bunches of tiny flowers on *taun* trees (*Pometia pinnata*) and on some nut-bearing trees were called *təwug*.

components, depending on the purpose or rite for which they are made, and they have spells (*bəlyigap*) blown or whispered into them as an essential part of their preparation. They have power to produce effects which ordinary food cannot have. Secondly, *wə'ati* (the singular form) is used to refer to certain objects used in rites but not eaten, and made mainly from plant materials. They too have spells blown or whispered into them as an essential part of their preparation, and have the power to produce effects which are not ordinarily present in things. The boy's *wə'ati* made for puberty rites of the *təpir* stem wrapped in pandanus leaves is a typical example. The *wə'ati* of the Tambin rites is a long cigar-shaped bundle wrapped with pinkish inner bark stripped from a tree called *lu wuniti* (*Plamchonia timorensis?*), containing many leaves and other plant materials. It is made in a closely similar manner to the body 'image' of Panu'ət for the treatment of illness caused by that spirit (see Lewis 1975, pp. 176–80 and pls. 5, 6a and b, 9), except that it is much longer and without a painted face and shell decorations. Something of the power of the spirit is concentrated or localised in the *wə'ati*. The big *wə'ati* of Tambin represents a temporary embodiment for the power of the spirit. The *wə'ati* for the puberty rites is a lesser parallel in form and size, which is not thought, so far as I know, to concentrate a particular spirit, though it concentrates power. I have tried to use *wə'ati* for the object and *wa'agəp* for the 'soup' to avoid confusion in reference. But a *wə'ati* of the sort made for Panu'ət or Tambin may be broken up and its components strewn about: then it would be referred to as *wa'agəp*. In a simpler version of treatment for Panu'ət illness (Lewis 1975, p. 180) the materials for its body 'image' may be collected and crumpled amorphously in a *rukat* container (i.e. not made into an object); then the materials may be called not Panu'ət but *panuŋgəp* (the spirit's name in plural form) and used with the same aim of healing. The *wə'ati* for the girl in the puberty rites, the decorative *rukat* filled with herbs and water, is what corresponds to the boy's *wə'ati* of the *təpir* stem as an object of special power and importance in the rites, but the Gnau refer to it as often by the word *wa'agəp* as by the word *wə'ati*.

Wə'ati and *wa'agəp* are things made by men containing power that may come from spirits. They represent manipulable and material forms of power or a spirit, concentrating or localising it. Spells (*bəlyigap*) are needed in their making. The Gnau also distinguish *gəplagəp*[12] which are scraped or pounded substances similarly made for the most part from plants, but they are used dry and not cooked, and they may be chewed, eaten or blown into the nose, or put into skin incisions or rubbed in the hair. The three — *bəlyigap* 'spells', *wa'agəp* 'cooked or wet substances', *gəplagəp* 'dry, scraped substances' — identify special man-made productions that harness, activate, concentrate or release mystical power (see also Lewis 1975, pp. 181–4).

12 *Gəplagi* is the singular of this word and the name of a tree with distinctive long oblanceolate leaves flashing silvery on one side.

I cannot explain the paradox that the generic term for flowers,[13] in which the people seem so little interested, is used for these special substances and for some material objects that localise power or a spirit. Unnamed but particular flowers are essential in the making of some of them.

When they give the *wa'agəp* to the girl or boy to eat in the rites for puberty, they take a little pinch of the cooked mixture, blow or whisper the spell into it, sometimes with a gesture stretching their arm right up as high as they can, stretched suddenly up onto tiptoe in a movement that begins with the arm bent, the hand upraised to lips blowing in the morsel, then an abrupt extension of the arm, as though it were blown upwards. This may be repeated three or four times. They say the movement is an expression of what they hope for; that the boy will grow up tall as the coconut-palm crowns rustling above him. The morsel is waved in a circle round above the head of the boy or girl (*lə'aiyəyəndən*). This gesture, establishing whom the thing or the effect is for, is done in various situations: for example, the mother should similarly wave her knife or axe over her son before she strikes the piece of firewood in front of him (see p. 94); it is also done for example, with the money paid for a puppy when the puppy is handed over to the buyer. The morsel of *wa'agəp* is then usually put into the boy's or girl's mouth in the special manner I described (pp. 79–80), back towards him or her, right-handed over the shoulder (*yig tapi'it* 'coming from the back'). The gesture is explicitly in imitation of the mother's method of pulling up a sitting or sleepy child by the wrist onto her back so that she can carry it on her back. They say the gesture in the rites expresses the hope that the boy or girl will get up, rise up, i.e. grow up. On many, many evenings I have seen a mother pull her drowsy child up onto her back, saying, *Tiyi! Tiyi! dəg təwupyi* 'Get up! Get up! I'll carry you', but they had to point the symbolism out to me before I saw it.

In the *wə'ati* and *wa'agəp*, as in the rules about *nəm beirkatidəm*, there is a symbolism of growth based on links to plant growth. The rules for both boys and girls about these things are almost the same. *Nəm beirkatidəm*, the *wə'ati* and *wa'agəp* are motifs open to various interpretations. Knowing now the linked associations with tender growth and young life and new life, and their contraries, the reader may find it appropriate, as I did, to learn both that a sick man will refuse to consume *nəm beirkatidəm* and that, in the past, a man who had killed someone was forbidden to eat anything except *nəm beirkatidəm* for the few days of seclusion in the rites called Lyigʌt, which followed immediately upon a killing. To have killed someone was a major achievement for a man; it demonstrated toughness and ability, and in most cases it was a desired and admired act.

---

13 *Wa'agəp* also means the coarse chippings of sago pith before they have been pounded or the starch in them leached out. I asked the Gnau whether they associated the *wa'agəp* of ritual with the sago chippings but they said, no, it was flowers they thought of in connection with it.

In discussing the restrictions on *nəm beirkatidəm*, I have not brought out so far with due emphasis the fact that the *wa'agəp*, though cooked with the *wə'ati* water, contains as its main substance shredded coconut and dried meat; it is essentially a food made of *nəm beirkatidəm*. In keeping with the symbolism, it is an act of giving materials linked with the maturing, toughened achievement side of a successful life. Both growth and achievement are required for a successful life and both are represented in the short rites of puberty. Acts of eating *nawugəp* (the hunting ash), smoking and chewing betel occur in the rites. I was told that the boys and younger men in pre-contact times were forbidden generally either to smoke or to chew betel with lime until they had proved their hunting ability and undergone the culminating hunting rite after which wild-pig flesh became taboo for them; nor were women allowed to smoke or chew betel with lime until their reproductive life was achieved and they had grandchildren (see p. 3 and Lewis 1975, pp. 93–4). Gnau people say that smoking is not good for growth, the smoke harms the vital centre (*wuna'at*) by its heat, yet young people smoke now and chew betel with lime, which their parents were forbidden to do. In those times, the ritual acts provided a foretaste of things to come with achievement and maturity and pointed towards them.

Achievement

When I first attempted in the field to find out what the phrases for stages of maturity meant (*naragəl, nauwərun nəsupat*, etc. – p. 139), I got three types of reply. One type, the one I have already reported, was a description of what the person looked like, or examples of individuals who exemplified the phase: this was a type of answer perhaps more an artefact of the situation of explaining something to me, a stranger, than the other kinds that they would give spontaneously to each other. Many men would far more naturally explain *naragəl* as meaning a man who refused pig and cassowary flesh (*minagao bəlu'ət tambini*), *nauwərun nəsupat* as meaning one who eats wallaby, eagle, hornbill. If the phrases were ones referring to women, or the question was referred to women, the answers instead would be of the type, 'She has given birth, she has had two or three children' or 'She has had children, her children are married and she has got grandchildren.' With reference to men answers combining the two were also common, e.g. 'He is married, has children, does not eat pig' or 'He has killed pigs and cassowaries, lots and lots of them, his sons have children.' There are three types of answer: one referring to the bodily state, another to hunting achievement and another to reproductive or family achievement. In effect the kind of food, the stage of development, the necessary achievement are so bound up as a cluster of associations that the directional quality of cause, a state and a consequence does not seem clearly set one way. Men fall much more readily into a way of phrasing the whole system of food taboos as a system set in terms of hunting success and the achievement of many kills. But the same man asked to state the conditions of the system as they apply to women (and in most cases with reference to the same foods) will refer them to marriage, reproduction and family development. And he may well present the conditions in the same way for men on another occasion if the context of the discussion has set him thinking on family lines. What is clear is that there is a sequence in these food restrictions and a sequence in human development, and that the two are linked. Both are formal patterns and they are put in parallel. The cause-and-consequence direction of what links them is not consistently set but may often go either way: the interpretation is open to opinion or reflection. The meaning given to development begins with a common feature, growth, with the sense of increase in size and strength, health and beauty; as the stress later comes to weigh down on achievement, men differ from women, and hunting and killing come more to the fore as criteria of male achievement, while reproduction and family development emerge as those of female achievement. Given the future, conditional, causative aspect that permeates the rites of puberty, people will often interpret any action in them in a future light, laying stress then on the achievements most valued. This makes their comments on the significance for boys or girls diverge and differ. Thus answers about the significance of almost any of the actions I have discussed so far (e.g. the *nəm beirkatidəm*, the *wə'ati*, etc.) may in respect of a boy point out their importance for his future success as hunter or killer, and not their relevance to growth and size. I received in fact many interpretations of the elements I have discussed already that related them to hunting success and gave that as the reason for doing them. This divergent future stress is what lies behind the different attention given by girls and boys to the restrictions on *nəm beirkatidəm* together with the pattern and connection aspects I have discussed.

The system of food rules related to development

I found in fieldwork that as, from desire to decipher a code, I kept searching for a clearer system to the food taboos of the Gnau, I looked to each restriction for an answer that would fix the rule satisfactorily and make it apt by some association; but the people frustrated those attempts. It seemed appropriate to me that men who had hunted well should in the end be able to eat the eagles and the kite and hawks that also hunt and kill the high-tree-living marsupials. This was a reason most people would give to explain why the taboo prevented younger men from eating them, for they were not yet sure of their success. But then I would find that women, too, could not eat these birds. Could they never eat them? But, yes! they could, when they had grandchildren growing well. The system of restrictions as a whole is shot through with exactly that kind of aptness from one vantage point but not another; it gives a tantalising sense that one has almost got it, and then what seemed to fit slides slightly out of grasp.

Just as with the eagle, I could obtain a series of rules in which the phrasing about them was largely in terms of success in hunting, and the restrictions were presented as though they applied to men only. It took specific questions about women, or it required asking a woman whether she would herself eat this or that, to find that most of them applied to the women too. The temptation is to make the rules as a whole sound more precisely fixed and apt than they seem to be in practice.

People would give lists of the animals or birds classified together for restriction as though they were like a family of the senior brother and his younger brothers. The senior brother was the most eminent example with strongly marked characteristics, the eagle, for example, or the cockatoo, the biggest lizard, the most conspicuous bird of paradise, but among the less important followers there was sometimes less certainty about whether some particular creature belonged there or not, or which qualifying characteristic should determine its alignment. Should the black palm cockatoo (*Probosciger aterrimus*) be put with the parrots because it is like them, or with the hornbill because its head and wings can be used as a back ornament? Where should the lines be drawn? Do predatory birds (the birds that kill) include the owls, or should the owls be kept separate because they are night birds that shriek or whoop? Do the frogmouths go with the owls because they are predatory night-birds or are the frogmouths separate from the owls because they look so different or because they call when a dead spirit passes? Should they be put with the birds that sing at deaths? Are all the spiny-backed lizards taboo because they wear 'hornbills' on their backs like senior men or because they have sharp barbs like killing arrows? The system has some clear points of association with ideas which most people mention. It has some striking animal foods with distinctive characteristics. It is relatively exact on the timing of the rules fixed to youth and extreme age, but liable to uncertain statement of the timing in the middle. It is clear about the most distinctive kinds of animal or bird, but more flexible on which other kinds also go with that distinctive member. In the middle ground and for the smaller fry, I think that the system in practice allows for variation in its details. And I should point out that my attempts to go through the whole spectrum of possible food with a few individuals took me through lists of mammals, birds, lizards, frogs, snakes, fish, crocodile, turtles, crickets, grasshoppers, mantids, grubs, beetles, butterflies, termites, yams, taros, bananas, nuts, squashes, etc., without finding any category for which there was not some rule or many rules connected with development. No two people gave identical rules and links. Additional little points of rule or association went on revealing themselves the longer I spent among the Gnau: the more I learned the less convinced I became of a system fixed and precise in detail.

I would give some additional reasons to the ones above for this variability in the middle ground and for the smaller fry. In youth a boy or girl is warned by his or her parents, instructed and corrected about what should or should not be eaten. Growing up, they become more independent. Parents are still their most appropriate mentors; and senior people generally should have a care that the younger people know what is good or bad for them. In the general view, these are the people who should tell them when they can start to eat something hitherto forbidden. But in practice, exactly whose job is it to tell that particular middle-aged, quite senior, man or woman that he or she can now eat this or that? They are active energetic members of the community. Their parents are dead. It depends rather on some senior person's force of character, sense of duty or zest for telling other people what to do whether he actually does so or not. One man would tell me that he was waiting for his older brother to tell him when. Another would say, I am waiting for my other daughter to have a baby that survives, then I will eat that food. I remember a number of occasions on which I have heard an older man during casual conversation suggest to some other less senior one that he should eat x or y food, that he seemed ready and old enough to try it; and the other then reply, 'No I won't try it yet, not yet, I want to wait a little longer.' A man is considered largely responsible to himself for observing these rules with care — it is his own success and health that are in question. Indeed people are not at all accurate or certain about the details of exactly what things the older individuals in the village will or will not eat. This is easy to find out by questioning people about each other and then checking. It is also crops up for observation quite often at food distributions or feasts when someone is given something he does not eat. With these points in mind, it becomes more understandable that the system of food taboos leaves room for variation in the details of observance, lapse, change or mistake intervening in transmission of the rules, and understanding of them and their timing.

A man is particularly responsible for his own and his immediate family's welfare. He is likely to pay attention to the care with which his wife and children observe the rules as he understands them. Similarly his wife is likely to know what foods he is permitted to eat or not. People tend to say that senior people of the husband's family at his hamlet, or her own parents if they are not dead, will tell her what she may not eat. But in practice the women told me more often, when I questioned them about something specific, that it was their own husbands who had in fact told them when. For example, Kalimao happened to say that she did eat the beetle grub that grows in sago palms (*nalgəp lawusəm*). I asked her who told her she could eat them. She said Matasi, her husband. Later I asked Matasi whether he ate *nalgəp lawusəm*. He said he did, that his father had told him he could soon after he had been through the culminating hunting rite by which pig meat became taboo to him. After that, he told Kalimao it was all right for her to eat them too. When I had asked Kalimao about why she could eat them, she had said, Because I have got two children now (she had given birth to two living children; she had had three others who had died in early infancy or just after birth). For Matasi the timing had been set by his hunting rite. The point of these remarks, and the example, is that I think they may provide insight into why so many of the taboos which seem primarily associated with hunting turn out to be ones that women observe too. The mode of transmission of the rules contains room for change of detail: over a long time, details may well be elaborated, changed or confused, and also particular items, once set as rules for men, may tend to come to apply to women too.

In the picture of the system given above, I have drawn attention to the blurring and shadows over detail. Its main outlines are, however, clear, and the distinctive creatures stand out with their characteristics. I shall now indicate the outlines without attempting to fix the detail. The whole system covers life from birth to death. From birth to about four years old is a phase that begins with everything forbidden except a mother's milk and ends with almost everything released (see Lewis 1975, p. 91), except for the creatures most associated with death or with killing. A phase of relative freedom follows which lasts until the approach of puberty, when the growing child should begin to observe the broad block of restrictions that must be in force by the time of the rites of puberty. They last from then on through the years of youth and inexperience. They are imposed more strictly and from an earlier age on first children than later ones, and on boys than on girls (see p. 95). The only food taboos that seem to be attached at the heart of the rites of puberty themselves are the one on *gənaŋgət* that I have mentioned (p. 154) and the *nəm beirkatidəm* ones. Some people also put the taboo on sago grubs (*nalgəp lawusəm*) as a taboo set in timing by the rites, and lasting until the phase of full maturity (*naragəl*). Though no one put the two together for me by stating a connection, I would note a possible reason for the aptness of this rule. A newborn baby in its first weeks of life should be rubbed with water in which *nalgəp lawusəm* have been cooked. It is a little rite done by the mother so that the child may lose any of the lanugo hair it may have been born with, and grow up with an admirably unhairy skin (*kə nyir pugarin* 'that he will be unhairy'). The grubs are long, fat, hairless things. The grubs are linked with the idea of hairlessness. A sign in men of being *naragəl*, which they remark on, is having a mature growth of beard and hair on the chest. Between puberty and reaching the phase of maturity, the grubs may not be eaten — the hair must grow.

The long middle phase of life contains the major experiences that test, try and toughen the whole man or woman, the whole person (*nəmblin*). It is the phase of marriage and reproduction, the serious work and competition of life, gardening and hunting. At marriage the most lovely of their birds of paradise (*gamulti*), the lesser one (*Paradisea minor*),[14] also the most common in their

14 This species is uniquely classified in Gnau bird taxonomy. All other bird pairs have one name applying both to the male ('husband') and female ('wife'), however sexually dimorphic the species. The lesser bird of paradise (*Paradisea minor*) is named *gamulti* and *durapəgan*. *Gamulti* is the adult male bird with the golden plumes. *Durapəgan* is the dowdier female and the immature male. According to an important myth, *Gamultɐg* (the Birds of Paradise), two sisters became these birds of paradise. There are many

land, is forbidden, as is the line of other birds that go with it (which include, as it happens, the other ones they know that we too class as birds of paradise, though they are so various in size and plumage). This is because they say the lovely birds (*gamulti*) are fickle, they were once women, they scream and squawk 'like women' laughing *latəkaki*, the high shriek of laughter, they flirt and dance their plumes in the treetops, they flit about from here to there, pursued by many consorts (the dowdy *durapəgan*). Therefore avoid eating the birds so as to keep, or keep to, your spouse, and preserve a faithful, steady marriage. This is a clear association. Some of the restrictions associated with reproduction have a clarity of perceived link established by timing because they come into force, not for all this phase, but only when pregnancy is declared; then they apply to the couple concerned until the young child has securely established its hold on life. The rules concern various creatures (some mammals, birds, reptiles) that live in holes (stated association: lest the baby may not come out); some high-tree-living marsupials (rarely stated: a link through height with treetops and a watching spirit of someone dead that happened to have the same name as the child has taken; risk of harm from that spirit); bird eggs; baby cassowary; any conspicuously big vegetable (association: so big, therefore a spirit may be interested in it or stay in it; risk of harm to the baby); the goura pigeon (association: its trembling crest, the baby shivering or having fits); big fruits such as large specimens of banana or pawpaw (association: the roots going deep in the earth, earth covering the child over); the single fish that was permissible no longer so, all fish forbidden (association: the fish 'breathing', gasping, open-mouthed; the sick baby gasping).

Gardening season and timing all point to a reason behind the rules forbidding those birds such as the bee-eater, the roller and some swifts (birds which in fact migrate) whose reappearance each year signals the time to begin covering over the *yammami*: do not eat them until your ability to garden successfully is sure (see Lewis 1975, pp. 54–5).

It is not until the end of life approaches that men or women see themselves as fit to eat those birds associated with the dead or death: those that shriek or whoop or drum at night (frogmouths and some owls); that call out loudly and sing for a death (birds that sing loud in the dawn chorus; the butcherbird and the coucal are among these — they are also linked with evil witch-like spirits in some myths as birds that warn of dawn coming); the black flycatcher (*Monarcha alecto*) that comes to sit on the death platform; the fairy wren-warbler (*Todopsis cyanocephala*) that whistles warning messages from the dead — these are forbidden until near the end. Some associate killing, talons, arrows, barbs

variations on this myth in the area. They say that *gamultag* (birds of paradise) were women, that *gamulti* is the 'wife' and *durapəgan* the 'husband'. But they also know from observation that *durapəgan* lays the eggs and that some *durapəgan* turn into (*watip*) *gamulti*. In all other bird pairs, they know the 'wife' lays the eggs. Individual Gnau men have pointed out this paradox to me and shown a twinge of doubt about the truth of what the myth tells and its assertion that *gamulti* were women and are the 'wives'.

and death with the rules that keep the chief birds of prey and spiny lizards forbidden until late in life. Some associate those kinds of frog that live round natural pools with spirits of the pools because the frogs jump into the pool to warn the spirit; therefore those kinds of frog must not be risked until late in life.

In the middle phase of life, progressive experience and sequence are the main themes — leaving rather blank, open or casual the association that people may choose to find in explanation of some rule; or they find none. The order in which some kinds of bananas are made free to eat is fixed and clear: *bəlai*, *bəladən, meiwasi, lyimaŋgai, wagər, gelkitu*, and last, *sutəwal* (and there are many other kinds less salient). They state the general association I mentioned with a myth (see p. 154) but not reasons in detail for that particular order.

The call of the goura pigeon (*wunimban*) sings out for game to come, as a log *garamut* beats out for men to come. The paths (*maniwug*) which the game follow are said to be cleared by a set of ground-walking animals and birds that go in sequence to make the path, the little ones first, followed by the larger ones up to the pig and cassowary. The notion of a sequence in making the path is parallel to the notion of progress in hunting achievement, and order along a path is associated with the rules about eating the animals.[15]

There are also the things associated with the hunting of tree-living marsupials, the restrictions about the kinds themselves and the birds that prey on them too, the smaller eagle 'that cooks hunting ash'. Within this hunting field there are a few rules observed by men and not by women. Above all, the rule that after the culminating hunting rite wild pig and cassowary flesh must not be eaten by the man, never again unless the man is willing to acknowledge that he will never hunt again. The goura pigeon, the maculate forms of the maculated phalangers (the spotted cuscus, *Phalanger maculatus* and the rare *Ph. atrimaculatus* which occurs in Gnau land) are forbidden to men, though not to women, while the whole-coloured forms of *Ph. maculatus* are free to be eaten. They told me no special reason for distinguishing between the whole-coloured and maculate forms.[16] I can imagine that it is apt to permit immaculate forms to the man who is *nəmblin* (newly whole) and to release the maculate forms only after he has become tarnished by experience; but no one I spoke to made that connection.

Marriage, reproduction, death, gardening, hunting, killing are then the main themes which appear in the associations of food taboos linked with the develop-

15 The parallel is internally contradictory: the first to walk the path is the first released from restriction; the last along the path becomes taboo at the end, having been before permissible.

16 The Gnau taxonomy of phalangers classifies the adult forms by different names, each according to fur colour and pattern, and provides different names again for the young. The classification of tree marsupials generally differs in pattern from the one they use for most other mammals. It is complex when connected with their understanding of the mating and family relationships among them.

ment of people. Compared to the rules about vegetable things, which had to do with the process of growth, rules concerning food from the animal world seem in general to be more often to do with achievements, with doing things in an active way.

The Gnau views on plant and animal life, with which I began this chapter, had about them something of a contrast between passive and active — what plants showed was life as a span, a passive, unchosen process of time, but life was in animals rather as the quality of moving, being active, purposive, aware. I think it is consistent with this understanding of two senses in the meaning of life that the animal foods more often point to active achievement as the reason for the rules, while vegetable foods point rather to the process of growth. Both belong in the full understanding of human development in life.

Differences of stress

The themes I have discussed apply to both sexes, and I have tried to bring out how a stress for one or other sex may come to differ. The motif of restriction on *nəm beirkatidəm* comes first as a rule for the individual alone to observe at his or her own puberty; at the first birth to a couple the rule is binding on husband and wife together. They must observe it jointly even though they are not allowed to touch each other or share the same house; it isolates them as a couple, requiring them to control their appetites for the well-being of the child that now links them. At puberty, I must not for my own sake; at childbirth, both I and my wife (husband) must not, and that self-control is demanded of us both for the sake of *our* child. Nowadays perhaps the habit of betel and tobacco gives the sharper edge of privation to that joint experience. Though this identifies the demanding force of the rule, I should note first that two or more young people may go through the puberty rites at the same time and so become *wusai* to each other; second, that at a first childbirth, the *wusai* should[17] likewise observe the *nəm-beirkatidəm* restrictions in sympathy with his or her *wusai* because they acknowledge the bond between them. What they say is that 'they think of their *wusai* and are sorry for him (her)': they do not say they do it for the sake of the child. Likewise close brothers or sisters may also observe the restrictions in sympathy with their sibling now become parent. Their observance expresses a fellow feeling and acknowledges a bond.

Marriage followed soon after puberty in the old days, and in recollection of that past people said that the Tambin rites came in a man's life usually when he had already become a father. Then in the seclusion in the rites, the restrictions on *nəm beirkatidəm* were necessarily an experience closely shared by a set of co-initiate men. Around the *gamaiyit* (men's house), an encircling fence (*waŋgi*) was set up with only one small hole through which to crawl in and out, closed

17 There is a difference of force in the rule: the difference between 'must not' and 'should not'.

by a mat of plaited palm leaves. The young men were confined inside together, shielded from eyes outside, and within obliged not to speak aloud.[18] That experience of restriction in the company and sight only of other men must have given a further, deeper, more mysterious feeling to the rules about *nəm beirkatidəm*, which only men could sense who had 'slept in the song spirit' (*latə bəlyi'it*). Men ordinarily sleep in the men's house (*lat gamaiyit*); but *latə bəlyi'it* is quite different, for that phrase (literally 'they sleep or stay in the song spirit') means to go into seclusion and keep apart from women when the great rites of a spirit are done, bringing the spirit into the village, localising and concentrating it in the men's house, where the men stay or sleep in its presence. The men were inside together and the womenfolk excluded. Outside, the mothers, sisters and the wives of the men who 'slept in the song spirit' would avoid *nəm beirkatidəm* in sympathy. From what they said I gathered that that expectation weighed more on mother and sister than on wife. Any of the three might, if they chose to — and here the stress was most on the sisters — go further and vow to eat only baked dry sago (*lawə'ut*), not jelly sago (*təbəgan)*, for that time, as though in mourning for the man.

Separation of the male sphere and secrecy

Men apart, sharing an experience and knowledge that must be kept from women, is my theme now. By its very nature, secrecy aims to separate those who know from those who must not. It draws a boundary. The choice to make secret is a choice in favour of some but against others, and commonly particular others. For secrecy to work, those who share knowledge of it must recognise the obligation that binds them all to hide it. If some, or perhaps even one, should fail in this, the purpose may be lost. Indifference does not go with secrecy. The device of choosing to make secret thus has power to establish the definition of some group within a group, and to demand commitment from its members. Secrecy is an eminently social thing. The secret may come to have a value that bears little correspondence to the significance it might have had, had no one thought to make it secret. Part of its value, maybe a large part or even almost all, is that it is an item guarded and reserved.

Gnau men generally consider that they should decide public matters and choose what is right for the community. They should protect and defend it from outside attack, fight out or settle disputes that occur within it, preserve or restore good relations with invisible powers in the world about them. Responsibility falls on them for these things which make up the serious and uncertain business of their lives and that of the community. Grown men take

---

18 They were supposed only to whisper during the whole phase of seclusion up to just before the eating of *teltʌg–nawugəp*, or else to talk in whistle-talk. All the Gnau are adept at transposing speech into a whistled mode and they use it also in some everyday situations.

control and deal with each other more or less as equals. Children are not granted that equality of standing or that responsibility, nor are women. A certain justification for this arrogation of responsibility and control, a certain confidence to face it, grows from participation in that part of the ritual life of men which excludes women and children. Commitment to the values held generally by men depends, no doubt, on a great variety of social and psychological influences, but the rites have a special place in creating it and providing impressive direction to male aspiration. By excluding others, making some knowledge and experience esoteric, they find a justification for their capacity to act in these matters and enhance the value of what it is they do. They choose what sorts of knowledge shall be restricted, what departments of life they refer to; they control access to the knowledge, they bind men together in a shared duty to keep it secret.

It is the definition of some knowledge (particularly that concerning spells and the preparation of magical substances) as essential but secret which establishes a measure of shared male control over all Gnau ritual life. As they see it, men have responsibility for making the rites for women and children (e.g. at a girl's puberty, a childbirth) effective just as clearly as they have for the rites primarily affecting men. Women and children cannot do these things for themselves because of those parts of the rites that only men know how to do; and in a sense, to the outside observer, they become so decisive and essential only because they have been defined as such and kept from common knowledge. Their value is created by secrecy and does not stem, as it would seem to the Gnau actors, from the intrinsic nature or power of those things.

Strength and readiness to use or face violent action, courage, steadfastness and loyalty were qualities required of men in the conduct of war, defence and dispute in old times. Their ritual life sought also to prepare them for this and to create values and bonds between men that might withstand testing danger and the fear for one's own skin; and to create this not as a matter for choice by some men only, but as a duty for all the individual men in a community. The community was tiny, its defence and security depended on the tens, not on hundreds, of individual men that happened to be born together, endowed or not as they might be naturally with strength, courage or the quality of loyalty.

These general points are necessary as a frame within which to consider the separate ritual life of Gnau men, even though the prohibition of warfare, successfully imposed by about 1950 in their area, changed the conditions out of which that form of ritual life had arisen. The rites have changed too in response (and I shall consider this in chapter 10) but not so far yet as to make the former circumstances irrelevant to an understanding of them. Suppression of war and the use of lethal weapons in dispute, removal of the more or less distant but abiding threat or possibility of attack are what is radically different now from the past — and I am thinking of the difference of daily life in a Gnau village; the guards for any women working sago; the few and protected entrances to the village; garden houses and garden work with weapons constantly to hand;

the danger of walking outside village territory or of sleeping at a garden house; the general insularity of life within the confines of a territory outside which one rarely went and inside which there was still a possibility of ambush or attack.

At puberty, a boy was first introduced as an individual into the sphere of exclusively male rites, and he still is, but where once the possibility of killing men in war, of fighting to kill and fighting in defence was partly the *raison d'être* for what was done, it is no longer. The interweaving of killing in the hunt, killing in war, the binding of men in loyalty and commitment to each other, has come apart so that hunting and success in hunting is left alone to carry more than it had to bear before of the desire for achievement, and to provide reasons for the sense of value in what is done. Success in hunting, the courage to stand as a boar charged, a sure and strong bow arm drew on the same qualities as were required in past times for war. The man who hunted well would also fight well. There was a circle of related effects. Why did we do the Lyigʌt rites after killing a man? So that we would hunt well and kill many pigs and cassowaries. Why did we do the hunting rites for a man? So that he would kill pigs, cassowaries and men. What decided the right to wear the hornbill with spread wings on the back and the hunting bag (*lagil bawug*)? The fact that the man had killed men and many pigs and cassowaries. By the hunting rites a man would do well in warfare. From killing an enemy and the rites which followed, a man would do well in hunting. That sort of argument was often presented to me by men who had known those times. The alternating vice-versa quality is still present in the way they view the virtue of ritual work. Great rites are put on and at the end they must be 'tried out' by hunts to show through success whether they have been done well enough, long enough (see p. 48). During their performance, older men repeatedly tell the younger men to go and sing in them; they rouse up sluggards to go to sing all night, reproach them if they want to leave early; and they urge them to greater vocal effort so that the young men will have success in hunting. A night is passed in singing; then on the next full day beyond the singing, the men should go to hunt. As the singing is kept up over months in long rites, days of hunting should alternate with nights of singing. Success in the hunt should be followed by a night of singing.

The *waipət* — the male headdress

In the boy's rites of puberty, the man's phallocrypt is first put on and he acquires the right to wear it. In old times the phallocrypt was a *wadən*, a short bamboo tube, now it is a *barwi'it*, the white oval shell *Ovula ovale*. Only relatively recently have contacts with the coast brought among them enough of these shells, before so valuable, so that all men can have one for a phallocrypt. The boy may also have his hair drawn up into the *waipət*, the men's headdress. In past times this was done, but the full right to wear it as normal dress was not granted to most men until after they had been through the Tambin seclusion. Men speak as though the order used to be *wadən* first, then *waipət*, corresponding to puberty, then Tambin rites, but some men, referring to the past, say they were granted the right to wear both *wadən* and *waipət* at puberty, though others say they wore the *waipət* only after the Tambin rites even though they did have it worked for them in their puberty rites. The change of appearance made in the puberty rites was striking and public in the past in a way that it is no longer, because then boys went stark naked, their hair unkept in long ringlets until the moment of the rites: neither women, girls nor men wore long hair loose.

The *waipət* as evidence and emblem of manhood has lost its power and presence for the eye. The headdress is abandoned, to be seen now only at the dances of major rites. As men sometimes say, we do not fight now, we sit down quietly, well-behaved, we keep the law of whiteskins and we are become like women, we have cut off our hair: we cannot wear the *waipət* of before when we were fierce. But the imagery remains: *waipəsen* '(man) of the headdress' can mean admirable, terrific, powerful, a man who has fully proved himself, as well as merely a grown man with the right to wear it. The first stage of its placing in the boy's rites of puberty was done, and is still, if it be done, just before the act of the mother striking a piece of firewood before the boy. The boy sits on the *wə'ati* to have the *waipət* made. He should be inside the *gamaiyit* away from women, but when I saw it, it was done beside the men's house outside. They began by placing a disc of plaited vine (*wagabati*) on the vertex of the boy's head and tying it into the hair. It has a hole in the centre through which the long hair is pulled in a bunch. That hair is parted and hunting *gəplagəp* rubbed into the hair and spells blown into it. All the other head hair would have been shaved off before, leaving only the long bunch at the vertex; but they tied a kerchief to cover the rest of the boy's hair when I saw it done. Thick crinkly leaves of *sipə dʌgrei* (dark crimson on one side, dark green the other) were tightly bound around the bunch at the base with a fine length of liane (*laŋgabupə gugibət*). A five-inch tube of bamboo (*gapə*) was fitted over the bunch so as to stand up on the vertex of the head with the hair inside it. This tube was the *waipət niŋgi* (literally, *waipət* child: a similar phrase *gamaiyit niŋgi* is used for the scaffolding to make the men's house roof from inside — see p. 70 — and I think the sense is 'inside supporting structure of the *waipət*'). It may be made of bamboo, but more usually the tube was carved from wood of *lu burben*, the kapok tree. The fine string of liane was drawn through the tube with the hair, and brought down taut over the face to be held in the boy's teeth so that the tube stood upright in position.

That is a bare outline of how I saw the first phase of putting on the headdress done. The points they stress about the procedure are that the boy should 'go up and sit upon his *wə'ati*' (*nəwup nəwum wə'ati*) while it is done; and that he must hold the fore-string taut in his teeth to keep the *waipǝt* standing up – if it should fall it would spell disaster in his future.[19]

Tearing the *lyimʌŋgai* leaf

As he sits upon the *wǝ'ati*, the *lyimʌŋgai* leaf is torn over him. I have described the leaf-tearing (pp. 47, 53) and its first performance in the myth of Dǝlubaten when the hero does it to create men. The action is almost the characteristic act of Gnau ritual and strikes the eye infallibly. In almost every ritual at some point the betel-splotched leaf with the hibiscus flowers stuck in it is held over something for which benefit is sought. But hardly anyone when asked to explain it thought spontaneously of referring back to the myth as Sǝlaukei does in the text I quoted on p. 54; instead they would say that it was done so that the rite would work well or the person be well. The leaf is held over the boy as the hunting *gǝplagǝp* is rubbed into his hair; under the leaf some hearth ash is put in a little piece of leaf as smoke from a cigar is blown across the leaf at the moment of calling out for benefit from the ancestors. The smoke is blown across to alert and ask the ancestors for benefit. One man said to me, 'It is like what you whiteskins do when you say a prayer in a church service.' Only the experience of trying so long with many people to obtain an interpretation or reason for the act of leaf-tearing, and failing to find a convincing explanation, could really produce the sense of revelation that I had when at last someone referred me back to the myth of Dǝlubaten. I had taken the myth down from dictation long before; there was laid out a full description of the first performance in which a type and example was set for men so that they should know how it must be done. But I had not previously thought of making the connection.

There is no intrinsic sense in the action itself that might reveal itself to the searching eye and deductive mind. It marks an appeal for benefit and a way to it. That is evident from the situation in which it is used. And for many Gnau people that is all they summon up and are aware of when asked to comment on it: it is a motif that keeps recurring in their rites and something done for good. The reason why it should be done in exactly that way does not occur to them, nor do they feel the need to question something that is set so clearly by custom and tradition. Yet nonetheless a few do see why: they link the action to its charter, the token to the type from which it originated just so, the type revealed and not otherwise discoverable. It is an example to me of how I exercised my imagination

19 Another omen of disaster, which seems to me like that one, is the omen of the *wailtaro*, the fight-aroid, which falls or droops suddenly and warns the mother's brother of disaster to his sister's son if he finds one that he has planted fallen so (see p. 100). The *waipǝt* is a sort of *summum* of the man: when a man is buried, a liane is tied to his *waipǝt* and, on leaving for the hunt to end the mourning restrictions, the mourning hunters give a jerk on the liane to call his spirit from the earth to accompany them and bring them success. In past time, when they smoke-dried the body on a platform, they tied the string to the three cardinal points of the whole man – his great toe, his penis and his *waipǝt* – and jerked on the *waipǝt* end to call his spirit to go with them.

to find an interpretation in the wrong places. The leaf-tearing also epitomises for me how Gnau people may differ individually in the understanding they have of what they do. To present the action as one whose correct or real meaning is given by the myth falsifies what the action signifies to most people of that culture now in the same way as it would seem false to turn to Panofsky's explanation for why we may raise our hats (p. 37) and say that is what the gesture 'means' in our society. To reveal a reason, to ask 'Well, what about the bit in the myth of Dəlubaten?' (i.e. to prompt them to it) does provoke a reaction of realisation on the part of those who had not noticed it before. Something hidden is revealed and it seems true and right. But though the interpretation can be pricked forth or suggested to someone who does not see it and is accepted by him, that does not indicate or constitute a 'subliminal' or 'unconscious knowledge' of it. Gnau people may more often see the link and message themselves because the myth and the ritual act with the leaf are still very much present in their culture. But, despite the strength of the reaction of revelation when the link is pointed out, I would not therefore attribute 'subconscious knowledge' to the reactor.

I would parallel the situation for the reader so as to show why I think that approach to interpretation false. The nursery rhyme 'Ring-a-ring-a-roses' is an old one. I read somewhere that it dated from the time of the Great Plague in England.

Ring-a-ring o' roses	blotches on the skin — the rash or 'blains' of plague
A pocket full of posies	plague buboes in the groin
Atishoo! Atishoo!	pneumonic plague
We all fall down	death

This reveals a terrible irony and a hidden message in the rhyme; a new sense of knowing exactly why the rhyme is so. But to speak of my having known that covert meaning or message unconsciously before, or of my having responded in any way to it, would be absurd however strong my feeling that it was right and 'explained' the rhyme when I came to learn of it later. If there was something behind it once (however, see Opie and Opie (eds.) 1951, p. 365, for strong doubt about that explanation), that something was wholly lost to me for all the time I knew the rhyme before my chance discovery of someone's suggestion about it. The discovery seems to fit, but the rhyme survives without the meaning for the thousand children who are playing the game and say the rhyme, or for their parents who hear them.

Hunting gəplagəp

The *lyimaŋgai* leaf is torn for the boy's benefit as the hunting *gəplagəp* are rubbed in his hair. The *gəplagəp* and this first application in his hair are done by men apart and point towards the series of rites that will be done in the future always by the men apart to mark his successes, and bring him future success, in hunting. These rites reveal to him step by step the full knowledge of hunting magic. The marks of honour a man may wear publicly are bound by them, the *lagil bawug* (the hunting bag), the hornbill with cropped wings spread and the special belt of cassowary quills, head and nose ornaments: and these were closely linked in the past with the honours that came from homicide, the neck torque of pig tusks (*dalyiwug*) and the hanging chest ornament (*wakapu*) of pig tusks. These rites for killing are outside my scope here: except to note the aspect of control in them exercised by senior men over their juniors through their knowledge of the secrets which they reveal only step by step in stages spread over the middle years of life of the man, whose right to learn them is conditional on their decisions and their judgment of the proofs he gives them through his success in hunting and, in the past, in warfare. The Gnau do not have a male ceremonial cult system of the same complex type with a sequence of initiatory stages as the Iatmul (Bateson 1958, pp. 123–37, 245), Kwoma (Whiting 1941, pp. 65–8; Hayes 1973, pp. 159–89), Abelam (Forge 1970a, pp. 270, 275–6) and other Middle Sepik cultures; but progress through stages in the Gnau rites for killing (in hunting and, formerly, in war) resembles them in manner by the progressive unveiling of secrets in a male cult (Forge 1967, p. 68). This system is one in which advancement was closely bound up with personal achievement in those things they honoured and valued most highly.

The first phase of making the headdress in the rites of puberty is followed by the spitting with betel juice, by the mother's act of cutting the firewood and by the giving of money by 'sisters' and 'father's sisters' (p. 96). Then the men take the boy away to the place by a stream or pool where they will bleed him and themselves in secret. When this and the second spitting with betel juice to cover the blood have been done, the second phase of putting on his headdress is completed. They put on the plaited disc (*siwan*) with tufts of cassowary feather circling it which fits round the base of the *waipət*, the *nəmblapə məsipə*, which is a sheathing tube woven of fine rattan from which attached skins of birds hang down in a cascade of brilliant colours falling to the back of the head. It fits over the bamboo or wooden tube containing the hair. A *woawul* of black creeper covers the forehead, contrasting with the tiny white shells (*tiyigət*) tied over it attached on strings to a fibre base (*sa'adutap*). The large heart-shaped leaves of *wail taro* on long stems were stuck in the centre of the *waipət* so that they curled down about the boy. The fight-aroids, *wailtaro* (*nɑlawug* in Gnau, but the names and kinds are particular to different clans), are the plants above all associated with fighting and the rites for killing, which used to be eaten raw; they burned the mouth and throat and made men fierce (see Lewis 1975, pp. 209–10). These, with some of the *nɑlapə* aroids of a kind used in the hunting *gəplagəp*, were tied so that *wə'ati wigan wiwagən kə lin niyab bəlu'ət* 'the *wə'ati* would go down on him, fall down on him that he might kill pig', i.e. the influence of the herbs curling above his head would fall and enter him and bring him success in hunting. Then he was given the *wa'agəp* of meat and blood and his arms were jerked down to make the joints crack and give him strength of arm. He returns to the village and there enters the men's house to sit again upon his *wə'ati* in seclusion away from women (see p. 80); inside he is given hunting *gəplagəp* blown from a cordyline leaf of *dauwalyi wɔda* up into his nose and spat into his mouth, just as they blow the same *gəplagəp* into the nose of a dog to make it a fierce hunting dog, relentless and unafraid to corner a wild boar.

The point I made earlier about a tendency in the ritual use of plants to associate them with the process of growth rather than with activities or achievements needs qualification, because, as in the case of the fight-aroids, there are many exceptions. Indeed the term used to indicate the materials from which hunting *gəplagəp* are made is *lu-lambət* which means 'tree-creeper' (see pp. 48, 49). A general theme behind the choice of *lu-lambət* materials is the idea that the plant materials used in hunting *gəplagəp* are the things pigs and wild game specially desire to eat and the man in receiving them establishes a link or identification with the game he will hunt and makes game come to him. The association seems to me clearer (by reason of my ignorance of what wild pig most love to eat) in some of the later hunting rites where men eat tiny bits of pig faeces and worms because the Gnau say that pigs rootle from desire for worms to eat. The line of forest-dwelling paradise kingfishers, for example, is taboo to younger men because the birds, like pigs, eat worms.

The *gəplagəp* also contain scrapings of a number of tree barks which have powerful scent and some aromatic herbs or creepers, as well as scrapings with the musk scent from a wallaby's scent glands (*dambən duwəlbəg*, literally 'wallaby testicles')' Men delight in this musk scent. And scent is closely linked to success in hunting. The food rules aim to ensure that a man's scent (*tamasiwug, tambisiparən*) shall be good, attractive and not scare game away. The kinds of forbidden yam are ones that have a faint smell reminiscent to the Gnau of tree marsupials: someone eating them would be known to the animals. The rules forbid the man, when young, many foods in order to preserve that 'good smell of youth' (*dalyipədel*) so game may come to him. In the end as the man eats more and more of those foods forbidden him before, he finds no game, for the animals know him by his smell and run away. So must a man avoid yams outside the season for eating them lest pigs should smell them in him and his hunting fail.

There are small pointers to symbolic identifications in many of the food restrictions to do with hunting, just as there are in many other food rules (for instance, the ones about the food restricted to parents with a baby or young child — see p. 163). But the dominant rule deriving from an idea of identification is the rule forbidding any man or boy to eat whatever he has shot himself. It is a cardinal rule, most rigorously observed; and for its understanding we must enter the last cluster of ideas I shall discuss in this chapter, which is the one that has to do with blood (*gɑŋgi*) and the secret act of penis-bleeding.

Blood identity and kinship

No man may eat anything that he has shot himself because by shooting it he has put something of himself into it. What they say is that his own blood is in it (*gʌŋgi arən watəpə*). The blood in him, in his arms that draw his bow and aim, follows the arrow and enters the kill. Things caught in a trap or killed by striking with a bush knife are not forbidden to him because his blood is not in them. However, they have extended the rule to cover things killed with a shotgun, where the actions of aiming and the arms holding it and firing are considered too similar to the bow action to allow a man to eat what he shoots himself.

To eat would bring disaster on himself – sickness, breathlessness, decrepitude, weak limbs, failure in hunting. His own blood is in the kill and therefore it must not be eaten. People should never eat their own blood. The Gnau teach their children not to lick the blood from a cut finger. When they caught me doing it they were slightly disgusted and appalled. They say dogs lick their own blood from cuts, but people must never do so.

They say further that a father must never eat anything shot by his son. His own blood is in his son, his son's blood is in his kill, his son's kill is forbidden to him. It would bring the same disaster on the father as if he were to eat his own kill. The father and the son are identified by blood.

He cannot eat his own blood whether it be in his own kill, the blood from his cut finger or his son's kill. Nor may the son eat his father's blood in the puberty rites because 'his father's blood is already in him' (*dadarən gʌŋgi arən watəpən*). His father's blood is explicitly forbidden him in these rites for that reason. This point is very clearly made. No one seemed to see a contradiction between this statement and the lack of restriction on sons or children eating what their father had shot. At no point during his father's life may he eat his father's penile blood. This is the essential rule. But I should note what seemed to me a curious thing about their statement of it, viz. that the rule was given categorically as the one that covered the eating or rubbing on of a father's blood, and the exception was not mentioned to me. Only when we were concerned with the details of the first-birth rites would men talking to me describe an act of penis-bleeding that seems to contravert the rule though they never considered it in that light.

The nuance that struck me comes from having questioned men closely about these rules, asking which men's blood was permissible for use to rub on the skin and to put in the *wa'agəp* for the boy's puberty. In this situation, ideally the blood should come from the *wauwi*, the mother's brother – that is the positive rule – but it may come from men in a variety of other relations. These are permissive secondary provisions in the rule and I give them in order of diminishing desirability of choice: lineage or clan 'fathers' or 'brothers' of the true mother's brother, senior men of the boy's own lineage or clan in his father's generation, the boy's clan 'senior brothers' (i.e. grown men of his own genealogical generation), the boy's own elder brothers if grown up. The primary

174

negative force of the rule is that it must *not* be blood from his father; secondarily, it must not be blood from any grown man in the category of 'younger brother' (*subin*) or 'son' (*nəŋganin*). When I put the question 'Could a man under any circumstances eat the blood of his father that bore him?' One man said, 'Yes, he can after his father's death. When he eats scrapings of his bones.' That answer is indeed quite correct in the sense that men do eat scrapings from their own father's jawbones in various rites. It was the only time I received an answer different from the straight sure reply, 'No, a man can never eat his father's blood.' No one referred me to the rites for childbirth. It was not that they wanted to hide the facts of the childbirth ritual from me, because they were quite ready to tell me about them. The nuance seems to me that they did not consider bringing them into an answer when asked about the rules in general.

In the rites for a first birth, the new father goes in company with a senior man of his clan (explicitly not his own father) on the day before the final celebration and they both bleed themselves. Blood from the new father is brought back hidden in a leaf. On the final day he enters his wife's house for the first time since her confinement; he throws a yellow *dapati* paste-apple into the house and she throws it back; he crushes it with his foot and throws it back in again; then he may enter in company with his wife's father. His wife's father holds the baby and the new father rubs some of his own blood on his baby's face. The husband gives the wife some of his own blood hidden in a betel quid to chew, and the remainder of the blood is put in the *dapati* and placed in the roof of the house. They say the baby's face is washed with blood to 'clear its eyes' (*natelən nambəg*) − in Pidgin, so that *pes bilong en i-klia, bai em i-kirap na sindaun i-gutpela* 'his face will be clear and he will get up and stay well'. The Gnau phrase and the act resembles the washing of one end of a bow in blood from a kill so that the bow will 'see game'. The feeding of blood to the wife is to give her strength and health for her own, and the child's, sake. The new father has already eaten the blood of the senior man who bled with him and for him at the bush so that he will have replacement of blood for the blood he gives to his wife and child.

The point of that description is that the father's blood is rubbed on his child's face, and the Gnau do not seem to regard it as an exception to the general rule that they think of in connection with puberty, nor as the same sort of act in regard to its purpose. The further question that must arise from that description is the question of Gnau views on consanguinity. For the acts of the father might seem intelligible as ones that give his blood to the first child and also put it into his wife, now become fully married to him by having given birth − an act symbolic of incorporation into his lineage, establishing a tie by blood.

But this is not so. The Gnau have what seems to me a precise theory of consanguinity. The father's blood is not in the child because of the act of 'washing his eyes' but because he begot him (her). In the euphemistic language many men use to speak of these things, the man's 'water' (*subat*, i.e. his semen, *bulpəg*) goes into the woman and 'turns and changes to become blood' (*wambəri watip gaŋgi*); then the blood 'turns and changes' to become the foetus. Some men say that the man's blood (changed semen) makes the foetus, and the woman's blood becomes the placenta (*gaŋgi wɔlit*, literally 'blood lake'); others say the male and female 'bloods' mix in the foetus but the placenta is made only of the woman's blood. These ideas are from answers to direct questions about conception, and I shall not go into detail on their ideas about the progressive formation of the foetus and the part played in this by the father's contribution of semen. However, the theory implicit in various rules and spontaneous statements is a theory of consanguinity. A child contains blood both of its father and of its mother. The first child is born of the whole blood (*gaŋgi nəmbli*) of its parents. The notion of entirety, of a whole and finite stock, *nəmbli*, successively diminished by each following birth, is the idea behind the rules of precedence according to birth order. Each succeeding child is relatively less the child of its parent's whole blood, relatively less *gaŋgi nəmblisa*. The married woman who has not borne a child is still whole, *wei nəmblisa*, like the man. As they have more and more children, their blood stocks are depleted by the children taking the blood, and they grow eventually old and feeble — *ta'aləm lagaiyel gaŋgi, dadaril, mandaril, lil lə'up wɔla'an, nəmbig lagəp gənaudel* 'the children take their blood from them, their fathers, their mothers, they go up steep paths, their knees and joints not (strong)'.

It is the same idea of a finite stock of blood which makes the Gnau hate mosquitoes and leeches, makes them think that blood-donors for transfusions ought to be very heavily reimbursed for their loss. But the loss from parents to children is part of the nature of generation and the succession of generations. It is sequential. The relationship of senior sibling (*gəmin*) to junior sibling (*subin*) depends on birth order. With patrilineal descent, the terms used between classificatory siblings are unalterable and depend ultimately on the birth order of a pair of brothers however many generations back that pair were born. But because the blood stock provides a theory of consanguinity and order, a curious anomaly can trouble that order. If a woman successively marries two men, her children are half-siblings. The children she bore to her first husband are necessarily senior to the children she bore afterwards to her second husband. It can happen that a widow with children marries a brother of her former husband, and if the second husband is in fact senior brother to her late first husband, the problem of terminology arises for the later children. The second husband being 'senior' brother *gəmin* would normally have children that were called *gəmin* by the children of the 'junior' brother, following the relative seniority of their respective fathers. But any subsequent children the woman has by a second husband must be *subin* to her preceding children, for they are relatively less the children of her whole blood, relatively less *nəmblisa*. And the decision taken by the Gnau is that the terms in this conflicting case should follow from birth order to the mother, notwithstanding the relative seniority of the second husband to the first by which otherwise they would have been called 'senior' to her first children because their father was senior. So the anomaly arises because people outside the family classify the children of a man by his relative seniority within the descent line and they continue to go by the respective fathers, but within the family the position is reversed and will continue reversed in later generations between the children of the sons, who will follow the relative seniority that held between those sons who became their fathers. In the case of a man marrying two sisters, a comparable problem does not arise. The anomaly results from the rule of patrilineal descent, coupled with the emphasis on relative seniority set by birth order, ultimately by order in birth to the mother.

Transfer of blood

This particular view of a stock of blood successively diminished may perhaps explain why the rules of transfer of blood allow the elder full sibling brother to smear his penile blood on his younger brother, but certainly forbid the reverse and forbid the father's blood also. If the prohibition on the father's blood followed simply from the idea of identical substance (blood the same as was already in his son) it might be hard to see why the elder brother's blood was not also forbidden. For he too must share in that identity with the parent. But if each succeeding child is relatively less the product of his father's 'whole blood', then a second child is product of part of what blood was left after the first child had been born and so on for each one after. Thus an elder brother's blood was never part of that which the father might have given him, while the blood which remains to the father is stuff which, were it used in the begetting of another child, would belong to a younger sibling. This argument, a rationalisation for their statement of the rules, is one that occurs to me and was not given by them. It would apply within the nuclear family. But blood from a father's younger brother may be smeared on his elder brother's son: the son is not like his father in this respect.

The stress is on seniority and responsibility. The rules of seniority are recognised within one generation and they also establish enduring positions of relative seniority between the patrilineal lines of all men of common descent within each subsequent generation; that is between all classificatory brothers. They behave towards 'elder brothers' (*gəmin*, singular; *gəmitap*, plural) in some ways as they behave towards men of the preceding generation, the generation of 'fathers' (*dai*, singular: *gatagəm*, plural). The stress on precedence skews the system, so that the father's elder brother is called by the same kinship term as the grandfather (FeB = FF = *mami*) and reciprocally yBS = SS = *baluan*. An elder brother is expected to look after and care for his younger brothers rather as a father would, and he may do so after the death of the father, sharing responsibility for their welfare with his father's younger brothers (*gategəm*). In the duty to provide blood, there is a general sense of care or benefit for the welfare of the younger generation, the juniors: the seniors give stuff of themselves to the young so that they may grow to maturity and strength as have the men before them — the *dai-gatagəm*, their fathers. I noted before (p. 44) that *gatagəm* is derived from an adjective meaning 'huge or big in size' and the word *dai-gatagəm* is also used in the physical sense of a 'big man', grown, mature and powerful. By smearing his blood on their skin and by giving it them to eat, he helps them to grow as he has.

The transfer of penile blood is an act transferring benefit, primarily for growth, and for health and strength. This is the general sense they give to it in the puberty rites, whether the blood be given overtly to boys, or covertly to girls; it also has this sense in the first-birth rites in the transfer from husband to wife, and from senior man to the new father; in the Tambin rites; and in certain rites for the treatment of sickness. It is pre-eminently the right ənd duty of the mother's brother to be the one to do it at puberty. The welfare of his sister's children is seen as his special concern. The blood he gives is good blood: his sister's son gets rid of the bad blood by bleeding himself first. In Pidgin, the Gnau say *kandere bilong en em i-gipim em blut bilong en bilong senis* (*-im blut bilong en iet*) 'his mother's brother gives him his blood to exchange (for his own blood)'. The mother's brother's blood in the *wa'agəp* will go into and fill up his blood (*wəlauwən gʌŋgi arən*). The usual Gnau phrase for this does not quite so clearly have the notion of replacing or exchanging for his blood: *wauwi nyigə'aiyən nyig gʌŋgi beiya nyitətapən* 'the mother's brother will wash him with the blood that will stay on in him'. The gift of blood established an enduring link or debt to the particular mother's brother(s) who gave it him. After the act, anything shot by that sister's son will not be eaten by the particular mother's brother who 'washed him' because, as he gave blood, so must something of his own blood be in the kill. That *wauwi* has the strongest claim to gifts of meat shot by that particular sister's son but ironically may not eat what he receives. The other *wauwis* may do so as they did not bleed for him.[20] The observation suggests that the gift of blood is an individual transfer of substance for benefit rather than an act on behalf of a group aiming to establish a consubstantial link or identification to the clan or lineage of the mother. The gift of blood by a particular *wauwi* does not alter the senior/junior placing of the sister's son (or daughter) in relation to his (or her) cross-cousins. That placing is already determined by the sister's (i.e. his or her mother's) birth order relative to her brothers (i.e. the mother's brothers, the fathers of the cross-cousins).

Their theory of blood transmission in birth involves both sexes. Both sons

20 But most people say that the mother's brother should not eat game shot by the son of his younger sister, though he may if it was shot by the son of his elder sister. The rule is curious because it seems to depend on assimilating the son to the mother in regard to the ruling following from senior versus junior status, for a man can eat food shot by his younger brother's son but not food shot by his younger brother. I was also told that people do not always bother about the rule concerning game shot by the son of a younger sister.

and daughters come from the blood of their parents. The issue of seniority is present in cross-sex relationships as well as parallel ones. So the related rules affecting some behaviours between brothers and sisters fit the same general pattern: for instance, an elder sister will not drink after her younger brother has drunk from a vessel, she will not eat sago or coconut he has planted or a domestic pig he has raised. The relative seniority between brother and sister is passed on to their children, who are cross-cousins: the rules continue to affect their behaviours and they are transmitted to their children in turn. The pattern is consistent but the force of the rules is different and weaker for women than for men. Men are always concerned by the question of who shot the kill; was it shot by a man of junior status (*subin* – younger brother, or *nəŋganin* – son, or a cross-cousin of junior status)? This is the ever-present concern. But most women will eat meat shot by a son or younger brother. A few choose not to for special reasons of caution or past experience. The idea of 'blood' in kills tends to be referred to by men and to be bound up with their concern for their hunting success and their relative seniority. There are the other customary observances depending on relative seniority, which have to do with domestic and family life. In general they matter more in relationships between men than in relationships between women, and they matter more the closer the genealogical relationship. The type is given in the relationship between father and son, elder brother and younger brother: here the list of rules is longest, care to observe them strictest. The type pattern can be found to govern or influence behaviours involving seniority in more distant relationships, but the number of rules, as well as some of their force and strictness, diminishes with genealogical distance.

Their idea of consanguinity therefore establishes the placing of a man or woman in relation to parents, siblings, father's and mother's lineage through birth and relative seniority. The gift of blood by the mother's brother does not alter placing in that scheme. It establishes a special tie between the mother's brother and the sister's son and indebtedness for benefit. The controlling concern for the welfare of his sister's child is a special charge on the mother's brother. But it is temporary and ends with his death in a way that the father's concern does not. Specifically a sister's son must *not* use bones from his dead mother's brother for any of the beneficial purposes for which he may use bones of his father. The sister's son must formally avoid certain contacts with the remains of his dead mother's brother, his grave, his men's house, etc.

The blood the boy (or girl) is given will 'stay in him (or her)' and do good for growth and well-being. The boy must be bled first before he receives it – *lyinəm lyiŋgupən gʌŋgi wɔləda taŋgi wəsuwipən kə lin wuyin* 'they strike him, draw out of him the bad tough blood so that it goes clear of him and he may be well'. They said it was incorrect of me to suppose they were getting rid of the father's blood so as to replace it by the mother's brother's. They were only getting rid of bad blood in him, such as might come from the boy's having eaten bad things which would interfere with his growth if left. The act of penis-bleeding to release bad blood makes a man feel cleaned and light (*nar matagəp, na'ab tambit, kə nyitiyi, nyir belpi* 'he is heavy, he strikes himself (i.e. penis-bleeds) so that he will get up, feel light'). Men may sometimes bleed themselves in illness in the hope of recovery (*ala nyipəl tambit* 'so to put off [i.e. change] self'). In doing it the first time for the boy at puberty, the men say they show him how to do something which is a secret he must keep from women and something which will help him in the future. To know the pain is a privilege and a responsibility.

Men need to know how to do the bleeding. They will have to do it to help others. Only they can do it. It hurts. The first time, the pain and the importance of the act, heightened by its secrecy, makes the penis-bleeding an ordeal, but also the focal point of the boy's puberty rite. His penis wound has hunting ash (*nawugəp*) rubbed into it and then the phallocrypt is put on him for the first time. He is spat with betel juice and decorated.

The link of blood to life, the sight of blood in killing, the pain of wounds are a matter of Gnau, as of human, experience. They, like many people in the world, have ideas about generation, the giving of life, what the stuff of kinship is, why children and parents, brothers and sisters may look alike, where the vigour of life and the strength to act lies, all of which they connect with blood. It is undoubtedly strange and precious stuff. Gnau men choose to use it in a secret and responsible way that they say belongs to Tambin. Tambin is the name of the myth, the great rites, the song and the spirit. They say that penis-bleeding is 'something of Tambin' (*nəm beiya Tambin*), that the action was first shown them through Tambin. The spells that are blown into the *kuti* (the bone awl) which they use to stab (*lapəsupəl* 'they stab, puncture them') the penis come from verses of the song of Tambin. But there is no act of penis-bleeding related in the myth, nor any hint of it. The relation of Tambin as narrative in the myth to the acts within the rites called Tambin is enigmatic. The myth does not describe an action to set the example, as the myth of Dəlubaten does for the act of tearing the *lyiməŋgai*-banana leaf (see p. 170). The verses of the song of Tambin which are relevant to the act are set by fiat as the ones of virtue for the performance of the bleeding. I did not learn of any interpretation of the myth of Tambin which exposes a justification or unveils a reason for the bleeding: the myth's connection with the ritual act of bleeding remains a mystery. I cannot go beyond it to explain it.[21] Except to note of it this: that the myth is a narrative open to the hearing of both men and women, the song is sung out loud,

21 The narrative of Tambin is in essence an account of how Tambin came to Rauit and was first sung there; then how Tambin continued his journey and was killed. What led to his death was that he tricked his two wives into thinking that he was ill, saying he could not go to sing Tambin with them at another village. He told his wives to go and they went. Meanwhile, inside his men's house, he pulled off his skin and hid it in a hand drum. He went and danced. He was tall and red and magnificently decorated. He did not look like himself, but one wife guessed. The wives went back to see whether he was still at home. In discovering his skin in the hand drum, they set light to it. He went mad at the other village where he was dancing (see p. 62). It is possible to assert a slender correspondence

but the act of bleeding is a guarded secret. If the myth or the song revealed that act, it could not stay secret in the same way.

Within the complex rites of Tambin, the young men are bled on the day of their entry into seclusion, so that they 'may be light, may rise up' (*kə lyir belwug, kə lyitiyi*). They are bled again in the complex series of events that precede emergence from seclusion, and the bleeding then is done so blood falls onto material from the *wə'ati* of Tambin — they bleed onto or into Tambin. After this second bleeding, they may receive blood in *wa'agəp* from their mother's brothers, or from other senior men, to go into them and give them its virtue and replacing quality. The bleeding at puberty is the first time that a boy experiences the pain of this act which is perhaps the central secret of men's ritual life, repeated in Tambin, in rites to do with hunting, with killing, with childbirth and sickness. It is practised as an act both for a man's personal preservation and well-being as well as to protect others (especially women and children) from the dangers of contact with himself after he has taken part in major rites and has been in the concentrated presence of a spirit or power. It is also sometimes later an act for the giving of blood, a precious stuff, to those junior to him whose well-being he would seek to foster.

It is a serious act that is valued and good, a secret shared by all men, but only men. I have sought to bring out some aspects of the separate ritual life of men which are (or were) bound up with the values men set on success in hunting and killing as male achievements. The boy's rites of puberty mark a point of entry to that ritual life and the status of a man, perhaps most clearly through the act of bleeding. The second revelation that so surprised me, which I mentioned at the outset of this chapter, I have reserved until now so that it should not undermine the general Gnau stress on men's ritual life as a separate sphere. During my two stays with the Gnau, I talked about the Tambin rites with various people many times. I depended on close questioning to form a picture of the rites because I could not see them done. It was only late in my second stay, from a chance remark about a particular woman, that I learned that a girl might be secluded in the rites of Tambin. Maka had been so. Nothing they had said before hinted at it, nor had anything I read about male initiation elsewhere in the Sepik prepared me for this. I had not asked whether a girl could go through them. I assumed from the way they spoke that the division of men from women was sharp and inflexible in this sphere. It reflects a strength of presupposition on my part, and the strength of received ideas put into me by reading.

I can think now of various items where the presupposition of so rigid a

between the Tambin rites and the story by stressing his withdrawal from women into the men's house, his change to redness, tall height and magnificent decoration, and the seclusion, spitting with betel juice, and the emergence from seclusion magnificently decorated. But that interpretation would seem to me a lame and vain answer, arising chiefly from desire to find something relevant to fit the myth and the rites together, and not from anything evident to the Gnau or true to the effect of the story on its hearers: they do not state those parallels.

181

division is false — for instance, women are sometimes allowed to enter the men's house (*gamaiyit*) and to learn hunting magic. In the major male initiation rites of Tambin, a girl might be put through the whole series of the rites and 'sleep in the song spirit' in seclusion with the young men in the men's house if, but only if, her father had no sons and chose to put her through them for lack of a son. She would have to be an eldest daughter, near puberty, but not yet having had her menarche. Then she might go through all the rites of Tambin with the young men except that she would not enter the house until after they had first entered, so that she could not witness the first penis-bleeding, and she would be taken apart later just so that she might not see the later bleedings. Everything in the major rites of male initiation may be experienced by a girl and shown to her except for one thing, the penis-bleeding. It conveys the special importance of the act as the male secret. But the real revelation of that chance discovery was that a girl might go through the rites at all, a discovery that destroyed my supposition of rigid exclusion of women from the special ritual sphere of men. It would be obstinate and blinkered of me to try to maintain that the motive force behind men's ritual life is the negative one of keeping women out, or of expressing a 'sex antagonism' or 'hostility'.

The spitting with betel juice

In the puberty rite of the boy, I described (p. 78) how he crouched between the legs of his mother's brother who bled over him. Both boys and girls are spat with betel juice and it is smeared all over them so that at the end of the rite they are shining red all over. A newborn baby is called *gaŋgiden* 'red person' or 'blood person'. The light, less pigmented skin of a newborn Gnau baby does sometimes look quite red or pink, and may shine with the blood of birth on it. Though the crouching boy being bled over, and the boy or girl spat red all over, suggested new birth to me, the Gnau did not agree that the acts reminded them of this. They pointed out that the boy does not necessarily have to crouch between the legs of his mother's brother for this, but that it is easier for the blood to drip down on him like this. Sometimes the blood is collected on a leaf instead for smearing on him. Neither boy nor girl is referred to as *gaŋgiden* at the time of his (or her) puberty rites; only a newborn baby is so spoken of, although the word can be used of older people to imply teasingly that they are 'ignorant as a newborn baby'. If asked specifically why they spit someone red all over in the rites, they answer that they do it so that the boy or girl will grow well.[22] It is, of course, a most striking public visible sign of completion of the rites and quite distinctive to them, since on no other occasion (except for young

22 A comment made by some in connection with betel-spitting is that it covers over and hides the blood smeared on the boy; also, a point to note, that the betel juice spat on the girl by the mother's brother serves as a vehicle to hide the blood he gives her (p. 109).

182

men in the second bleeding of the Tambin rites) does a person get spat over and smeared completely red. Spitting betel juice is a technique used for the transfer of magical substances or substances of power in many situations. The verb used for this spitting (*lasual* 'they spit them') has the same root *-su-* as is used generically of all ritual acts of spitting or blowing ritual substances or spells so as to transfer their effect to a person or into an object. Such spitting is done, for example, on the *lyimʌŋgai* leaf (p. 47), into the crushed and crumpled leaves to be put in the *rukat* to make the girl's *wə'ati* (p. 150), in hunting rites as the way to transfer the *gəplagəp* (dry ritual substances) to the man. In the puberty rites, the spitting provides a way for many men to transfer some personal benefit to the boy or girl, to transfer something of their own quality to them. So many senior men will spit the boy or girl on this occasion, respecting the order of mother's brothers first (see p. 94), and also, if possible, getting particularly powerful or successful men to do so as well. When I was present at the rites, I was sometimes urged to spit the boy or girl because, they said, they hoped I might thus transmit something of my (to them) large size to the boy or girl that they might grow as well as I had. The smearing of the betel juice, like the smearing of the blood, is a way of spreading its virtue, and the strong pressure on the *dəglit* platters used to smear the thighs and legs, arms and trunk seems to rub it in. The boy or girl must leave the smeared betel juice on the body and not wash for some days until the red has disappeared from the body, rubbed off or rubbed into it with time.

The spells and spirits

As the betel juice is spat on the boy or girl, the men standing round may chant verses from the Tambin song called *nʌnt gapati* (the bird spell), *nʌnt wɔras* or *nʌnt dyulin* (the shooting-star spell). Both these verses are used as the base of the secret spells whispered or blown into the *wa'agəp* the boy or girl is given to eat just afterwards. The secret spells have additional names and trills added to them and have a special power or virtue. They are done with serious and intense concentration. I was struck by the way one man said to me rather proudly just after the rites for two boys were ended, how he felt exhausted by the effort of doing them, as though the concentration was demanding and took something out of him. He conveyed to me his sense of the special value in the spells by his later touching concern to teach me them secretly so that I might know them for the benefit of my own son when he should come of the right age to need them.

Nʌnt gapati and *nʌnt dyulin* are spells which are also used in the hunting rites. In some of the boy's puberty rites I saw, the man would finish the act of giving *wa'agəp* by pulling down on the boy's arm, choking the spell in his own throat and making the 'ghrough ghrough' noise of a shot pig's grunt of agony as he flapped his own foot down hard on the ground. These actions are the same as the actions done in the hunting rites where explicitly they say they do them so that the hunter's arm will be strong and his arrow fly straight. The pig noise and the foot-thumping are to make pigs turn and come to him. This sense is given them in the rites of puberty for boys. But if asked why they sing the verse for a girl, they would say so that she will grow well. There is some variation in whether or not they sing the verse aloud, and some variation too in the actual verse chosen. For as well as *nɑnt gapati, wɔras* or *dyulin*, some men say they use a different verse, *nɑnt bulti* — the snake (Python) verse — for the spell they blow into the *wa'agəp*. This verse, *nɑnt bulti*, they associate with the myth of Bulti Taltəwun. The verse itself comes within the song for Panu'ət sung at the building of a men's house, and not from Tambin. The myth belongs to an ancient site, Maiyi Wɔlgam, and there is only one small lineage at Rauit with strong ties to that place. The narrative relates how the Python hero of the myth made children suddenly grow up (see p. 107). This provides a reason why the verse spell is thought apt for the puberty rites, and some people, not only those belonging to the lineage connected with Maiyi Wɔlgam, use the spell in question. As so often with Gnau religious ideas, it proves difficult to draw clear boundaries and say that the things done in this rite belong only to that spirit. The rites of puberty do throw out pointers to the rites of Tambin, to their other *rites de passage*, to rites of hunting. Some of what is done in the puberty rites draws on the power of spirits, but which named spirit is not clear. As a verse or spell comes from the great rites of Tambin, people may answer that Tambin is involved in the efficacy of what they do; but they are much more likely, in referring to the power underlying efficacy, to call it *malət* (spirit) and not to name it. The water that they use for the *wə'ati* for mixing with the aromatic herbs, leaves and other substances for growth, for cooking the *wa'agəp* in, must come not from any pool but from a natural pool, one of the pools inhabited by a spirit (*malət*). Again if some power or efficacy be in this water, it is the power of an unnamed spirit, though one also associated with ancestral spirits attached to that land.

The invocations to spirits are directly addressed to the ancestral dead of the boy or girl's father and mother, and they say out to them that they are accomplishing the rite for their descendant, and request that the boy or girl may grow well. These invocations are made when the leaf is torn over the headdress of the boy; over the *teltɑg–nawugəp* (the leaf and ash salt mixture); when the betel-spitting is done and the *wa'agəp* given. After spitting the betel juice, the men who have done it take a mouthful of water and spit it out in a fine spray to either side of the boy or girl, calling aloud to their ancestors. The fine-spray-spitting is a marked form for opening an invocation to ancestors. The rites are addressed to spirits of the dead who may respond to the appeal by watching over the boy or girl and helping him or her to maturity. But this is a broad indefinite understanding of the presence of watching spirits of the dead, which pervades how the Gnau conceive of the continuing interest of the dead in what their descendants do, and the diffuse benefits and protection which come to them from their ancestors. It is not a view so specific to the performance of the rites of puberty that I ever heard anyone attribute someone's small stature or poor growth to failure of his ancestors to respond to the appeals contained within the rites. In the vicissitudes of someone's later life, the attentions of ancestors may well be given as a reason for particular outcomes in fortune and misfortune, in success or failure. The spirit's actions and attentions are given to explain a particular event, rather than the general direction and progress of someone's life.

The rites of puberty are not solely secular but draw on powers associated with great spirits and unnamed spirits; they are addressed not only to the world of the living but also to the dead. And the men have responsibility for their proper performance, a responsibility and capacity to fulfil these duties restricted to them, and given value by secrecy. At the end of this detailed discussion of the manifold associations thrown up by what is done in the rites, let me repeat that of all public rites along the course of people's lives, the rite of puberty is the only major public event which all people must undergo personally as the individual who takes the centre of the stage. They require public observance for each and every individual in a way that only death can match among the Gnau. Though the rite itself is short and takes only a few hours to do, it contains within the general theme of human development pointers to much else in Gnau understanding of the course of human life, its direction, the powers, values and aspirations that should guide it.

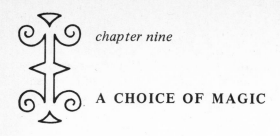

chapter nine

A CHOICE OF MAGIC

The search for cognitive content and possible symbols in other people's rites outweighs concern for what people may feel about them. I think this neglect may distort their just interpretation. Anthropologists sometimes treat rites rather like a set of clues or a test to be solved by finding answers that all fit together. It is as though the cry 'It fits' would convincingly repay the effort and the ingenuity. Rites come to seem like riddles or crossword puzzles. But if the actions were not clues, the rites not intellectual games . . . ? If there were no right solution . . . ?

Smell, colour, noise, actions that hurt, exhaust, excite, satiate seem clearly designed to act on the senses and emotions. They provoke responses. They do not necessarily suggest solutions to problems or answers to questions. There may be no set message to be deciphered. Among the variety of responses evoked, some people may think of answers to satisfy an intellectual impulse. The question is whether there is only one correct solution or rather many partial answers. The search to find a 'right' solution presumes that a problem has been set, or an answer provided in the rite. That a problem or answer in that sense exists may be imaginary. What the analysis may explain sometimes is why the actions chosen are suited to provoke or elicit the responses they do. If there were something to find in the rites, it might resemble the chimera or the hydra rather than the unicorn.

The appeal made by rites both to emotions and to intellect can be chimerical. It underlies a common uncertainty in interpretation of symbols and their magical efficacy. With statements of the type 'I must stay here in the village because my mother's brother wants to catch some bats roosting in a tree on his land. I must stay in the village now so the bats won't fly away' (cf. p. 100 above), we are tempted to ask ourselves whether they believe it literally, or whether they are only talking symbolically. Is it a literal statement of magical belief in a mystical connection, or a statement intended to be understood symbolically? If we answer that they mean it literally, we may go on to worry about how they could come to hold such false ideas about cause and effect in the world. Implicitly, to believe in it literally would be incompatible with thinking of it as a symbolic

186

statement at the same time, if we restrict ourselves to the actor's point of view, and exclude the observer's. Couched in terms of intellectual understanding, the question seems to ask us to choose either one answer or the other. But if people are not always absolutely committed to what they say they think, if the relations they may have to their statements vary, sometimes because of changes in their emotions, then the answer about literal belief or symbolic statement need not involve an either/or choice. The power of some symbols lies, I think, in their dual appeal both to the mind and to the emotions, and in the dissonance they may set up between clear reason and hot emotion.

Do they really believe what they say? I hope to explore this question now more vividly by a particular example to do with the relations between the mother's brother and the sister's son when they have gone wrong. I once asked someone to tell me about the duties and obligations of the relationship and he told me about them by describing various imaginary situations. One of these was about how the mother's brother might revenge himself on a sister's son who failed to honour his obligations. This is a translation of what he dictated to me.

Wauwi speaks to his sister to make her take away the children (*ta'aŋ*) — to his sister who has died [in the subsequent part of the text he changed the spirit addressed to the *wauwi*'s father] — he speaks to his dead ancestors about the children, saying, 'You, So-and-So [naming the ancestors], come, stand at my back while I cut down this tree and call out the name of the son of So-and-So [his sister]. He [ZS] went to the coast [the plantations], got things and earnings there, and came back. But he gave me nothing. He came back, he hunted and killed pig, animals, birds, but he gave me nothing. He did not know me [ignored me]. I shot game, I gave it to him. He got things but he kept them to himself. He planted yams and taro, bananas, *pitpit*. He kept them to himself. Now I call out his name and may he die.' [The *wauwi*] takes the skull of his father or ancestor, he goes, puts marks on it, and places it up resting here like this [just behind him], he makes an offering platform, breaks a branch of areca nut, prepares sago jelly, gets a coconut and puts it on the platform.

The tree stands here like this [in front] — a great tall tree [on the *wauwi*'s land]. Then the *wauwi* goes and makes marks for the eye, nose, lips and chin [of his *mauwin* 'sister's son'] — marks on the tree. He speaks: 'Father! Ancestor! I cut down this tree and I name the son of So-and-So. He got things and he kept them to himself, [put] nothing for his mother's brothers and their sons.' Then he stands here like this, he puts things on the platform. He puts the sago jelly, the meat with it, the areca nut, the dead spirit's skull, and the coconut, he prepares tobacco in a leaf, he breaks off some betel pepper leaves, puts them out and some lime. Then he speaks to his spirits, saying, 'Father! I am giving you this coconut, the areca nut, I have prepared sago jelly for you, cooked you this possum and you must draw the son of So-and-So to you. You two together can eat the sago jelly. You can cook him the meat, give him coconuts, get him areca nut, and prepare his tobacco for him, and the betel leaves for him to put in his string bag. The two of you can sit together now. I am going to cut down this tree: you hold him fast and wait. In a little you will see the tree about to fall, then you throw him first [in front] and follow him — hold him well! You can look after the son of So-and-So now. He gave me nothing. If he had not been like that, then we might have stood together still. But I send him to you now. He is not mine but yours. You look after him now. Strike him down! Draw him to you so that he may learn to shoot game and give some to you.' The tree crashes over, destroying the image (*malǝt*) of the ZS. Later in the night, the [*wauwi*] sleeps and dreams of his father, who speaks to him: 'I have drawn your *mauwin* to me and gone away with him.' The *wauwi* answers, 'He's yours! Pull him to you and go off — he's not mine but yours! I have sent him to you.'

The man dictating to me told me that this is a way by which the mother's brother can kill his sister's son. This was confirmed by others. But do people act on it?

At the main stages of the sister's son's development, I have described how the mother's brother used to receive a payment of shells as wealth. Shells are now devalued — they call them in Pidgin *rabis-moni* or even just *rabis* 'rubbish' — and payment is made with money. The shells lost their value because men brought back box-loads of them from plantation labour. Before then the people had had few shells. The problem of how to accommodate to an upsetting new situation faced the Gnau very soon after their first contact with white men. The problem was that by two years' work young men could acquire enough shell wealth for bridewealth and independence. By the time that the glut of shells began to turn treasure into rubbish, they had a solution to the problem. They had to dispossess the young men of their wealth. The solution lay in the parallels they could see between plantation labour and their Tambin initiation rites. In the Tambin initiation rites, the young men were secluded in the men's house for many months; inside they talked in whispers or whistles, not speech; they could leave it only by a secret hidden path, their heads and trunks hidden by a thick leaf-frond covering. From the public point of view they disappeared as though they had died. They were fed and fed. And they reappeared at the culmination of the rites, fat, shining, in finery they had not worn before. They made a great gift of wealth to their *wauwi* who had hunted meat for them during their seclusion. Plantation labour was two, or even sometimes three, years' long. The men who went were lost to sight and sound. But they came back, dressed in shirts, *laplap* (a cloth wrap), shorts; sleek, well fed, their hair peroxided, their skin shining and scented with the pink perfumed oil of the trade store. And the wealth in their *pinistaim paus*, the bright red box with a lock of the labourer returned *pinistaim* 'finished time'? Here is a text on the disposal of plantation earnings from that long response I quoted from before:

His [the *mauwin*'s] father speaks, saying he must tell his *wauwi* to come to see the things brought back by his *mauwin*. He has gone to the coast and they will honour their obligations. The *wauwi* looks at the things; then he says, 'You can keep the bush knife, I will take the axe.' Or, if there are many *wauwis*, the older one will take the axe, the younger one the bush knife. And the boy's father says to his brother-in-law [i.e. the *wauwi*], 'You take your money, take the axe.

You decide, you say whether to leave me some, or if you will take it all your-self — if all for you, that's all right, I shall not be angry with you. I am good [generous]. It is as you wish, give me some only if you choose to.'

The text describes an imagined situation and indicates the ideal. But by con-vention, the *wauwi* usually gets (gets perhaps rather than takes) only about half of the total money brought back. But given that a man goes to work at plan-tations only once or twice in his life, and that there is no other way for people in the village to earn so much money, it is a great gift.

I would like to quote now two letters from a father to sons at the plantation. I served as scribe in the village. The letters are terse, to the point, and they come from a man of no practice in composing letters. They were dictated in Pidgin. To his son:

Dear Seri,

When you are ready to come back, you must not throw your money away on things. Bring it all back. Buy an axe for Maitata who 'washed' you [a euphemistic reference to penis-bleeding], and buy one for Dukini [the younger brother of the sender], but don't buy finery and things. Your 'finish-time' box, that's all right, you can buy it. Your monthly clothing issue, get it then put it away to bring back to the village for gifts. Give it to your mother's brother. Now, as everyone knows, the *wauwi* gets his *mauwin*'s stuff. They get the *mauwin*'s stuff in the 'finish-time' box. These are the things you will bring back with you and your *wauwi* will get them. I have got what Dabasu brought back, we got £18. Well Paitu got £3, Dukini £5, I got £6 and Palen £4. Of this they are putting aside £5 to go to Paitu [Paitu belongs to the generation following the sender's: Paitu is in the same generation as Seri, the sender's son] and I gave my £6 to Belei [Seri's wife]. That's what we did with the money from Dabasu. Tukri didn't get any. Later perhaps we can change it and put a small part for him. We are waiting for when Weiri dies [Weiri is the sender's sister, a redoubtable, spry widow, voluble and in excellent health], and when we bury her, then we will get the money and share it all out. I, your father Səlaukei, I am telling you what to do about the things you are going to bring back.

To a classificatory son:

Dear Lelei,

I, Səlaukei, write to you. Your uncle Wɔgwei has arrived back at the village. When you and Seri return you must not land at Nuku. You must land at Yankok. Recently coming through Nuku, Dalukil's son Waimo got back. He did not come and give the money well [generously, properly — *em i no kam gipim moni gut, nogat, haitim long en*]. No! he hid it from him. His father took it and hid it away, put out £5. 10s. 0d. for us, and we also got a mosquito net, a towel and a *laplap*. That's all for now, Lelei.

The first letter presents duty in a brighter light — what it is good to do and to receive. It is hard but right to give. The second letter states that people do not always do right, the money and the things may not be offered entire, and there can be suspicion that a part is hidden, a portion granted but begrudged.

But if we paused to ask about Dalukil's son, we would find a whole involved story and tragedy behind it. Dalukil as a young woman about nineteen years old, loved Wɔlaku, though he was already married. Her father was fiercely against the idea of her marrying him, especially because he believed the spirit of Wɔlaku's father (the man was dead) had caused his own wife's death. His wife had fallen from a *tulip* tree that Wɔlaku's father had planted. So there was a row between Dalukil and her father over the young man Wɔlaku. She ran off in the night to Mandubil, the next village on the other side of the river Galgəbisa. In the early morning, her father found she had gone. He followed after her crying and weeping out loud that she must come back because he needed her help to look after her younger brother and sisters. The village she came from and Mandubil were at the time involved still in the long series of killings between them, but her father supposed he could go there as he had many clan kin at Mandubil who would give him safe passage. Perhaps he did not stop to care. He carried only his axe. But three young men had gone out from Mandubil to ambush him close to the river as he came crying. The one who shot first was the one who had decided to marry Dalukil, and he did. He is the father that Səlaukei suspects in the letter of hiding the plantation earnings. Dalukil after her flight that night did not make the two-hour journey of return to the village where she was born for many years, perhaps as many as fifteen years, not until her children were well grown.

Her father's death was avenged in the eyes of her 'brothers' when they killed a Mandubil man, but not until a few years after her father's murder. Her children grew up, but not because Dalukil's 'brothers' in her natal village made any move to benefit them. Had she come with the children to seek such a thing for them, the children might have been killed. I was told of an instance which had happened at about that time, when the child was a baby pulled away from the breast, held upside down by a leg, and stabbed through with a big arrow in front of the desperate mother.

What I wish to consider is this: the man who married Dalukil, though he murdered her father, and by so doing orphaned her brother, yet sent to her remaining kin shells in bridewealth for her soon after through a woman intermediary. Though her brothers did no service to benefit her son or help him grow, they got some of his plantation earnings. Of course great changes had occurred in the time lying between Dalukil's flight and her son's return from the plantation — killing had been stopped and the villages could visit each other freely.

The symbolism in duties and the point of it: uncertainties and their resolution

The people who find themselves in a given relationship develop more or less complex feelings about each other out of their various contacts. These develop and differ in the detail of each case. Left to grow quite unguided from circumstances and character, there would be great variety in the sentiments of different people who chanced to stand in that relationship. Alternatively, its desired quality might well be known. If this were known only as some precept such as 'Love and respect your mother's brother', it would still be difficult for the individual to know what to do about it. Without any teaching or rules to say what kinds of action showed love and respect, the actions of one man are open to another's misunderstanding. The question is how clearly the desired sentiments are formulated and how clearly they are linked with particular actions. If it is clear, the action can be used to show the sentiment. But a particular action may be set as a duty without establishing a dogma about what sentiment it shows; this then remains open to individual supposition. Custom can determine how some actions should be done, but in terms of kind and detail it says little about the vast variety of circumstances in which people may face each other in everyday life. The push and pull of their interests and personalities in this are bound to be accompanied by assessment of each other in terms of the values associated with the relationship. Doubt or resentment built of various small things, complicated, hard to judge, hard to make public because their significance would not be generally accepted, may be set to rest or forced out into the open by making use of the attention given to performance of certain duties and their accepted significance. It is easier and clearer to throw down and break a sister's son's gift, asserting it to be too small, than to try to explain about and list a whole string of minor snubs or derelictions which, taken singly, are not serious and even taken together could be construed in various ways. The performance of set duties can serve to show up or indicate with objects and actions what otherwise might remain amorphous, uncertain or petty. Something about the state of relations can be objectivised; but only in specified and restricted terms which tend towards all-or-none, black-or-white statement. This statement is clearer, less ambiguous, but only if, or because, the terms by their fixity and formal ruling allow for little in the way of qualification or shading. What should be done by the sister's son when he first returns from the plantation is decided in bold outline, not in minute terms that say, act for act, object for object, what obligation is recognised in each and what feeling it bespeaks. Money by its divisibility makes it possible to measure and finely grade the wealth presented in a way that was not possible with shells. Differences in amounts stand out clearly — money is counted — but what such differences shall mean is not established.

Dalukil's son gave £5. 10s. 0d. of his plantation earnings, a mosquito net, a towel and a *laplap*. Dabasu, the other sister's son in the first letter, gave £18. What sort of titration of recompense, sentiment and duty is this? Does £5. 10s. 0d. represent what is due to some irreducible principle of Gnau kinship and the £12. 10s. 0d. of difference represent £10 of recompense and £2. 10s. 0d. of affection? Had he made over all that he brought back, would he have fulfilled some ideal? Given what had happened in the past, why did they bother to give anything at all? To Dalukil's husband and Dalukil's son did £5. 10s. 0d. seem generous, a gesture full of good intentions? To Dalukil, a gesture of remorse and desire for reconciliation? How did they expect Səlaukei or, more precisely, Dalukil's brother to receive the gift? Səlaukei and Dalukil's brother took it ill, which I doubt Dalukil's son intended them to do, though he may have guessed that in whatever he would do there was some risk of this, because the action was bound to make them think again about what had happened in the past. The feelings they had about all that past infected their judgement of his action. There were no rules to say just what he should do to make his intentions clear to them.

Other people said they expected that Dalukil's brother might use one of the ways to harm his sister's son which was described in the text I quoted earlier about a *wauwi*'s revenge. The money affair made them think again of what could be done. I learned of nothing from which to suppose the brother did in fact try to use the method. But the suggestions that he might use it are interesting. Did the people who suggested it not stop to think that surely he must have tried to work this technique for dealing death in the past, when he had reasons more sharp and bitter for doing so then than now — the wound was not so old then? If it had not worked then, why bother with it now?

Beliefs, actions and illusions

We talk of the 'beliefs of another people' and it is a catch-all phrase. 'Belief' is used not only of absolute faith and unalterable conviction. The things someone says, what he feels, what he does, do not have to stand in any simple relation of consistency to each other. Words come easily, they are said quickly and cost small effort in the saying. While human actions can and do change — even the inanimate world — doing things is harder and slower than speaking about them. By a direct act of violence, a Gnau man might kill his sister's son (I told you of the baby who was killed) but the Gnau also say he could have killed him by words and actions which are not so direct as stabbing, spearing or shooting him.

In the statements about revenge by magical murder, the words and actions are said to lead to the death of the sister's son. The man who would do these things must know that too. In the bare light of this knowledge, it must be judged that he intends to kill. Why kill by magic where one might kill by violence? It is true that to kill with the arrow or the spear is now forbidden; that to kill by magic might be kept secret; that to kill by magic makes a shade of one's dead an accomplice in the act and thus part responsible; that to kill by magic does not carry the immediate danger and difficulty of the violent act. But what of its certainty? Surely the hate so hot and bitter as to spur a man to try to kill his sister's son would seem enough to fix his attention on the effects of his actions, and make him face the question of delay and his intention unfulfilled?

In asking why a man would seek to kill by magic when he might kill by violence, I want to know about his choice. He says that he would kill, but between that and the act, on the one side, of attempted violence or, on the other, of spoken phrases and cutting down a tree, is there just one self-same will to kill linking what he says to what he does?

This is a lurid way of asking a question about beliefs and symbol. If we take their statements literally, and if we presume a true intent to kill, our answers about a man's choice will have to do with the relative economy of effort, the secrecy, responsibility, and the dangers that decide him on his choice. In magical revenge, it happens that I suppose he will almost surely face a failure and that the strength of his intent to kill should force him to try and explain it. But that is an issue to one side. If we assume his true and literal belief, either the violence or the magic must seem to him equally effective ways to satisfy his desire. Before that ferocious desire, there are two ways open, and to our assumed literal and convinced believer, it is not that his words and his cutting down the tree are symbolical, because to him they would not be a symbol (however they may seem to us) but a substitute for the act of violence. For secrecy, the safety of his skin, shame, difficulty and danger, he might prefer to substitute magic for violence.

Now suppose we slacken the certainty of his belief, impute less of the literal to his statements, allow him some measure of recognised and voluntary illusion, a half-belief, then the magical action may become that much more an act that stands for what he would like to do but does not really dare, or does not wholly desire. It is a substitute but a partial substitute. It does not bear quite the same relation to fulfilling the desire as setting out to kill the man with a bow and arrow. It is in part symbolic to the man himself. There is a difference in the recognition of symbolic action as one looks from outside at the beliefs, makes tentative play with exotic materials, knowing that one's own beliefs are not involved, or instead seeks to grasp and understand the experience of someone for whom these things are part of the real business of his life and involve his own knowledge, the things he learns and is asked to believe. It seems evident to me, if I think about the implications of the things people sometimes said to me, that there is some voluntary illusion recognised in their assertions about these beliefs. For example, a younger man, who happened to be the one who first told me about one of the forms of a *wauwi*'s revenge, ended his brief account by saying that he had the right kind of hole on his land, that some day he might do the magic, not because he wanted to kill his *mauwin* but because he wondered whether it would work. Of course, he said, if his sister's son did fall ill, he would immediately unstop the leaf in the hole and end it. People must differ individually in how they view the truth of what they assert in common with the others of their community, and differ too in their inward reflections as impulse and motive wax or wane to allow them a degree of detachment which is inconstant, and alters how they think about it (see Kräupl Taylor 1966, pp. 109–19).

193

Assertion, affirmation and promise

Some kinds of conviction involve assertion only. To believe that a god has set the stars in their courses and therefore they must move as they do for ever does not present a believer with the same possibilities for doubt as does a belief that entails a promise or a prophecy. If you do this, then that will happen. There is an infinite and complex gradation in the particulars of belief between those of pure assertion and those affirming the promise of immediate and material effect (see Janet 1927 and Ellenberger 1970, pp. 331–417). The complexity lies partly in the strength, closeness and detailing of the link which binds the affirmation to its promise. The link may be defined clearly or not so clearly – this is part of the matter – but feelings may also affect how individuals regard the link. These may differ. It is one thing to talk in an airy or theoretical way about what is possible in vengeance, but another to brood with aching unappeased spite on what to do.

Conviction and false knowledge: the part of reason and the part of feeling

Evans-Pritchard showed why he could not prove to Zande people that what they said about witchcraft was false (1937, esp. pp. 475–8). He unravelled and ordered the premisses and logic that would defend those beliefs by reason rather than sentiment. Indeed he put the case for the defence by reason so well that a defence on grounds of sentiment might seem superfluous. Sentiments and individual feelings are clearly involved in such beliefs. Some anthropologists (Evans-Pritchard (1951, p. 46) was one of them) have said or implied that such matters of sentiment and feeling lie in fields belonging to the psychologist – a bridge leads to these fields but only the asses of anthropology would cross it.

I have no wish to find myself with long hairy ears, yet I would give attention to the part of sentiment and feelings in belief. These contribute, as well as reasons, to the preservation of false knowledge and the incorrigibility of shared illusions. My concern here is with the variable interplay of reason and feeling, and to see how it is complicated when we speculate or ask about the individual's private attitudes to prevailing public beliefs. I do not suggest that one aspect of explanation (through sentiments and feelings) should supplant or displace another (through reasons): the one does not exclude the other, but they interact in various, inconstant ways particular to circumstance and occasion. The relations people have to their assertions are psychologically complicated, and these relations are not solely dominated by reason. As outsiders, our curiosity is especially pulled to those assertions sometimes made by members of another culture which we regard as errors or false knowledge. We see these errors according to the knowledge which we share with members of our own culture. In seeing them, we do not have to take a view that isolates each of us as an individual with an understanding no one shares. The errors we see as outsiders are errors that within another culture are common to everyone, i.e. socially shared, normal and openly asserted, indeed perhaps sanctioned as right thinking. The individual, within that community of knowledge, is faced with real events which may put doubts into his mind. To bring these forward he must be prepared to separate himself from what everyone else says he believes. And it requires courage to assert oneself against the others of one's whole world, and stand alone confronting them with doubts. Whether it is worth doing depends a great deal on what is at stake for the individual — this is a matter for his feelings and interests as much as, or more than, cool reason.

Whether some belief tends towards pure assertion or an affirmation linked to a promise can alter for the individual as his feelings weigh down the balance on one side or another. To an individual faced with some particular situation in which his immediate interests are at stake, the weight may fall on the promise entailed rather than on the assertion, but this is not so for other people. As their concerns are not involved, they may not share his grounds for doubt. The issue of shared assertion as against an entailed but empty promise can be seen in a Gnau belief linked with the rules against speaking a *wauwi*'s personal name. I stumbled against the requirements of this rule almost every day of my field-work. I knew their stated belief and I must have been the casual witness of thousands of situations in which some individual had to interpret the rule in his conduct.

The rule is tacit, part of common knowledge, imperative and unconditional: do not speak the name of your *wauwi*. In the ordinary dealings of life, no one needs to talk about it. Everyone lives by it. As a child begins to speak, the rule is already in force for him. The child still stammering, imitating noises, people round about repeating *wauwi*, smiling, pointing, encouraging, so that, for the child, *wauwi* comes among its first and most loaded words. As for the infant, so for me; it was only later, after I had sensed the rule as something imperative and almost absolute, that it came to have anything conditional about it. I learnt that someone who spoke the personal name of his *wauwi* might be fixed by a certain little snake (*bulti məlwati*) as he walked along a path. He would be fixed, unable to move before the little snake unless he gave it all his shell valuables and finery, stripped himself bare. It was suggested to me that nowadays, for instance, I or someone like me wearing shorts, should empty his pockets of any money and drop his shorts down before it. *Bulti məlwati* is not, they say, poisonous. Nor did I discover or hear of any man who had had to face this disturbing predicament.

But countless times I have pressed someone in another predicament, that of identifying a name to me which was his *wauwi*'s. Obtaining genealogies was the problem. There were ways round it: someone else present might say the name for him; or he might say something like 'You know — thinggumme, the father of X, or the husband of Y, or the son of Z'; or he might begin the name and hint 'Wei. . . Wei. . .', or say it dropping out a consonant or two' 'Wei. . . Wei—il'; or he might twitter it very soft in whistle talk, or he might put his mouth right up to my ear and breathe it out just audible, we two in secret at my house. There were some men who could be pressed to say the name in private to me and others who would not budge and we just had to leave it until someone came up who could tell me. I do not know for sure, but I doubt strongly that any of these men put by me in this predicament gave a thought to the possibility of trouble with a little snake on a path in the future. Their attitude about speaking the name I would assume was close to what some people in our society feel about saying four-letter obscenities, except that the sentiment complex involved had to do with respect and moral duty, not sex and filth. The prophecy or promised condition about the snake which they can assert as a reason for obedience carries little or no emotional weight. It is mere assertion. But the act of speaking the name does do something to the speaker's feelings. We may reason that an obscene word refers to a bit of the body, or to sex in action, which we forbid people to dare expose in public; that to say the word is a bit like showing the thing or doing it, but of course it is not quite so bad, though still offensive to the more delicate-minded. We know that just about everybody else knows the words. We know that if a newspaper were to print 'The Hon. Member said "F. . . the Minister"', then every reader would know what foul word he was supposed to have uttered. But all this reasoning and recognition does not convey that shock which the word said out straight and clear can produce in the right circumstances. An account of the rules and beliefs about the wicked speaking of forbidden words which tells only about reasons and cognition and leaves out sentiment and affect fails to convey what such beliefs and rules mean to those who try to live by them.

The significance of symbols in real life

I have asked whether it would be right to call the actions of a *wauwi* who tried to kill his *mauwin* by saying words and cutting down a tree symbolical to him (the *wauwi*) if we supposed that he truly believed they were as fully a way to kill as hunting down the man with a bow and arrow. If the two ways were seen by the *wauwi* purely as alternative techniques, the one able to be substituted for the other, there need be no difference of intent to kill behind a choice of one or other technique. But if we suppose that his actions are recognised by him as symbolical, we must in turn recognise that his choice of the magical revenge involves some alteration, perhaps a deflection or a hesitation, in his intent to kill.

The issue here involved can be made more general. The issue is that of symbols and their significance in real life (see Jaspers 1963, pp. 330–40). When we use the word 'symbol' we refer, at the very least, to one thing which *stands for* something else. I have argued that if one thing can fully serve in the

196

place of another, it is not that one thing *stands for* the other, but that one thing *substitutes* for the other. Symbolic equivalents are not so equal as substitutes. In metaphor, the illusion of identity is voluntary. The Gnau know, as we do, that on many grounds neither the banana plant nor the bats nor the tall tree is the same as a sister's son, but they are prepared to neglect many conspicuous differences for the sake of one (or a very few) attributes in which they see an identity. Indeed it is because there are so many differences to be neglected or discarded before the metaphor makes sense that the sole or few attributes of that identity in metaphor stand out so clearly — more clearly — and so metaphor may serve as an instrument for discovery.

What the metaphor is in the sphere of speech, the symbol is in the sphere of things, i.e. the sphere of objects and actions. There may be mere symbols too in the sense of mere metaphors, where the illusion is voluntary and passes for unreal. Both the terms 'metaphor' and 'symbol' stand for something which is not used in its barest literal sense or for its proper purpose. Both describe methods which are used to give concrete expression to ideas. An object that can be seen may be transferred to an entirely different concept that cannot be directly perceived. Our reason thinks of something for which there is not any corresponding direct object or action to perceive. But to say that there is no corresponding concrete object or action to perceive is not the same as saying that the thing thought of is not real. The subject of this discussion has been the relationship of mother's brother to sister's son. It is not easy to point to an object or an action and say 'That is a relationship.' But the relationship is there.

By certain rules of recognition, the Gnau can assign two persons to certain relative positions, one termed *wauwi* and the other *mauwin*. The rules of recognition allow them to predict that if a male person is born to a certain woman then he will be *mauwin* to certain men. If none of these men survive, or even if none of them happened to have been born, it is still known who (where) would have been his *wauwis* if they had been alive or born, because they would have occupied the specified position.

To know the terms for the positions and the rules to decide when they are occupied by persons does not yet entail any knowledge of the nature and content of the relationship between them. In Gnau society, persons in these two structural positions should have a relationship of a particular and valued kind. The relationship is complex, desired and enduring, and I believe they think of it as a kind of whole or entity or thing. It is not the kind of thing which can be seen, grasped, touched or smelt, or heard as a whole. It can be thought of in terms of the qualities of the relationship and its particular duties and attributes. It is enduring. It exists also at times other than solely those when a particular duty is done and seen to be done. The relationship is given or axiomatic, its desired qualities are formulated in ideal terms by people who see them as good and right (on the moral nature of kinship see Fortes 1953, pp. 35–6, and Fortes 1969, chs. 5, 12). As ideals, they go beyond what can be simply pointed to and seen. The nature of the relationship is not shown in a single concrete experience, but it may be more accessible in symbolic form.

When we take the particular symbols, and ask 'Of what are they symbols?' we find no actual object or action referred to except in the form of the ideas of the relationship. The enduring qualities desired in the relationship are moral and involve sentiments of concern, love, respect and recognition of the special value of the other person. These are things which cannot be simply or directly seen and described. The symbols help to make them known. Human ideals and values and counter-values are pre-eminently the sort of things for which people require symbols, because they are insubstantial and abstract. They are hard to grasp and apprehend. But the values and ideals are felt as real; they have personal validity for the people who hold them. Symbolic thinking amounts to more than just thinking in images. When we consider other people's symbols from the outside, our own beliefs uninvolved, make play with exotic material and images, we are liable to miss their true seriousness. If it were suggested that I might be able to build up from the detail of many observed situations such accurate, well-witnessed and vivid scenes of daily life that you might approach an understanding of the sentiments involved like to that of the people themselves, I would still not have pointed out a great difference in your second-hand understanding compared with that of the first-hand actors: that seriousness of real life, that experience of feelings which one's own real life involves, would be missing.

The symbols help people to apprehend these sentiments and values. The sentiments and values have personal validity for the people in the society; they are real to them but not simple or directly graspable things. The symbols or symbolic actions are concrete, actual objects and actions. They help them to understand the ideas which the objects and actions stand for. But people are prone to take the symbolic objects or actions for the reality they stand for (the felt reality of the sentiments and ideas). In other words they mistake the concreteness and substantial nature of the objects or actions for the reality of the sentiments and ideals they feel. They take symbolic reality as if it were the reality of direct apperception. So the symbols come not to stand for something else (an ideal or sentiment that goes beyond the object or action), but to be equal to the sentiment or the idea itself. That is, instead of being a symbol, it becomes a substitute or the thing itself; to our outsiders' view, it becomes for them an object of superstition. We may still, from our external standpoint, call these things symbols, but for the actors they are not any longer.

Part of the purpose of this chapter has been to bring this issue forward, and to suggest that people do not take the material performance of their duties as substitutes for the moral sentiments and ideals desired in this relationship, but do indeed see them as symbols or tokens of something that goes beyond the materiality of these required actions. Despite the face value of what people say, we can perhaps see better why the *wauwi* chooses the magical mode of revenge, desiring not wholly the death of his sister's son but that he should come to heel and return what he owes. The *wauwi* may cut down the tree and the secret may out; and rumour or suspicion may scare a sister's son into a sense of his duties derelict but so endangering that he will turn and seek to make them good. There can be appeal against the curse; but the arrow loosed from the string is irrevocable. There may be much subtle and individual variation in how particular people regard their beliefs. Belief is not always a matter of absolute conviction: emotion and feeling as well as reason enter in the link between assertion and conviction, and emotion and interest can alter that detachment which might enable someone to see certain objects or actions as symbolic or instead mistake them for reality.

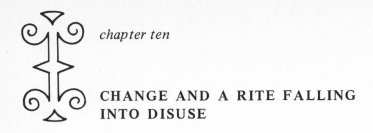

chapter ten

CHANGE AND A RITE FALLING INTO DISUSE

The people at Rauit and other Gnau villages continue to perform the rites of puberty for all their children but they do not do them exactly as their fathers used to. They know this. The question which I shall consider is why they have changed them.

Their social world was entered by strangers not much more than two generations ago. The old men in the village remember when first they saw some 'Malay'[1] hunters after birds of paradise who travelled south of the village but did not come into it: they came from the west (from Dutch New Guinea, as it then was). They carried guns and showed the Gnau salt (the Gnau mistook it for their semen — *bulpəg*), matches and tin plates which, to the Gnau, shone like the moon and they called them *gə'unit belgap* 'fingernails of the moon'. Between that time and my most recent visit in 1975, with Papua New Guinea become an independent country and villagers discussing whether to try to join together to buy a truck when the road comes, much change has invaded the general character of their lives. It has extended the scope of the social world in which they live.

The knowledge and experience of their fathers no longer provide sufficient basis and training to face the present and the future. Between what they need to know now and the culture of their fathers lie changes produced by events from outside, for reasons they have no full means to understand. Changes set constraints and possibilities to which they must adapt on the basis of partial information and sometimes garbled understanding. New things affect or penetrate their lives in many sorts of ways. They range from what seem small details, like the use of matches or the annoying new kinds of grass found on paths and in gardens, to things with diffuse extensive effects on their culture like the stopping of warfare, the spread of cash or Pidgin English. I would not pretend to be able to weigh up precisely how such disparate forces have influenced the conduct and maintenance of their ritual institutions, or the rites of puberty in their particular detail. I would pose the question of selective

1 They learned their name as *Məlyi'ai* in Gnau — I suppose they were Indonesians.

maintenance and change in the rites rather differently for its bearing on some aspects of ritual function and significance.

In common usage, sometimes the word 'ritual' may imply action done insincerely, stereotyped action followed mechanically or thoughtlessly (cf. Gombrich 1966). The connotation derives from the fixity of ritual, the lack or denial of choice of how to act in the given situation. 'Information can be received only where there is doubt: and doubt implies the existence of alternatives — where choice, selection, or discrimination is called for . . . signals have an information content by virtue of their *potential for making selections*. Signals operate upon the alternatives forming the recipient's doubt; they give power to discriminate amongst, or select from, these alternatives' (Cherry 1966, pp. 170—1). This view of information in communication theory (essentially a quantitative one) also lies behind the principle applied by some linguists to meaning, viz. that meaning implies choice (Lyons 1972, pp. 70—3). By analogy therefore the lack of freedom to deviate from the acts enjoined for the ritual, or to change them so as to fit some particular message or occasion, would deny those actions a power to communicate information which otherwise they might have had. Bloch (1974) has reasoned from this to urge that the formality of ritual is a device by which the units of ritual come to 'drift out of meaning', and lose their potential to inform or carry messages, gaining instead the social and emotional force, illocutionary force, deriving from traditional authority and its exercise, from respect for it or submission to it.

It would follow from this that we ought to pay attention to the ifs and buts in people's statement of the rules for procedure in ritual. They may imply choices and a potential for conveying information denied where there are no alternatives, and the first step taken must inevitably and always lead to the whole sequence. Social changes of the many kinds that have happened within a short time to the Gnau impose the need for adaptations. They call into question how what their fathers taught them may be relevant to their present circumstances. What they choose to preserve of their ritual institutions, what they alter or adapt, may therefore reveal something more about the aims they give or gave for doing them, also perhaps something more about what they mean or meant. Change has come within a short space of time. Past practice can still be remembered and compared with present practice.

They know they have changed the rites of puberty. They do not do them quite the same on each occasion. Not only are some parts left out but also there have always been subsidiary rules such as the ones to provide for substitutes if the mother's brother should not choose to act or the mother be dead, choices of which particular man would hold the boy, bleed for the girl, etc. What they did for Geryik (see pp. 75—7) was not the same as what they did for Wowulden (pp. 77—8). The reason they gave for putting on a *waipət* head-dress for Wowulden was that he had never had any schooling, had not gone to mission services — his father set him an example in keeping away from such things. When it came time for him to have the rite, they urged that he should follow the traditional way and have the *waipǝt* and the hunting *gǝplagǝp*. He had been brought up as a *buskanaka* 'a bush native'. The choice involved discrimination on their part of what belonged to their heathen (*haitan*) past. For they argue that the reason for the differences in how they do the rites now is that they are no longer *haitan* or should not be so. Part of what they used to do was intended to make men fierce and headstrong, ready to fight, and it made them so. Now, however, they must sit down peacefully, obedient to the general law that restrains their independence, so some parts of the rites must be given up.

The attitudes to that past are ambivalent. In one frame of thought the contrast of the present with the past is one between a time when they were wilful, self-sufficient, fierce, impetuous and feared, and now, when men are like women, submissive and docile, and puny. In another frame of thought, they contrast the old men who do not understand what is going on around them with the younger men who do. These are the ones who must decide for the future, they have the *savoir-faire*, and understand how to deal with administrative officers, speak Pidgin well. The old men are bewildered and stupid (*long-long*): they urge them to waste their efforts and time in making yam gardens to give away in exchanges, instead of growing rice and planting coffee to 'pull in the one shilling'. If the dichotomy should seem partly one of age, nostalgia for the past, versus enthusiasm for the future, it is nonetheless an ambivalence partly shared by the older men who also feel that the younger men should take on the jobs of councillor and committeeman; should decide for them, not the old men themselves. The younger men must go out to find money, try new enterprises, build a fence for cows; these are things the village needs, and they themselves do not know about such things, nor would they be competent to make a success of them. The younger men, contrariwise, also boast of the village in the past, of the men like heroes, their impetuous fierceness, the game that once abounded, and what great hunters men were then. If most young men desire to see change at home and the arrival of things they have seen at the coast, they also swagger when dressed in the headdress, scent and feathers of the past, and speak with pride of the magnificence of their rites if they should put them on, gloat with satisfaction on the number of yams they have planted to present to their affines.

The choice to adapt is an explicit one in respect of some things they have abandoned: for example, the decision not to use the *wailtaro* aroids which were connected with fighting and killing, the decision to forget that success in killing and fighting was intertwined with success in hunting as motive for some parts of the rites for boys. Other changes have probably retrospectively coloured what they did before — for example, the abandoning of the men's headdress. In the old days, they say the recruiters used to cut off the men's hair and headdress before they marched them off for the plantations dressed in a new *laplap*. The change of appearance was a pointer to the other things to which they were going off. It came to be an outward sign of conformity with what was new. As the people living round them gave up traditional dress, so the headdress implied the lack of contact with progress. And in the end retention of the headdress almost came to be a mark of defiance by those few men who still persisted in wearing it, refusing to go with the tide. They gave it up at last, though even now it is not hard to tell by appearance who were among the last to give it up. In retrospect, the headdress is associated with past times, with a wilful rejection of change, and with the qualities of fierceness and fighting that were important then.

They have had to suppress or give up some of the values of the past: men have had to divert a stream of ambition and pride away from fighting success to hunting success, and even so, the possibilities of travel, of using shotguns, organising beats, and the growing scarcity of game, have altered some of the character of hunting. For women, things have changed less. The rites of puberty are done much the same as they were before except for differences of decoration dependent on conformity to the general change in appearance – they no longer shave off their head hair, or wear nose ornaments or leg-bands as they used to. The changed significance of shells as valuables has led to the shell pubic apron (*timalyi'ep bifaŋ*) being borrowed and worn as a decorative sign, instead of a new one being given to each girl; trade beads (called *wapeiyagas* in Gnau) are put on the arms and neck for decoration instead of shells and shell arm-bands. In terms of function, money substitutes for shells within the rites in the presentations for the first children. The old colonial shillings, which had holes through them, were tied to the *waipət* or hung from ears in the rites, but they are no longer.

An explicit emphasis on traditional practice is strong and is highlighted in the rites. It is bound to the sense of following what their fathers taught them. A child does not come to look like a grown-up through being decorated, but like someone of the past, people who are dead. Nowadays, that aspect is pointed up by the possibilities for doing otherwise. There are other vessels that might be used to cook the *wa'agəp* in, so the decision to take a clay pot (*malpə*) for it is more explicitly a conscious choice to follow past precedent, and it may cost a little effort to obtain one, given the relative scarcity of clay pots now. That it may require a little effort, or seem strange to have to bother, pulls attention to the choice and what might be a reason for it. It may serve to prompt a question like the question of the *Ma nishtana* inscribed in the Haggadah to be asked by the youngest child at table on the Jewish Eve of Passover, 'Why is this night different from all other nights?' to which the answer begins: 'We were Pharaoh's bondmen in Egypt: and the Lord Our God brought us out therefrom with a mighty hand and an outstretched arm.' The sense of an identity and attachment to a past becomes more explicit in a situation where things have become different, and a general conformity with progress and change abolishes those distinctions of identity, appearance, style of life that used to mark the people of this area of tiny, almost autonomous, village polities. What becomes heightened is the turning to the past for guidance, to a past not shared by others as the present is, a past providing grounds for some pride in a particular identity that is compromised and diminished in their present circumstances. This, at least, is how I understand the mood of joyful declaration expressed in excited behaviour, particularly by the older men, immediately after completing the bleeding, spitting and decoration (see pp. 77, 79, 84). What they had done was something good which came to them from their fathers as a heritage, not something picked up or borrowed from strangers, but properly theirs, something set for them ancestrally and for no one else. The relation of what they did was the relation of token to type, and the type was what helped to give them a distinctive identity. As if they were to forget their language and speak only a Pidgin English indistinguishable from that of other people round them, so if they should give up all their ritual institutions they would lose much of what makes them a people different from the others round them, who look the same and live the same. I suppose that men generally have some impulse or desire to discover a distinctive identity for themselves; and finding it, will take pride in it. The quotations from their conversations that I have translated in chapter 3 convey this much more powerfully than words of mine.

Another sense of time and change is granted by rites. It comes out of the formal rules for performance which, having first established a pattern for repetition, then require actors to fulfil the roles. The fixity in what should be done, which would link the present to the past denying change, serves also to heighten realisation that things are not exactly the same as before, for the people who fill the different roles must change. I was once the child who asked the question *Ma nishtana* and this is now my son who asks it. By the fixing of a form for repetition so as to identify what is to be done now with what was done before, demanding attention to correct performance, memory is alerted and may be made sensitive to change and continuity in a way that usually escapes us in the inconstancies and turns of ordinary life. Actions are, as it were, stilled and caught by memory as by a snapshot; and when they come to be repeated, the old picture and the new are not quite the same. The power of repetition to evoke a sense of change and continuity may work with force occasionally in ordinary life in the way that Proust described in connection with the madeleine, and his stumble on a paving stone (Proust 1954, I, 43–8, III, 866–7). But my point may come over more clearly from this passage about school visits to a museum (the Museum of Natural History, New York) in *The Catcher in the Rye*:

The best thing, though, in that museum, was that everything always stayed right where it was. Nobody'd move. You could go there a hundred thousand times, and that Eskimo would still be just finished catching those two fish, the birds would still be on their way south, the deers would still be drinking out of that water-hole, with their pretty antlers and their pretty, skinny legs, and that squaw with the naked bosom would still be weaving that same blanket. Nobody'd be different. The only thing that would be different would be *you*. Not that you'd be so much older or anything. It wouldn't be that, exactly. You'd have an overcoat on this time. Or the kid that was your partner in line the last time had got scarlet fever and you'd have a new partner. Or you'd have a substitute taking the class, instead of Miss Aigletinger. Or you'd heard your mother and father having a terrific fight in the bathroom. Or you'd just passed by one of those puddles in the street with gasoline rainbows in them. I mean you'd be *different* in some way. I can't explain what I mean. And even if I could, I'm not sure I'd feel like it. (Salinger 1958, pp. 127–8)

Rites which fix by rule a duty to repeat them may exploit that power of evocation and the pleasant emotions or nostalgia that people often feel with past experience recollected. Familiarity may partly lie behind the pleasure they derive from doing the rites, the sense of continuity that may produce a kind of confidence by establishing points of attachment or stability in a changing world. At the same time, things are different, and those changes the Gnau have made to how they do them, the appearances of the people taking part, do all point only the more strongly to the differences for those who knew the rites in the past; for they are meant to be the same, are called the same; yet they are not.

The rites of puberty have as their central theme that of successful growth and development in the individual. Many of the values connected with that theme, such as the desire for good growth, marriage, children, remain little altered by the social changes of the last generation or so. The reasons and grounds for doing them have been less affected by change than the grounds for doing some other of their rites. The differential response in ritual to the pressures of change can be seen by comparing the maintenance of the rites of puberty to the near-abandonment of the rites of Tambin for initiation of the young men.

The Gnau experience of change is no doubt similar in general type to that of many other inland people in New Guinea. The old men remember the Malay bird-hunters. Then in the 1930s recruiters began to work in the Lumi area nearer to them and they heard of them from neighbours. By 1936, a recruiter had come as far as Nəmbugil and Də'aiwusel, but not to Rauit or Mandubil (Marshall 1938, pp. 57–65). In September 1935, a big earthquake caused devastation in the area. After it a man with hair 'like cassowary feathers' passed through their village – Masta Kon (*konkon*, a Chinese man). In 1938, G. A. V. Stanley came; he was surveying for oil and he is remembered as the first whiteskin they ever saw – Masta Mak (the man who set up marks). In 1938 or 1939, six Rauit men left the village to find a recruiter and they worked in the gold fields at Wau. They returned. Another batch left to find work. Then came the terrible epidemic of dysentery in which many died (Lewis 1975, pp. 67–8; 1977). The men who had left to find work did not return because the war in the Pacific had begun (1942–5) and only after it was ended did the survivors return to recount their adventures. In the meantime, the village heard rumours of the war; they saw a monstrous and terrifying thing fly over the village, heard the explosions of a few bombs dropped near villages to the north of them. But no Japanese or Allied soldiers came into Gnau territory.

In retrospect, the earthquake and the epidemic of dysentery marked the turning point of time, and they speak of them as signs that were foretelling change to come, though they did not understand their message then. The men who returned after the war had been told at Aitape to teach the new order of law in the village, and one was given a hat in sign that he was *luluai* (the appointed village headman) and responsible for order in the village. But things went on much the same. The patrol post was set up at Lumi by 1949 and a first patrol was sent to Rauit to apprehend some village men who had murdered a man and his wife belonging to another village. The patrol was not properly armed. It reached the village, was threatened, and retreated. In 1951, a strong patrol returned and outfaced the village. The patrol camped on the highest hamlets (Pakuag and Wimalu) for some time while men who had abandoned the village came to menace them at nightfall and shoot at them. The patrol burnt the weapons they found in the men's houses, and also some houses, but left without bloodshed. From that time dates the decision of the village of Rauit to submit to the new order. The first census of the village was made in 1952.

For a while after that, the difference in life in the villages was that they knew they must not fight or kill other people, that they ran the risk of gaol if they should disobey. Men could leave to find work and money at plantations in spells of contract labour that lasted for two years or more of total absence and silence. Head taxes were imposed. They had to find money to pay them. A patrol would visit them about once a year to census them, hear disputes, check on order in the village and see that they complied with instructions about how houses should be built, paths cleared, people buried, latrines made, and perhaps to fine them. The patrol office at Lumi had to organise another show of force in 1956 when mutinous Gnau villagers refused to pay the tax.

Then in 1958 the Christian Missions in Many Lands came to found a large missionary settlement on flat land close to the river Opan at the base of Anguganak Bluff, near the village of Yankok. The mission was called Anguganak Mission. (Anguganak is the proper Au name of the village on the bluff above it; I refer to this village by its Gnau name Nəmbugil to distinguish it from the mission station.) The mission was planned as a large one. An airstrip was cleared and gradually a whole establishment built. For villagers in this area, it was the major sign and agent of change in their lives, bringing among them white families, opportunities for work and trade, schooling, etc. The airstrip, a hangar, a trade store, an assembly house for religious services, a sawmill and workshops and houses for mission personnel were built over the years. When the mission was set up, one of the missionaries who came there was a doctor, and under his direction the mission set out to provide a medical service for the local population. Trained nurses came as mission personnel to help with the work of the hospital he built. He began to train a few local men as aid-post orderlies later when the school had begun to produce people who could read and write in Pidgin.

The Anguganak station made itself a central place in the area. The mission required garden produce for its personnel and the hospital and the school, so a marketing system was introduced by which surrounding villages were allocated different days on which they were to bring produce for sale. Villagers found they could obtain money by selling food. They found limited opportunities for earning cash by taking jobs and doing casual labour. The trade store was the source of new goods. The airflights to and from Anguganak brought mail and took some men off to plantation labour and brought them back. In short the station was the centre of evident local changes and news. There was, and is, much coming and going there by people with something to sell or buy, some business there, or just curious to see what progress was and to chat with people of other villages. It is a place where villagers may meet and mix on neutral ground, and there was no such neutral ground before the mission came. At Ningil, which is a few miles further north, a Catholic (Franciscan) mission was also established in 1958. It is on a rather smaller scale and without a hospital.

The villages surrounding each mission station have tended to benefit materially according to how close they are. The villagers nearest have tried to make the most of their opportunity to get jobs, which they felt belonged by right to them and not to people further off. The mission personnel, aware of such competition, inter-village rivalry, jealousy and individual greed, tried to steer a difficult middle course between such claims, strongly felt by those nearest them, and the wish to be fair and do something to help a wide range of people. The Gnau villages are not among the villages which have been most involved in mission work and influence. The three Gnau villages cannot be reached from either station except by climbing the steep, sheer Anguganak Bluff, and for a long time there were no easy paths up it. One of the Gnau villages is on the top edge of the bluff closer to Anguganak Mission than the other two: it has had more contact. Rauit and Mandubil people say that they feel disadvantaged compared to other villages because they have not benefitted, being so much further away and the path tiring. Yet they feel that they have a rightful claim to benefit because, when the missions were first established, they sent men down to work to clear them and make the airstrips.

The Franciscan priest visited the Gnau-speaking villages once every one or three months, and after 1960 a local Catholic catechist from a village elsewhere in the Lumi sub-district was placed in each village. The catechists in the Gnau villages for one reason or another did not manage to settle down and stay very long. Evangelical teaching by the C.M.M.L. began at Rauit in about 1965 and consisted of a day visit once every month or two, but these stopped in 1968. A few boys attended school at Ningil or Anguganak but none regularly for long from Rauit or Mandubil. From 1963 onwards a nurse from Anguganak Mission came to visit each village about monthly to weigh and immunise babies.

Administration by annual patrol and census with *luluai* and *tultul* appointed in each village continued until 1967. In October 1967, the first elections for local government councillors were held in the area. As the villagers took part in the Lumi Local Government Council, the *luluai* and *tultul* system was abolished. Villages were combined in groups of two or three to elect a councillor and committeeman who were expected to oversee local affairs and attend the monthly meeting of the Lumi Local Council. In 1964, the villagers had voted in the first elections to membership of the House of Assembly. In 1971, a patrol office was opened at Yankok near the Anguganak station. Outwardly village life and subsistence remain relatively self-contained apart from the experience of plantation labour and the attempts to earn cash by planting rice, which most men try, but without great enthusiasm or success, for such rice as they produce must all be carried on their backs down to Yankok for sale. A few are trying to grow coffee.

But the appearance of New Guinean administrative officers among them, and the pace of change in self-government, has awakened greater interest and speculation about change than was apparent before in the Gnau villages. Independence was celebrated at the Yankok patrol office in 1975. Work on the all-weather road from Wewak on the coast to Lumi, so long planned and awaited, had come close to Yankok by then. The road was planned to pass by the station. The Gnau villagers decided with some consensus that they must send boys for schooling lest they should find the sons of rival villages set over them administratively. This move was largely organised by the younger men who have young sons. Because they have known the priest of Ningil Mission for many years — he built it and has visited their villages over the years, whereas the mission personnel of Anguganak station often change and they rarely go to the villages of Rauit or Mandubil — the people of Rauit chose to send the boys to Ningil Mission school though it is further away and the children had to board there in the week. The Gnau have vacillated in their choice of which mission they will adhere to. It seemed in 1975 that at Rauit and Mandubil they had decided to become Catholic rather than Christian Brethren, while at Dǝ'aiwusel the reverse obtained. A potential dichotomy of villages by religious affiliation was appearing then which did not necessarily follow linguistic boundaries. The missions each created an organisation of participation through Parish and School Councils, an organisational structure additional to, and partly seen by villagers as alternative to, the Local Government Council Structure. From the villagers' point of view, many of the matters they felt it appropriate to discuss there were similar.

Throughout the time since contact, men have been going off for spells of contract labour at plantations on the coast or islands; this has been the main source for their knowledge of the outside world. The adventures of life at the coast have been a continual topic of revelation, shock, comment and vivid story-telling. Life at the plantations is lived by different rules from village life. The views they formed of white people based on their observation of mission personnel were at variance with the views they came to through contact with white people in towns on the coast, or at the plantations. They have by now seen white men drunk, met them in brothels, drunk with them in the same pubs and on occasions brawled with them. Plantation life exposed them to quite different New Guineas from the ones they knew; it required new patterns of co-operation and organisation. It involved groupings for work under *bosboi*; the organisation of support in fights by district of origin; and more recently, weekend sorties to pubs to get drunk under the care of sober companions; beer- and rum-drinking races and competitive exchanges between batch intakes at the plantations; the creation of fictive kin ties with families in villages neighbouring on the plantations; dances; machines; the sea; music; clothes; buildings; ships; films — a ferment of things there which are beyond the experience of those who never leave the village. In 1974, the first two women of Rauit village ever to leave with their husbands went with them for work on a plantation.

Almost all the men have been to work at a plantation: the exceptions are restricted to men now over fifty years old. The young, who have not gone but have passed puberty, grow impatient to be off. Usually a little drama of departure takes place with the coming of the New Year. I quote from my notes.

The puberty rites of three girls at Pakuag were done in the second week of January 1969. The people had been hunting before for a few weeks in the bush. The day after the rites some young men came to ask me to write a letter for them saying here were the ten men from Rauit whom the Bongos *bosboi*[2] at Nuku had asked a year ago to come. They said that Weibi, the Mandubil councillor, approved of their going off. Last year there had been discussion whether the Nuku *bosboi* had any right to recruit from Rauit, and people had said recruiting was wrong. The *lo* 'law' of the Lumi Council now was that men wanting to go must get permission from their councillor and then present themselves. Some of those now wanting to go were still obviously adolescent. Only one had been before, although whenever a group leaves they choose to send one or two men who have been before to look after them.

2 *Bosboi* here refers to the New Guinean assistant or agent of a white contract-labour recruiter.

The next morning early (16 January), three adolescents from Pakuag walked through the village with their string bags over their shoulders, a coconut, a bamboo tube of sago flour and they set off down the road towards Mandubil. The men sitting eating their morning meal at Watalu (the lower hamlet) made some vague joking remarks about them going off to the plantations. Noise of shouting and dispute from Pakuag. It was Duapo shouting at her married son Matasi that he must not go. Three more young men, with Matasi, went by. A flurry of talk in another part of Watalu. Ramaka, a white towel flamboyantly round his neck, a bamboo tube of sago and a coconut over his shoulder, came by. He had reached Saoga's house, when Dabasu, lowering and determined, came striding down the slope from Pakuag to fetch his young brother back. Seeing Ramaka, without a word he grabbed the bamboo tube and smashed it and the coconut with an axe he carried. No resistance from Ramaka, his clan 'son' (i.e. classificatory [e]BS). Dabasu, lowering and still silent, went on after his younger brother who had by now ten minutes' start. The older men sitting in the dayhouse at Watalu enjoyed this scene hugely and were cracking jokes about it. Ramaka, after a discomfited pause, also silently set off behind Dabasu, empty-handed. Ramaka's smashed food was on the ground. His step-mother went to pick up the broken bamboo of sago flour. A man, laughing, yelled out, 'What are you picking that up for? Leave it for the dogs. Are you a pig to eat food off the ground?' The woman picked it up, disdaining to give him answer.

Within twenty minutes, Dabasu was back with all the young men who had set off. They sat down on the floorboards of a half-built house. I had expected Dabasu to rant and yell at them. Instead he began with a rather sensible lecture to the effect that he wanted them to go off in an orderly fashion, to see the councillor at Mandubil first. Then followed a more wandering discussion with Dabasu reiterating what everyone says, that if a man wants to work on a plantation to find 'one shilling' (*wansiling*) for himself and family, that is his affair (*samting bilong laik bilong man*).

Two or three hours later, nineteen men left for Nuku without going to the councillor. As people said, they were sorry to see them go off, the women especially. Mothers would beg their sons to stay, but the old men are permissive; at least they say it is something for a man's own choice: if he wants to go, let him. The Pakuag young men had said when they were brought back by Dabasu that they were going off just because they were fed up with hearing their elder brothers at Pakuag, especially Dabasu and Daisimbel, taunting them, ridiculing them that they were sitting around at home doing nothing, that they had not gone off to the plantations yet. The others commented that Dabasu had gone off after them to drag them back so as to make it clear that it was not the older men who were chasing them off, but that if they went, it must be because they wanted to go.

The next day, a group of mothers and sisters set off after the young men carrying food for them. They caught them up outside Nuku. The men told them who had been chosen by the recruiting agent and the women cried for the ones who were going, left the men recruited to wait, and returned a few days later with the disappointed ones who had been rejected because they looked too young. A few young sisters daubed on mourning clay for their brothers who were going off.

A week later came a rumour that the Lumi *bosboi* was looking for recruits. Men from two other hamlets set off. From Bi'ip, a group of men who had missed the Nuku departure had been getting tobacco and food ready for this. They had wrapped up their bows and arrows for long-term storage the evening before. Women from their hamlets made a great gathering just outside the village on the path to wail at their departure. Tuawei went through them saying he was going, not to the plantation, but just taking a message from me to Yankok. This was to trick his mother who had indeed spoken to me a few days before about her fear that he might run off. The group in fact returned two days later, having found out on the road to Lumi that all the places had been filled already. This was a relief to some of their mothers or wives, notably one wife with four young children, one of whom was newborn. The group had taken a side road to Lumi, not the main one, because of fear of sorcery. People on the road had asked to buy game from them finding that they came from Rauit. One man, laughing, said he had sold a bit of flying fox that was near to stinking, but the people there had wanted the meat so badly. The trip had not been a complete fiasco.

During this time and just after, there was all the little detail to discuss of who went off, the trickery of how they went and why. K., who had only come back two months before, did not want the wife his father had arranged for him to marry. She went back to her father to wait. S., who was quite a senior man, went ostensibly to accompany the women, then swapped in place of his lineage 'son' M., refused because he looked too young and small to the recruiting agent. W., already married for three or four years with no plantation spell to his credit, was very keen to go: his wife with a baby and the payments he would have to make due to come up. D. went off to look after some of his clan 'sons', but also the threatened policeman came to fetch his wife just after he had gone because she would not bring her malnourished child voluntarily for supplementary feeding to the hospital. K., a middle-aged man, had nearly gone off, had stood up to go, but his decrepit mother and aunt screamed at him about his responsibilities towards his seven children and he felt 'ashamed' and sat down. R. had had a ticking off from his father for being a loafer the week before, the ticking off connected perhaps with a girl's rejection of him as a husband, etc., etc.

Following the departures there are gatherings of sympathy with the families which have lost a son. People sometimes put on clay when they go to these as for a mourning visit. They do the same when someone goes to gaol. Sisters may vow to eat only dry sago (*lawə'ut*) while their brothers are away — again

a similarity to mourning. It is only very recently that they have begun to exchange rare letters with those away for two years at the coast; before that it was
a long period of silence with no news.

In the last chapter I mentioned (pp. 188—9) how the Gnau found a certain
parallel between plantation labour and their initiation rites which they drew on
to invent rules for the disposal of plantation earnings. On the surface the parallel
is one of elements like the absence, seclusion, the silence and invisibility of those
who go, for they disappear completely from the village scene. The anxiously
awaited moment of their return is marked by their mothers, sisters and wives
going to meet them in joy, dancing their feet and crying as they draw them back
into the village, just as they used to do at the moment of the final celebration,
the magnificent coming out from Tambin seclusion, and resembling it even to
the extent that some mothers wear the finery of men for it, holding bows to
call their sons back to them and honour them. They return at the end, changed
and grown up. The new clothes of the returned plantation-worker, his hair
maybe peroxided, the scent, all are *bilas* 'finery' in their eyes. They look sleek
and filled-out. Many of the near-adolescent and younger men have grown up and
are more mature after the two years away. They do not look the same as people
remember them. But the people also seem to have an impulse to think them
changed and grown up which struck me most when I returned after five years'
absence to be greeted over and over again by remarks on how I had grown, how
much bigger, fatter and stronger I looked, more like a man. They think of the
special food men eat at the plantations — all that *tinmit* 'corned beef', *tinpis*
'tinned fish', *rais* 'rice' — luxury foods at home — when they want to explain
why men grow there. It is rather like all the fresh meat they used to be given to
eat in Tambin seclusion.

There are other items in which what they do suggests a parallel to things
they did in Tambin. The actions are designed from a sense of appropriateness by
function, rather than from any explicit intention to make the experience of
plantation labour an imitation of the rites of initiation. The matching came after
the making. It is a matter of common prudence to send with the young when
they first go some older men who have been before. But in accordance with
established patterns of responsibility, these older men should be father's younger
brothers or clan 'elder brothers' or the 'mother's brothers' to go with them to
look after their safety and guide them there. The same motive once guided how
they saw the role of senior men looking after the young men during Tambin
seclusion, guiding them through that period because they were experienced in
it. The mother's brother protected his sister's son at certain moments from the
rigours and pain of beatings by nettles. Seeds of a parallel perceived lie behind
the actions of the men who feel it appropriate on first arrival at the plantation
to bleed themselves from the penis into the sea. They say they do it to keep
well there, but the timing of the action resembles that of the initial bleeding

on entry into seclusion in the rites of Tambin. Some men bleed for their sister's sons at the plantation and give them the blood there. This is a more explicit imitation of what they did in Tambin. A batch of men going through a shared experience, and forming a bond of friendship in consequence, is another element in which to see a similarity; it is reinforced by the organisation of work-lines or gangs at the plantation. Chat about plantation life is frequently punctuated by the lists of those who went together, just as they give lists of those who went through Tambin together. They do not become real *wusai* to each other by virtue of having worked together, but the friendship bond of being a *wanwok* 'one work' does endure. I remember a rare visit we made to a distant village in the Maimai bush where, saying that we came from Rauit, one member of our small party was mistaken for a *wanwok* by a man in that village. My Rauit companion rather meanly did well out of the generous hospitality shown him in consequence. By addressing the other as *wanwok*, the Rauit man found it easy both to dissemble his initial ignorance of the other man's name and to act like the right man. It provided a fine story afterwards.

Viewed from one perspective, the various elements I have mentioned suggest that the people have used the pattern of practice in the Tambin rites to help them to understand and adapt to plantation labour. The rules about protection, care while there, the earnings, the ways they greet returned workers, represent some little movements to recast the new experience into a familiar mould, a kind of assimilation by which the stress they give to the growing up of young men who go away becomes more understandable. There are, of course, other very clear reasons why men want to go away to work, the adventure of dis- covering new things, the need and desire for money which they cannot earn at home, the wish to do what they have heard so much talk about and to equal the experience of other men. These provide sufficient motive for their actions and perhaps reasons why younger men should go before they have got large families to look after at home. They are strong and energetic, and anyway the plantation owners want strong young men for hard, unskilled labour.

But we might also consider what has been the influence of plantation labour on practice of the Tambin initiation rites. The timing, absence, and the pressures which led them to see correspondences, or to mould them so, did something to assimilate the two experiences to a common pattern. With the resemblance in pattern half apparent, the question of a similarity in function arises. They argue that they have not really given up the rites of Tambin, it is only that they have not done them recently, partly because they know or think that the adminis- tration and the missionaries would disapprove. Before, in the 1950s, when they began to prepare for them they were told to stop by a man who had been active and influential in the cargo movement (see Lewis 1975, p. 133). They think other villages would consider them to be showing once again how heathen they still were if they should do them. In the early 1960s and early 1970s, they prepared to do them, but some upsetting deaths decided them to stop. They also say the rites are harder to organise now when there are always some men away at the plantations; one father wants them to wait for the return of his son, another wants them to start because his son has just come back. Then again, the rites require a lot of time, organisation and the devotion of much effort. Already the men spend so long away at the plantation.

But these are not reasons that would stop them from doing them if they really wished to. I think the truth is rather that plantation labour has come to substitute for the rites of Tambin and substitutes for them in terms of function and experience. If the general purpose of the rites of Tambin was once to prepare them for their future lives and to form in them, and attach them to, values that should guide them as men through maturity, then it may be that they sense now that the Tambin rites no longer truly fulfil that purpose. The values and feelings evoked, created and instilled by experience of the Tambin rites belong to a past world. They do not fit a young man for the future as they used to. But plantation labour does so better: it provides them with a heightened sense of their present circumstances, revealing more about the course of change and the conditions to which they need to adapt. If Tambin once served to some extent to mould men's values and give direction to their striving and prepare them for it, now plantation labour, which like those rites is a dramatic formative experience, substitutes for them. It substitutes not because the people have set out purposefully and with hard-headed realism to analyse their present situation and reform their institutions, but because the labour experience meets their needs better. The needs, though strongly felt, are but half formulated and understood by them. The experience of plantation labour answers to them, releases a response in a way that Tambin can no longer do. The situation is one of flux, not plain and simple, nor motivated by a single impulse or purpose. It is more a question of whether doing something is worth the bother and the effort. If, as observer from outside, it seems to me that the first spell of plantation labour serves a rather similar function to the one once served by initiation in the Tambin rites, and therefore it has come to supplant the rites and substitute for them, it does not seem so to them. The two things are obviously not the same. When the time for the return of the men who have been away comes near, the mood of excitement and anticipation reawakens people in the village to think of putting on again the rites of Tambin. It is just because the young men are going to come back that the conversation of the older men flickers with doubts about whether they are not failing in their duties both to their fathers and ancestors, who left them something to carry on which they have not, and to their sons to whom they have not shown something that they learnt was precious, a source of pride and strength (cf. pp. 48–57). So at this time of waiting and in that mood, they generate the plan to put the rites on again lest they be lost and their sons left empty-handed. That is why I have heard the whole song of Tambin sung, for they began to practise it, and on two nights they sang it through

214

caught by the swell of enthusiasm, guilt and good intent; but the mood petered out in the various distractions of the arrival of the men come back.

The rites of Tambin are also explicitly addressed to the great spirit Tambin, a form of worship by which the spirit is brought into the village, localised and concentrated there. The rites provide a means of access to that spirit and its power which the Gnau share; it is something they know how to approach and do which others do not. If they abandon the rites, they abandon something that contributes to their identity as a distinctive people. Perhaps because the rites and the beliefs about the spirit Tambin are too closely linked to the former way of life, and bound up with the identity of the Gnau, too specific to them, they cannot bend so easily to fit a greatly changed situation; and so they break. If by reason of changed needs, the spell of labour at the plantation comes to substitute for performance of the rites of Tambin, they substitute something common to the experience of the people in all the other villages around them for something that they had before which was distinctive to them. It involves a secularisation of their experience and institutions, a disenchantment of their world, and some loss of their identity. The contrast between the puberty rites which continue and the Tambin rites that are disappearing seems to reflect a difference decided by function and the ability to provoke or release a response: for the one there is no comparably effective substitute; for the other there is. The response is not determined by message and meaning, for the rites do not 'convey information as railway trucks carry coal' (Cherry 1966, p. 171). It is not by some conscious rationalising choice that they are changing, but in response to the inroads of experience, new experiences that supplant those they found and knew before through the rite. In the effort to assimilate that new experience, they have tried a little to make it match the old. Thus insidiously a habit or regularity of work has almost come to substitute for a rite. A rite, some religious beliefs, some part of their former individuality are in the process of being lost. They are adapting to a different world and its demands.

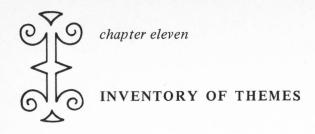

chapter eleven

INVENTORY OF THEMES

A mother feeds her child: we think we understand her action. It is a matter of experience that the sense of understanding other people's actions draws continually on familiar and subjective elements by which we attribute to others states of mind, desire, motive and purpose that we can recognise in ourselves, or feel we could. They help to make these other people's actions intelligible. We impute understanding of the purpose or feelings of the actors to them. It is often implicit and intrinsic in the verbs or words we use to describe human behaviour (e.g. 'announce', 'give', 'feed', 'welcome', 'answer', 'punish'). This is generally so in the description of human behaviour, whatever the writer and his purpose — novelist, historian, anthropologist, journalist, psychologist or philosopher. Description and interpretation of human behaviour are often bound together. Wholly objective descriptions of human behaviour (and 'pure' descriptions of social actions *a fortiori*) are very hard to provide.[1] We do not register human behaviour in a simple objective fashion but we continually seek to recognise and translate it as we perceive it into terms of understanding if we can. We do this without thinking in everyday life; many words we use to think or speak about human behaviour imply such understanding willy-nilly. But it is also a matter of everyday experience that we sometimes find other people's actions hard to understand. The effort of attempting to and failing makes by contrast the interpretative element, which is usually present but implicit, more explicit. The mother feeds her child: a clear description of her actions might suffice for understanding. We draw on a familiarity with that sort of action that

1 See Harris 1964 for a proposal and a theory of how this might be done in the study of culture. His proposed descriptive methods resemble those of the animal behaviourist. Any anthropologist who sought to put them into practice in the field would have to abandon the study of all but a tiny segment of behaviour. The attempt to build up a full analysis of any culture by those methods defies my imagination and belief. The proposal is a theory exemplified in the description and analysis of Mrs Harris frying potatoes. Hinde (1976) discusses how relationship and social structure might be discovered or attributed from data observed with the rigour and objectivity of the animal behaviourist. Chapple and Coon's past — perhaps little regarded — *Principles of Anthropology* (1947) made a brave attempt to formulate the subject matter and content of anthropology in terms of a consistent behaviourism.

216

gives us confidence in guessing what her purpose and feelings are likely to be. But when we see Gnau men smear a girl bright red with betel juice we do not have the same sense of understanding their actions. What people do in rites is often difficult for the stranger to account for satisfactorily, either to himself or to others, in terms of interpretative understanding.

We might say casually that we understood the mother's action as she fed her child. But if we changed our aim so as to make her actions the object of a study seeking a complete explanation of them, we should see the unending immensity of the task and the variety of knowledge we should need in order to be able to account for the reasons and the causes of her actions in terms, say, of maternal feelings, recognition of hunger, food and the properties of matter, etc., and for the particulars of time, place, the manner in which she held the child, her experience and so on. We must accept that a total understanding of her actions is a dream set in a hierarchy of explanation whose various aspects would demand quite different methods of inquiry and explanation. The kind of question that one chooses to ask or to try to answer about her actions will decide a level of inquiry at which some grounds for the actions are to be presumed, and other aspects neglected, excluded from analysis, and not explainable at that level. Each discipline is distinguished by the kinds of question it seeks to answer and the methods by which it tries to make itself competent to do so. Nadel (1951) and Lévi-Strauss (1950) have each tried to identify how they would place social anthropology within a hierarchy of scientific knowledge about human behaviour, and the whole hierarchy of sciences, physical, biological and social.

What is common to all the social sciences and distinctive in them is concern with social action. We cannot abstract any particular individual from his social and historical context: we do not know an isolated non-social man, or human nature without culture, for the natural state of man is social.[2] Therefrom comes the difficulty of separating what is distinctively individual from the social component in human behaviour, and the inverted danger, when considering social action, of supposing that social forces exist independently of individuals and reifying them as things mystical, mysterious and apart from people (on which see, for example, Goldenweiser 1933, pp. 59–67).

People act from desires and motives; they use means to gain their ends in a calculating way. They must take other people into account when they act. They are concerned with what other people will think of their actions and how they will respond to them. Understanding these internal dimensions to human action is a necessary part of understanding social action and its causes. The distinctive emphasis on subjective understanding of the meaningful connections in human action was clearly made by Weber for the social sciences and also by Jaspers in

2 On the psychological aspects of society, and the insufficiency and error of a science of psychology which putatively abstracts the individual from his social and historical context, see Fletcher 1971, sect. 3.

his treatise on psychopathology. 'Sociology is a science which attempts the interpretive understanding of social action in order thereby to arrive at a causal explanation of its course and effects' (Weber 1947, p. 88). By seeking to understand people's purposes and motives, and the meanings they give to their actions, we may learn some reasons for what they do. The social scientist cannot, like the natural scientist, disengage himself from concern with the subjective dimensions of human conduct. But there are also aspects of human behaviour which show regularities or features which vary concomitantly with others and are associated in a way that may be studied objectively and without regard for the subjective understanding of the actors. Durkheim (1938) sought to provide the rules of method by which these sorts of causal connections might be found in the study of social behaviour. Jaspers (1963) distinguished such causal connections from the meaningful connections within a general frame of theory and method in the explanation of human behaviour.

In his discussion of Mauss's *fait total social*, Lévi-Strauss (1950, pp. xxiv–xxx) gives a special place to social anthropology within the social sciences, by virtue of the otherness and strangeness of the societies and cultures studied. We cannot see our own society objectively because we were born in it and have taken in unaware its biases and assumptions. Our own society of reference is only one among a multitude of possible other ones. If there are attributes of the human mental constitution which determine our social actions and cultural perceptions just as the modalities of sensation determine ineluctably how we perceive some aspects of the world, we may recognise their properties and variety better through the study of what is unfamiliar, for it presents us with the effects and expressions of these attributes, or the outcomes of their operations, as objects for study. Subjective study will not reveal them to us: by introspection we cannot hope to detect the unconscious determinants and constraints on our own social action and perception: these are, by hypothesis, biases and assumptions we are unaware of. The anthropologist, having dissected and separated his data, may ask himself at the end of his analysis whether he can now draw them together and still understand them subjectively as an experience that he might accept in himself, for he must recognise that the other man and his actions, which he has taken as an object of study, and taken apart to try to understand, is another man whom he might have been himself, and that that other society is a society in which he might have been born, whose values and assumptions he might have held. We have a common human constitution.

These general remarks suggest (1) that we must try to find out what purpose or motives people give for their actions and what meanings they attach to them and (2) that these, if they are sincerely given, may be understood as reasons for their actions; but (3) there will always be causes, as distinct from reasons, for their actions of which the actors are unaware; and (4) the explanations that actors may give for what they do may not be sufficient explanation for them, because (5) people cannot necessarily formulate accurately in words explanations

218

for what they do, and do not necessarily have unbiassed or comprehensive insight into their own motives and purposes, nor do they always need to pay attention to them, or examine them in the course of everyday life. Therefore, the anthropologist observing them (6) may seek to interpret independently why they speak of their motives and purposes in the way they do, why they choose to emphasise or formulate their meanings in a particular manner; and (7) may seek to find causes for them which the people do not recognise, as well as those effects or consequences of their actions and declarations which go unrecognised by the actors. But (8) the anthropologist must also note that his recording and observation of behaviour and speech involves selection and a form of translation in which it is very easy to introduce interpretation of motive and purpose unwittingly as well as explicitly. His perception and understanding are also selective and potentially biassed. The aim of theory is to help him formulate the questions he asks more explicitly so that he will not mistake the level, significance, assumptions and limitations of such answers as he may think he finds (see Collingwood 1944, ch. V, on the logic of question and answer). The aim of method is to find an appropriate way to answer those questions he may have in mind.

The act of classifying types of social action is purposive and will set limits to the kinds of answer that may come out of an inquiry that assumes those categories (see Nadel 1951, pp. 129–36). That is a first reason for examining what criteria lie behind calling some types of social action ritual actions. Familiarity may enable us to understand some actions that other people do by imputing a purpose or meaning to them (as in the example of a mother feeding her child). As observers we do not feel a need to ask for reasons for the familiar things they do, nor do we feel a need to comment on them and interpret them when we describe them. When ideas or actions are strange, we make an effort to find reasons and obtain explanations. The pull towards difference and strangeness may distort the balance of our observations and analyses: what is familiar and the same as what we know in ourselves and at home risks being understood and passed over without comment. Observers vary in how they pay attention to similarities rather than to differences. The criterion of rationality does not enable us to distinguish ritual action from other sorts of action. The attempt to use it requires us to treat social action as though we, the observers, were able to judge it and the relations between ends and means objectively. Many social actions do not fall simply and clearly into only one field or type of activity: the actor's motives and purposes may be multiple. What distinguishes custom is the awareness on the part of the actors of convention or rules socially agreed on, and ritual must fall within the field of custom. Within that field, the types of social action are various and range from actions that seem brief matters of politeness to the complex, long sequences of certain religious rites. A classification of actions within that field might involve the construction of ideal types, and the deliberate selection of certain features of social action to make a model of which an understanding and causal explanation is sought. I have not tried to classify custom into defined types or to construct the ideal type of ritual. Instead I have directed my attention rather to the question of deciding how, when we observe something we are not familiar with, we should direct our efforts at interpretative understanding. I argue that we require positive grounds before we assume that we need to look for a symbolism or expression that is not apparent or explicit in the minds of the actors or in the reasons that they give for what they do. We require positive grounds so as to avoid a waste of misdirected effort, and the lures of too-free choice that may lead us in unbound speculation to light on what we want to find. What seems strange to an outsider, and appeals to him for further examination, must be measured against his habits and experience. If we depend on what preoccupies him, or on what is evoked in his mind, we depend on something that may differ greatly from the responses of the people he set out to study. We should pay attention to their conventions of performance, the intensity of the demand to follow a set pattern, the rules governing participation. Obligations of status and relationship, and connected values, may be linked with these rules, or be epitomised in them. The people's customs may be linked to their values as practice is to theory. We should identify the type that set the pattern, the direction of address in the performance (to the public, the performers, a watching spirit, etc.) and the forms in which those addressed may respond. These aspects of communication, seen from the actors' perspective, help to distinguish between genres of custom, to weight what we must give attention to. I have tried to indicate something of the differential effects of such alerting devices through my description of what I saw when the rites were done.

The fixity or formality of procedural ruling may lead to actions coming to have an explicit meaning that without the ruling they would not have. Operative actions (see Skorupski 1976, pp. 93–106) bring about a consequence which takes effect when the action is performed in due form by the right person(s). The ability of the person to perform a given operative act in given circumstances is a matter of his social characteristics. The right to wear a phallocrypt is conferred on a boy by duly going through the rite of puberty. The rite sets up and cancels certain rules in respect of the person who undergoes it. And the rules specify who may appropriately act in the various roles in the rites, setting the conditions for their performance by specified social characteristics. Action within the rites may be done with an explicit view to the incurring or discharge of an obligation. The obligative character of these actions is emphasised by formality. These aspects of purpose and meaning in their actions are given by the rules: by fixity of convention they introduce a possibility of understanding them and deviations from them. Discussion of this epitomising function was developed mainly in chapter 5 with reference to the maintenance and discharge of rights and obligations in an oral culture, and to the attention given to performance in the rites; then developed with reference to deviations from the rules and the uncertainty of interpretation in chapter 9. A second argument related to the fixity of ruling is concerned with how fixity may affect a possible cognitive or propositional meaning ascribed to ritual actions by the actors. It is a facet of the larger general problem of interpreting the meanings of the rites.

Here the main stresses in my argument on understanding and interpretation are, first, that the anthropologist is not free to speculate according to his fancies on the meaning of the rites, for then he may tell about himself and his preoccupations rather than those of the people he would wish to understand, and secondly, since 'meaning' is a word of such easy virtue (see Cherry 1966, pp. 114–17; Leech 1974, pp. 1–27), we would do well to be wary of its temptations. It is useful to distinguish expression from communication and to examine in what sense we may speak of code or message or communication in ritual. Styles of ritual vary in the clarity with which the meaning of any symbolism in them is taught or identified. It is a matter of empirical observation that people may give varied interpretations of the meaning of their actions; or may be uncertain about them, or say they cannot find one. We may say that people perceive a meaning or intend one, but not that things apart from people have meanings in themselves independently of someone's understanding them. By a curious usage, some anthropological writing seems to imply that rites or symbols have a meaning in themselves objectively present, sometimes even a single correct meaning, waiting there to be detected. Or else they imply that it was once someone's intention to set that meaning in the rites, and they recover it. The argument may be related to the notion of transmitting messages. Such arguments on the communication of messages in code seem to me tenuous when there is no evidence on the part of the actors who do the rites that they understand or interpret them so. The 'meanings' provided may be a revelation of the anthropologist rather than the people.

The analogy of ritual performance to a play suggests that we should consider response to stimuli as well as that intellectual component we might call the propositional meaning or communicated message. If we do this, we do not become entangled with putatively 'unconscious' meanings darkly understood but unverbalisable by the actor, yet recognised by the observer. We accept that people respond to the events of ritual with feelings of enjoyment, excitement, puzzlement, pain, etc. and that rites may be designed to produce such feelings. Such responses may weight the attention people give to what they do and the extent to which they try to make sense of them in intellectual terms. I have tried to show how different responses are produced and vary with experience in the discussion of *nəm beirkatidəm*. Aptness of association, and variation in how explicitly people recognise the associations, the evocative power of things used or done, lead to variations in response and detected meaning. The fact that responses and meanings may be evoked variously, may be left open or unfixed, is an empirical observation. The assumption that there is a single (right) meaning given intrinsically by the things used or done would leave quite unanswered the further problem, raised in relation to penis-bleeding, that peoples of other cultures give a different or specific meaning to the act. Why some should see it and not others is a question to be answered. Meaning is present not in things but in people's minds. The Gnau clearly understand as symbolic some of their actions and expressions. The variety of meanings that may be attached to a single set motif (or symbol) was well studied by Boas and his pupils in the field. They took some decorative motifs which could be found among many different Plains Indian tribes, investigated them and reported how symbols may be very abbreviated and conventionalised, may be quite arbitrary in terms of representation, i.e. an idea may be attached to a symbol by convention and not because of any imitative representation or iconic power intrinsic to the motif; the same motif may be given different meanings by one individual in different settings; different individuals within one tribe may give different meanings to the same motif in the same setting; different tribes may fix different meanings to the same motif (Boas 1955, pp. 88–143). To attribute then a single right meaning intrinsic to the object or action flies in the face both of evidence against it and of common sense.

Clearly, cultures differ in the ways they teach, diffuse or control the interpretation of their rites and symbols as something to be clearly established, or left open and unexplained, or made mysterious, or kept secret. And within one culture, kinds and items of knowledge may differ in how they are taught. Compare the detail of Gnau knowledge concerning the rules on blood with the transmission of knowledge about food taboos. The theme of learning in Gnau culture recurred at various places in the book. An interpretative understanding should depend on finding out about the responses of people to their actions first. The supposition that some things people do are natural signs or symbols to which a meaning may be attributed independently of what they say was discussed in chapter 6. It is a special case of the problems involved in asserting that something has a meaning when people do not state it or do not perhaps accept it. The curious uses of meaning in relation to expressive actions or responses for which the people provide no statement that resembles the meaning offered by the anthropologist seem to me to stem in part from a desire to find an intellectual or cognitive component in everything that people do at the expense of neglect of the emotional, expressive and functional components. This aspect was discussed in relation to the way in which emotion affects the interpretation of symbols in chapter 9, and in relation to the functions of ritual, and substitutions for them, in chapter 10. They are matters of expression and response to stimuli rather than of intellectual understanding and the communication of messages. In part the argument in chapter 10 is related to the formality and fixity of ritual procedure and the question of the propositional or message content of a rite. Bloch (1974) has argued that formality and fixity of sequence is a device that tends to drive out such propositional meaning in ritual. It may be so or not, depending on the style of ritual instruction and the conventional-isation of attached meanings. If, as with the Gnau, the meaning of certain motifs is left relatively open and unstated, we may see variety in their responses to them (as for instance in relation to the *nǝm beirkatidǝm*), and the way in which motifs may be used within rites to impose pattern, and by repetition may link different rites, provoking new responses with changed experience of them. The ways in which the media of ritual may be used to evoke such responses, depending on aptness of association, the gating and ungating of attention, pattern and placing, selection within a limited range, were discussed in general in chapter 2 and then applied in analysis of the Gnau rites of puberty in chapter 8.

Some of chapter 7 aimed to show how the balance of an interpretation for one society may be corrected by considering the relative emphases given to certain cultural themes when compared with other societies nearby. It is a cross-cultural expansion of the view that accurate interpretation can be furthered by knowledge of style, or of a limited range or spectrum, and choice and emphasis within it. The anthropologist is likely to distinguish themes and emphases in the culture he studies sometimes by matching what he finds against the standards of his own culture. If there is some striking contrast to his own standards, he may mistakenly suppose that the feature which arrests him is something that the other culture also pays special attention to. If he were to find that societies surrounding the one he studies all have the feature he was struck by first, he might alter the particular significance he was tempted to give it from study of the one society alone. To put the point hypothetically, we might imagine our-selves giving great significance to nakedness in relations between the sexes if we found ourselves asked to comment on the Gnau and had no standards other than those of Victorian England: we might come to view the significance of nakedness differently after we had learned that people generally in New Guinea wore little in the way of body covering anywhere on the island. In chapter 7 what I partly had in mind was the proposed interpretation that rites of a sort similar to the Gnau rites of puberty express sex antithesis, hostility or antag-onism. It is possible to select aspects of what they do and see them in this light. But to propose this as the dominant motive behind them would seem false to me, a form of distorting reductionism like that of the view that would explain the religious impulse and religious behaviour as a sublimated expression of repressed sexuality. William James scorned it (1902, pp. 10–16). It would leave what is distinctive in the religious genius and impulse out of account. He considered that one could, by selective quotation, show just as well that the religious expression came from the sublimated impulse of greed and hunger. To foist the interpretation on the data would express the preoccupations of the writer, or the intellectual fashions of his times, rather than account for the distinctive quality or character of religious experience.

In any reductive analysis a great deal of the particular must be lost. The point is that though there are elements of antithesis between the sexes recognisable within the rites, and men seek to control public action, an interpretation that stressed this as the dominant motive or theme expressed within them would misrepresent their character and the understanding that Gnau people have of them. The themes they state provide a more powerful guide for understanding them. When social changes come we see in their response some aspects of the continuing force of this understanding for them, for which no functional substitute has been provided; we also see that rites are not immutable, nor is their interpretation, and that new circumstances alter how the Gnau see themselves, what they did and what they now have to do.

REFERENCES

Abbie, A. (1960) 'Physical changes in Australian Aborigines consequent upon European contact', *Oceania 31*, 140—4.

Allen, M. R. (1967) *Male Cults and Secret Initiations in Melanesia*. Melbourne University Press, Melbourne.

Barth, F. (1961) *Nomads of South Persia*. Oslo University Press, Oslo.

Bateson, G. (1958) *Naven*. Stanford University Press, Stanford, Calif. (first published 1936).

Beattie, J. (1966) *Other Cultures*. Routledge and Kegan Paul, London.

Berndt, R. M. (1965) 'The Kamano, Usurafa, Jate and Fore of the Eastern Highlands' in *Gods, Ghosts and Men in Melanesia*, ed. P. Lawrence and M. J. Meggitt, 78—104. O.U.P., Melbourne.

Bernstein, B. (1965) 'A sociolinguistic approach to social learning' in *Penguin Survey of the Social Sciences*, ed. J. Gould, 144—68. Penguin, Harmondsworth.

Bloch, M. E. F. (1974) 'Symbols, song, dance and features of articulation', *Archiv. Europ. Sociol. 15*, 55—81.

Boas, F. (1955) *Primitive Art*. Dover Publications, New York (first published 1927).

Bruner, J. (1957) 'On perceptual readiness', *Psychol. Rev. 64*, 123—52.

Callan, H. (1970) *Ethology and Society*. O.U.P., Oxford.

Carlyle, T. (1831) *Sartor Resartus*. Chapman and Hall, London.

Chapple, E. D. and C. S. Coon (1947) *Principles of Anthropology*. Jonathan Cape, London.

Cherry, C. (1966) *On Human Communication*. M.I.T. Press, Cambridge Mass. (first published 1957).

Collingwood, R. G. (1938) *The Principles of Art*. O.U.P., Oxford.

(1944) *An Autobiography*. Penguin, Harmondsworth.

Douglas, M. (1970) *Natural Symbols*. Barrie and Rockliff, London.

Durkheim, E. (1938) *The Rules of Sociological Method*. Free Press, New York (first published in French, 1895).

(1912) *Les formes élémentaires de la vie religieuse*. Alcan, Paris.

Ellenberger, H. F. (1970) *The Discovery of the Unconscious*. Allen Lane, London.

Ellis, H. (1936) *Studies in the Psychology of Sex*, vol. I. Random House, New York (first published 1906).

Evans-Pritchard, E. E. (1937) *Witchcraft, Oracles and Magic among the Azande*. Clarendon Press, Oxford.

225

References

(1951) *Social Anthropology*. Faber and Faber, London.

Firth, R. (1951) *Elements of Social Organization*. Watts, London.

(1967) *Tikopia Ritual and Belief*. Allen and Unwin, London.

(1973) *Symbols: Public and Private*. Allen and Unwin, London.

Fletcher, R. (1971) *The Making of Sociology*, vol. 2: *Developments*. Michael Joseph, London.

Forge, A. (1965) 'Art and society in the Sepik', *Proc. Roy. Anth. Inst.*, 1965, 23–31.

(1967) 'The Abelam artist' in *Social Organization*, ed. M. Freedman, 65–84. Frank Cass, London.

(1970a) 'Learning to see in New Guinea' in *Socialization*, ed. P. Mayer, 269–91. Tavistock, London.

(1970b) 'Prestige, influence and sorcery' in *Witchcraft, Confessions and Accusations*, ed. M. Douglas, 257–75. Tavistock, London.

Fortes, M. (1953) 'The structure of unilineal descent groups', *American Anthropologist 55*, 17–41.

(1966a) 'Religious premises and logical technique in divinatory ritual' in *Ritualization of Behaviour in Man and Animals*, ed. J. Huxley, *Phil. Trans. Roy. Soc. London*, ser. B *251*, 409–22.

(1966b) 'Totem and taboo', *Proc. Roy. Anth. Inst.*, 1966, 5–22.

(1969) *Kinship and the Social Order*. Routledge and Kegan Paul, London.

Fortune, R. F. (1932) *Sorcerers of Dobu*. Routledge, London.

Frye, N. (1971) *Anatomy of Criticism*. Princeton University Press, Princeton, N.J. (first published 1957).

Gellner, E. (1970) 'Concepts and society' in *Sociological Theory and Philosophical Analysis*, ed. D. Emmet and A. MacIntyre, 115–49. Macmillan, London.

Gerth, H. H. and C. Wright Mills (eds.) (1948) *From Max Weber*. Routledge and Kegan Paul, London.

Ginsberg, M. (1961) *The Diversity of Morals*. Heinemann, London.

Goldenweiser, A. (1933) *History, Psychology and Culture*. Knopf, New York.

Gombrich, E. H. (1960) *Art and Illusion*. Phaidon, London.

(1963) *Meditations on a Hobby Horse*. Phaidon, London.

(1965) 'The use of art for the study of symbols', *American Psychologist 20*, 35–50.

(1966) 'Ritualized gesture and expression in art' in *Ritualization of Behaviour in Man and Animals*, ed. J. Huxley, *Phil. Trans. Roy. Soc. London*, ser. B *251*, 393–401.

Goody, J. R. (1961) 'Religion and ritual', *British Journal of Sociology 12*, 142–64.

Griaule, M. (1965) *Conversations with Ogotommeli*. O.U.P., Oxford (first published in French, 1948).

Harris, M. (1964) *The Nature of Cultural Things*. Random House, New York.

Hayes, R. T. (1973) 'Sorcery and power among the Kwoma of Sepik New Guinea'. Unpublished M. Phil. thesis, University of London.

Hinde, R. A. (1976) 'Interactions, relationships and social structure', *Man*, n.s. *2*, 1–17.

Hogbin, I. (1970) *The Island of Menstruating Men*. Chandler, Scranton, Pa.

Huizinga, J. (1965) *The Waning of the Middle Ages*. Penguin, Harmondsworth (first published 1924).

References

James, W. (1902) *The Varieties of Religious Experience*. Longman, Green, London and New York.

Janet, P. (1927) *La pensée intérieure et ses troubles*. Maloine, Paris.

Jaspers, K. (1963) *General Psychopathology*. Manchester University Press, Manchester (first published in German, 1913).

Kaberry, P. M. (1941) 'The Abelam tribe, Sepik District, New Guinea', *Oceania 11*, 233–58, 345–67.

Kräupl Taylor, F. (1966) *Psychopathology*. Butterworth, London.

Ladd, J. (1967) 'Custom' in *Encyclopedia of Philosophy*. Macmillan and Free Press, New York and London.

Laycock, D. C. (1973) *Sepik Languages*. Pacific Linguistics Series B, no. 25. Department of Linguistics, Research School of Pacific Studies, Australian National University, Canberra.

Leach, E. R. (1964) 'Ritual' in *A Dictionary of the Social Sciences*, ed. J. Gould and W. Kolb. Tavistock, London.

(1966) 'Ritualization in man in relation to conceptual and social development' in *Ritualization of Behaviour in Man and Animals*, ed. J. Huxley, *Phil. Trans. Roy. Soc. London*, ser. B *251*, 403–8.

(1968) 'Ritual' in *International Encyclopedia of the Social Sciences*, Macmillan and Free Press, New York.

(1976) *Culture and Communication*. C.U.P., Cambridge.

Leech, G. (1974) *Semantics*. Penguin, Harmondsworth.

Leenhardt, M. (1947) *Do Kamo*. Gallimard, Paris.

Le Roy Ladurie, E. (1974) 'Homme–animal, nature–culture, les problèmes de l'équilibre démographique' in *L'unité de l'homme*, ed. E. Morin and M. Piatelli-Palmarini, 553–602. Seuil, Paris.

Lévi-Strauss, C. (1950) 'Introduction à l'œuvre de Marcel Mauss' in Mauss (1950), ix–lii.

(1955) *Tristes tropiques*. Plon, Paris.

(1958) *Anthropologie structurale*. Plon, Paris.

Lewis, G. A. (1974) 'Gnau anatomy and vocabulary for illnesses', *Oceania 45*, 50–78.

(1975) *Knowledge of Illness in a Sepik Society*. Athlone, London.

(1977) 'Beliefs and behaviour in disease' in *Health and Disease in Tribal Societies*, Ciba Symposium no. 49, 227–41. Elsevier–Excerpta Medica–North Holland, Amsterdam.

Lyons, J. (1972) 'Human Language' in *Non-Verbal Communication*, ed. R. A. Hinde, 49–85. C.U.P., Cambridge.

MacKay, D. M. (1972) 'Formal analysis of communicative processes' in *Non-Verbal Communication*, ed. R. A. Hinde, 3–25. C.U.P., Cambridge.

Marshall, A. J. (1938) *Men and Birds of Paradise*. Heinemann, London.

Mauss, M. (1938) 'Une catégorie de l'esprit humain: la notion de personne celle de "moi"', *Journ. Roy. Anth. Inst. 68*, 263–81.

(1950) *Sociologie et anthropologie*, P.U.F., Paris.

Mead, M. (1970) *The Mountain Arapesh*, vol. II: *Arts and Supernaturalism*. Natural History Press, New York (first published in 1938, 1940).

Meinertzhagen, R. (1914) Christmas card.

Mounin, G. (1970) *Introduction à la sémiologie*. Ed. de Minuit, Paris.

(1972) *Clefs pour la sémantique*. Seghers, Paris.

Murray, G. (1946) *Euripedes and his Age*. O.U.P., Oxford.

References

Nadel, S. F. (1951) *The Foundations of Social Anthropology*. Cohen and West, London.

(1954) *Nupe Religion*. Routledge and Kegan Paul, London.

Ogden, C. K. and I. A. Richards (1923) *The Meaning of Meaning*. Routledge and Kegan Paul, London.

Opie, I. and P. Opie (eds.) (1951) *The Oxford Dictionary of Nursery Rhymes*. O.U.P., Oxford.

Panofsky, E. (1970) *Meaning in the Visual Arts*. Penguin, Harmondsworth.

Piaget, J. (1932) *The Moral Judgement of the Child*. Routledge and Kegan Paul, London.

Proust, M. (1954) *A la recherche du temps perdu*. 3 vols. Gallimard, Paris.

Radcliffe Brown, A. (1922) *The Andaman Islanders*. C.U.P., Cambridge.

Royal Anthropological Institute (1951) *Notes and Queries on Anthropology*. Routledge and Kegan Paul, London.

Salinger, J. D. (1958) *The Catcher in the Rye*. Penguin, Harmondsworth.

Sapir, E. (1934) 'Symbolism' in *Encyclopedia of the Social Sciences*. Macmillan, New York.

Skorupski, J. (1976) *Symbol and Theory*. C.U.P., Cambridge.

Sperber, D. (1974) *Le symbolisme en général*. Hermann, Paris.

Steiner, F. (1967) *Taboo*. Penguin, Harmondsworth (first published 1956).

Tambiah, S. J. (1968) 'The magical power of words', *Man*, n.s. *3*, 175–208.

Tanner, J. M. (1955) *Growth at Adolescence*. Blackwell, Oxford.

Tatarkiewicz, W. (1963) 'The classification of the arts in antiquity', *Journal of the History of Ideas 24*, 231–40.

Taylor, D. M. (1970) *Explanation and Meaning*. C.U.P., Cambridge.

Tinbergen, N. (1953a) *Social Behaviour in Animals*. Methuen, London.

(1953b) *The Herring Gull's World*. Collins, London.

Turner V. W. (1959) 'Muchona the Hornet, interpreter of religion' in *In the Company of Man*, ed. J. Casagrande, 333–55. Harper, New York.

(1965) 'Ritual symbolism, morality and social structure among the Ndembu' in *African Systems of Thought*, ed. M. Fortes and G. Dieterlen, 79–95. O.U.P., London.

(1968) *The Drums of Affliction*. Clarendon, Oxford.

Wark, M. L. and L. A. Malcolm (1969) 'Growth and development in the Lumi people of the Sepik district of New Guinea', *Medical Journal of Australia 2*, 129–36.

Weber, M. (1947) *Theory of Social and Economic Organization*. Free Press, New York.

Whiting, J. W. M. (1941) *Becoming a Kwoma*. Yale University Press, New Haven, Conn.

Wollheim, R. (1970) *Art and its Objects*. Penguin, Harmondsworth.

Yates, F. A. (1966) *The Art of Memory*. Routledge and Kegan Paul, London.

INDEX

229

Index

mother's brother–sister's child, sibling relationship; lineage

knowledge, 36, 48–9, 50–7, 112–20, 141–2, 170–1, 192–9; of Gnau, 121; of rules, 89, 97–9; of taboos, 158–66; *see also* belief; cognition; secrecy

Kräupl Taylor, F., 65, 193

Kwoma, 2, 111, 131, 172

Ladd, J., 12

lammergeier, 18, 25

Laycock, D., 132

Leach, E., 10n, 11, 15, 16, 35–6, 146

learning, *see* knowledge

Leech, G., 221

Leonardo, 2, 116

Le Roy Ladurie, E., 123

Lévi-Strauss, C., 2, 4, 217, 218

life, 136–8, 163–5, 180–1

lineage, 62–3, 93, 94, 96, 174–80, 190; *see also* kinship

lu-lambɔt, see herbs

Luria, A., 64

lyimaŋgai leaf, 46–7, 48, 52–3, 83, 99, 102, 106, 110, 154, 164, 170–1, 180

Lyons, J., 201

MacKay, D., 19

Madən, 42, 67

magic, 10, 23, 45, 49, 101, 102, 114, 126, 167, 186–99

Malcolm, L., 107n

male–female opposition, *see* secrecy; sex

Malinowski, B., 15, 23, 26

marriage, 90–1, 94–5, 99, 101, 107, 108, 123, 150, 162–3, 176–7, 190

Marshall, A., 205

Mauss, M., 113, 218

mauwin (sister's son), *see* mother's brother–sister's child relationship

Mead, M., 2, 111, 126–32 *passim*

meaning, 17–19, 34, 37–8, 97–101, 104–5, 110–20, 132–3, 141–6, 170–1, 201, 215, 219, 221–6; explanation by Gnau, 57–70; gating of, 31, 105; intuition of, 5, 6, 27–8; unconscious, 1, 5, 171; *see also* interpretation

Meinertzhagen, R., 18

men's house, see *gamaiyit*

menstruation, 2, 3, 4, 14, 81–2, 106–8, 110–20, 121–33, 148–50

mental set, 116

Mesmer, F., 14

metaphor, 31, 36, 67, 94, 99–101, 106,

111–13, 154, 196–9; *see also* code; motif; symbol

missions, missionaries, 77, 206–9

moon, 99, 122–4

mother–child relationship, 74, 92, 94–5; in rites of puberty, 77, 84, 94, 169; *see also* childbirth

mother's brother–sister's child relationship, 89, 99–105, 109, 122, 193–6; blood imagery in, 135, 174–82; developmental cycle of, 90–2, 101; magic in, 187–99; penis-bleeding in, 75–6, 175–8; rights and duties in, 97, 101–2, 190–2, 197–9; spitting in, 83, 178–82

motif, 134, 142–6, 148–58; *see also* code

Mounin, G., 33, 71, 117

Murray, G., 23

myth, 47, 50, 57, 61, 62, 107–8, 122–4, 125n, 154, 170, 180, 184

Nadel, S., 1, 10n, 14, 19, 24, 27, 217, 219

nawugəp (ash/salt), 40–1, 54, 79, 82, 87, 109, 180; see also *teltʌg–nawugəp*

Ndembu, 17

nəm beirkatidəm (dried things), 73, 82, 86, 103, 109, 135, 140, 146, 148–58, 165–6, 221; *see also* washing; wet/dry

nəmblin, 138, 164, 176

nettles, 104, 151

Ogden, C., 113

operative acts, 96, 220

Opie, I. and P., 171

orphan, 81

Osgood, C., 5

Panofsky, E., 37, 53, 171

Panu'ət, 40, 56, 58, 68–9, 125, 156, 184; song of, 59–67

Pascal, B., 12

penis-bleeding, 2, 75–6, 78–9, 86, 87, 92, 106–20, 128–33, 150, 174–82, 221–2; *see also* washing

phalangers, 69, 122n, 164, 173

phallocrypt, 75, 79, 95, 168

Piaget, J., 118

plantation, 90, 92, 188–92, 205, 209–15

plants, 68–9, 136–9; *see also* herbs

pollution, 3, 14, 95, 111–12, 124–33, 150, 153; *see also* sex; washing

Proust, M., 204

puberty, 2, 81–2, 90–7, 107–8, 123; *see also* development; growth; menstruation; penis-bleeding; rites of puberty

231

Index

purpose, *see* intention

Radcliffe Brown, A., 27
rationality, 13–16, 19–20, 190–9; *see also* intention
response, 33–4, 37–8, 98, 109–10, 114–20, 145–6, 150, 186–7, 190–2, 214–15, 221; *see also* emotion; expression
Richards, I., 113
rites of puberty, 53, 55, 73–88, 134–85; for boys, 75–81; boys' v. girls', 106–11; change in, 200–5; for girls, 81–5; interpretation of, 134–85; naming of, 57, 106, 107; organisation of, 81–2, 93–7; in Sepik, 4, 126–33; synopsis of, 86–8; *see also* development; puberty; Tambin rites
ritual, 6–37, 57–70; address in, 8, 89, 92; alerting quality of, 7, 19–20, 25, 46, 68, 97, 190–2, 220; v. art, 9–10, 15; as aspect of action, 16–19; audience in, 22–4, 26, 45; change of, 200–6; v. code, 32, 33, 35–7, 117–19, 221; concept of Gnau, 39–72; v. custom, 11–13; definition of, 7, 16–17; exclusion of women in, 125–6; explanation of Gnau, 57–70; fixity of, 7–8, 19, 59–67, 92, 97, 143–4, 190–2, 204–5; as kind of action, 9–16; v. language, 8, 9, 32, 33, 117; learning of, 20, 27–8, 50–7, 59–67, 222; meaning of, 34–5, 37–8, 221; naming of, 42; as performance, 8, 10–11, 22–4, 26, 33–5, 62, 143, 220–1; pride in, 52; public v. private, 21–4, 26–7, 89, 97, 185, 194; and rationality, 13; and routine, 11; secrecy in, 166–8; sequence in, 35, 41–2, 143–4; v. technique, 13–16; *see also* custom; rites of puberty
Rorschach, H., 116
rules, 11–13, 19–20, 25, 37, 89–105, 143–4, 204, 220; on blood, 174–82; change of, 200–5; and duty, 97, 101–5, 160–1, 190–9; on food, 146–8, 158–66; and implicit symbolism, 190–2; on names, 195–6; on plantation earnings, 188–92; for rebuilding men's house, 41–3; as sequence, 35, 41–2, 95, 135, 143–4, 146–8, 162–6, 171–2, 176–8, 201; variation in, 92; *see also* custom

sago, 40, 58, 70, 166, 211
Salinger, J., 204–5
Sapir, E., 35
scarification, 3, 131

scent, 173
secrecy, 20, 47, 76, 79, 109–10, 132, 135, 166–8, 180–2, 183
sentiment, *see* emotion
sex, 111–13, 124–33, 134–5, 165–8, 180–2, 223–4; *see also* cold/hot; pollution; secrecy
Shereshevski, S., 65
sibling relationship, 94, 153, 165, 174–9
siwug sirbəg, 93, 103, 154–5
Skorupski, J., 96, 220
social change, 169, 188, 200–15
song (*bəlyi 'it*), 41, 42, 47, 52, 58, 59–67, 166, 168
sorcery, 52, 57, 76, 126, 128
spell (*bəlyigap*), 25, 43, 47, 56, 63–4, 79, 80, 156, 180, 183–5
Sperber, D., 143
spitting, 25, 43–4, 47, 76–7, 83–4, 87, 90, 94, 110, 172, 180, 182–4
Stanley, G., 205
Steiner, F., 72
stimulus, *see* response
symbol, symbolism, 1, 17, 25, 32–3, 97–101, 104–5, 106–20, 141–6, 186–99, 220–6; actor's v. observer's understanding, 6, 186–7; clear v. ambiguous, 30–3, 67–70, 97, 180; of duties, 190–2; in expression, 26–8; Gnau explanation of, 57–70, 141; 'natural', 5, 27–8, 110–20; in representation, 29–32, 59–60; v. substitute, 29, 111–20, 193–9, 214–15; *see also* code; communication; expression; interpretation; meaning; metaphor; motif

taboo, 2, 72, 82, 85, 86, 90, 92–3, 95, 96, 99–101, 109–35, 146–8, 158–66; see also *nəm beirkatidəm*
Tambiah, S., 11, 15, 23, 36
Tambin rites, 3, 50, 90, 96, 104, 108, 140, 141, 142, 148, 151, 154, 156, 165–6, 169, 172, 180–2, 183–5, 188, 212–15
Tanner, J., 107n
Taylor, D., 119
teltʌg–nawugəp, 82, 87, 109, 140, 149, 150, 166, 184
Tikopia, 9
timalyi'ep bifaŋ, 84, 88, 95, 110, 203
Tinbergen, N., 115
token, *see* type
tradition, *see* custom
Trobrianders, 23
Turner, V., 16, 18, 22, 32, 35

232

Index

CAMBRIDGE STUDIES IN SOCIAL ANTHROPOLOGY

General Editor: Jack Goody

235

* Also published as a paperback